REPRESENTATIVES
AND REPRESENTED

REPRESENTATIVES AND REPRESENTED

**BASES OF PUBLIC SUPPORT
FOR THE AMERICAN LEGISLATURES**

SAMUEL C. PATTERSON
University of Iowa

RONALD D. HEDLUND
University of Wisconsin-Milwaukee

G. ROBERT BOYNTON
University of Iowa

With an Introduction by

JOHN C. WAHLKE
University of Iowa

A WILEY-INTERSCIENCE PUBLICATION

JOHN WILEY & SONS, New York • London • Sydney • Toronto

Library of Congress Cataloging in Publication Data

Patterson, Samuel Charles, 1931-
  Representatives and represented.

  "A Wiley-Interscience publication."
  Includes bibliographical references and index.
  1. Legislative bodies—United States—States—Case studies. 2. Iowa. General Assembly. I. Boynton, George Robert, 1935-   joint author. II. Hedlund, Ronald D., 1941-   joint author. III. Title.
JK2488.P38   328.73   75-20232
ISBN 0-471-67080-4

Printed in the United States of America

10 9 8 7 6 5 4 3 2 1

PREFACE

This book has been in the making for a number of years. The basic data were gathered in the latter half of the 1960s, at a time when little research had been done on support for political authorities and regimes. In the years since our research was designed, there have been a number of studies having to do with political support. We have not sought to reconcile our findings with other studies, nor have we tried to generalize beyond our own study design. Modes of conceptualization and methods of analysis vary sufficiently that such a reconciliation would constitute a major theoretical and empirical synthesis in itself. Rather, we present in this book our own findings in regard to support for the state legislature, based on our conceptualization of the problem. We leave it to others and to another place to put our work in the context of studies focusing on other legislative bodies or other political objects. We think our work stands on its own and is best presented in its own terms, at this stage in research on support for legislatures.

Nevertheless, we are painfully aware of the limitations and shortcomings of our analysis, and we take full responsibility for these in the hope that the work will be seen as merely one step along a rather ambiguous and torturous road to better understanding of the ways in which the American state legislature is embedded in a matrix of attitudes and perspectives held by constituents and political leaders. In pursuing this research, and in our cogitations and ruminations since this analysis was foreordained by our original research conceptualization, we have been educated a great deal by our colleagues. John C. Wahlke has been a steady inspiration to us, as well as our other colleagues at the University of Iowa—Gerhard Loewenberg, Chong Lim Kim, and Joel Barkan. From the University of Kentucky, we have been stimulated by the commentary of Malcolm E. Jewell and have benefited from face-to-face criticism and consolation when he came to the University of Iowa during the 1974–1975 academic year as a visiting scholar in the Comparative Legislative Research Center. And we appreciate the help at various phases of our analysis of Wilder W. Crane, Brett W. Hawkins, and Meredith M. Watts, Jr., of the University of Wisconsin, Milwaukee. David Brady (University of Houston), Paul Friesema (Northwestern University), and F. Ted Herbert (University of

Oklahoma), former graduate students at the University of Iowa, were immensely helpful at one stage or another of the project. For logistical support for the analysis of our data, we have had the continuing assistance of the outstanding staff and facilities of the Laboratory for Political Research in the Iowa Department of Political Science, and we were especially helped by Norman Elliott. We also wish to express our thanks to David M. Kovenock and the Comparative State Elections Project of the University of North Carolina at Chapel Hill. In preparing drafts of our manuscript, and in skillful typing of the final version, we thank Karen Stewart and Bonnie Fauls. For her work in preparing the index, we thank Polly Ann Patterson.

The research reported in this book was supported along the way by grants and other research assistance from the National Science Foundation, the Social Science Research Council, the Research Department of the Des Moines *Register and Tribune*, the University of Iowa Graduate College and Computer Center, and the University of Wisconsin, Milwaukee, College of Letters and Sciences and Graduate School. We are especially indebted to Glenn Roberts, Director of the Research Department and the Iowa Poll of the Des Moines *Register and Tribune*, and his staff, for indispensable help at the very early data-gathering stages of our study.

SAMUEL C. PATTERSON
RONALD D. HEDLUND
G. ROBERT BOYNTON

Iowa City, Iowa
Milwaukee, Wisconsin
June 1975

CONTENTS

TABLES

FIGURES

REPRESENTATIVES
AND REPRESENTED

INTRODUCTION
JOHN C. WAHLKE

Except for the materials discussed in the final chapter, the data presented, analyzed, and interpreted in this book concern political events, persons, and institutions in the state of Iowa during 1966–1967. This is not a book "about" government and politics in Iowa at that time, however, but a case study of one particular aspect of it: support for the Iowa legislature.

The case study format enhances rather than limits the potential power and interest of these findings. For it is not the specific bits of information about Iowa legislative support circa 1967, whatever their intrinsic interest, that can expand our knowledge about the governance of men. What we can learn depends ultimately on the extent to which we can account for what the information tells us; the extent to which the Iowa findings can legitimately be generalized to other times, other places, and other political systems; and how we can link these explanations and generalizations to our knowledge of other, broader questions about political systems and behavior.

In short, to borrow the words of another author about another book, this one should be read as a "tentative 'theoretical case study.' "[1] A first step toward such an understanding is to consider the book's locus in the general field of legislative research.

PERSPECTIVES ON LEGISLATURES

It is often said that the development of legislative study, as of political science generally, spans three "stages"—"institutional," "process-oriented," and "behavioral" (the "postbehavioral" revolution heralded by David Easton so far appears to have had little influence on legislative study).[2] The statement is inaccurate as literal intellectual history, and its typology sometimes generates as much polemical heat among political scientists as it sheds intellectual light on political phenomena. But it can help to highlight some of the differences among

1

Table 0.1 Some Frequent Connotations of a Familiar Typology of Legislative Research

Types of Legislative Studies	Main Object of Interest	Key Political Concepts	Main Kinds of Questions	Typical Modes of Reasoning, Kinds of Evidence	Characteristic Conceptions of Research
"Institutional Studies"	Legislative Institution: Structure Function	Institution(?) Legislation	Descriptive Classificatory Evaluative, prescriptive	"Formal": Legal Logical (Definitional) Historical Subjective insight, judgment	Case study: U.S. Congress; British Parliament Literature, Lore Documents
"Process-Oriented Studies"	Legislative Process: Decision-making Functioning	Power, Influence Representa-tion (?)	Factual ("realistic description") Explanatory (?)	Inductive Empirical	Case study: U.S., British Parliament Documents Aggregative Data (roll-calls, biographies)
"Behavioral Studies"	Legislators: Attitudes Behavior Legislative Decision	Representation Legislation Political System (Input, Output, etc.) (?)	Factual: Descriptive Relational Explanatory Theoretical (?)	Logico-empirical: Inductive &/or Deductive Empirical	Case study: U.S., other nations Cross-sectional, Comparative Study Aggregative data (roll-calls, biographies) Survey data Electoral data

the various (but not necessarily contradictory or incompatible) legislative studies now available.

The most important points of difference commonly associated with the classical trichotomy include: (1) the principal concern of the research (i.e., the set of broad questions that particular research efforts are designed to answer); (2) the key political concepts and variables used to orient and formulate the questions for research; epistemological premises, including (3) the kinds of questions asked and (4) the kinds of evidence and reasoning processes used for accepting or rejecting the answers found; and (5) research design and methods (i.e., primarily broad research strategies and intellectual conceptions of the research process, rather than just specific tactics and techniques for collecting and manipulating data). Table 0.1 presents a very gross and simplistic picture of the different connotations most commonly suggested by the three constituent terms of the schema in question.[3]

As the table suggests, legislative study as a distinctive field of attention in American political science, where it first appeared as such, was for a time characteristically preoccupied with rather formalistic depiction and evaluation of the structure and function of legislative bodies. Attention was given mostly to enumerating such details as the number of chambers, the powers and duties of presiding officers, committee chairmen, and other legislative officials, and methods of choosing them; the authority and ''functions'' of the legislature, in the sense of its legally assigned powers and duties; and constitutionally prescribed methods of choosing its members. It was usually taken for granted that the principal mission of a subject body was ''legislation,'' which was taken to mean the formal business of proposing, debating, amending, resolving, and enacting. Hence legislative procedures were often minutely and painstakingly examined. ''Representation'' referred mainly to the formal provisions for choosing legislators—for example, the time and manner of electing them, the legal requirements and qualifications for election to office, the franchise governing such elections, and perhaps extrapolation from these data to such formal properties of the system of representation as the numerical ratio between enfranchised electors and legislators.

To study a legislature not uncommonly meant to describe and classify such formal properties of it, to judge the arrangement as more or less good or bad in the light of an a priori conception of the ''good'' or ''right'' way to organize such bodies, and perhaps to prescribe some changes in the relevant constitutional and legal provisions that might bring formal structure more into line with presumed proper or ideal structure. ''Data'' consisted mainly of constitutional and statutory documents, legislative records pertaining to structural and procedural characteristics (by-laws, rules of procedure, etc.), and historical antecedents of these. The method of "proof" used to arrive at prescriptive and evaluative propositions was generally logical deduction from the a priori principles and logical extrapolation from the structure and functions formally described. In any case, there was characteristically scant systematic observation of day-to-day activities of legislators or voters, of the content of bills, resolutions, or laws processed by them, or of any empirical, observable material other than the documents on which institutional description was mainly based.

Although some scholars did try to set down generic accounts of legislatures in approximately the terms just described, the more frequent form of legislative study was straightforward description/prescription with respect to a particular system, usually the Congress of the United States or the British Parliament.[4] Besides the formal documentary data that provided the main grist for such studies, researchers commonly surveyed and summarized the assorted literature and lore of their predecessors. Their principal analytic tool was the subjective judgment, insight, and imagination of the individual analyst, usually applied in unsystematic and unreplicatable but nonetheless intelligent and sometimes brilliant fashion.

One must by no means infer from the foregoing sketch that all or most institutional studies of legislatures were false starts on wrong roads, of no value then or later. On the contrary, more often than not they were comprehensive, thorough, and highly informative. They provided not only interesting and useful information about the formal characteristics of specific legislative bodies, but also a sense of their historical development and of institutional continuity and stability, as well. Equally important, although not recognized for some time, they contained an implicit conception of the legislative institutional structure as a set of effective, channeling constraints that shape and pattern the behavior of legislators in important ways. Institutionally oriented scholars were generally interested not in the activity of legislators in the legislative arena, but in the shape and character of the arena itself. They therefore tended to ignore the behavioral implications of their descriptions of institutional structure. Indeed, they neglected what seems to be an obvious empirical question: to what extent and in what way do formal institutional properties and rules influence the behavior of role incumbents of the institutional group? If anything, they took it for granted that official behavior naturally or automatically conforms to formal rule and abstract description. Later reflection and study suggest that the "structure" of a legislature effectively inheres not in the verbal abstractions of analysts or in the formal rules enacted to govern the behavior of the group's members, but in the dependably repetitive patterns of behavior displayed by almost every legislator involved. Apparently, these patterns are more or less responsive in part to the formal prescriptions, although they manifest also common informal rules and understandings about what constitutes appropriate institutional behavior.

Although the institutional outlook was chronologically prior and was clearly predominant throughout almost a half-century of legislative research, there is less chronological difference and more substantive overlap among studies representing the other two approaches. Process–oriented studies began to appear somewhat earlier and were the prevailing kind in the 1940s and 1950s. But behavioral studies emerged almost as early, even though their spread was not quite so rapid. Similarly, although studies best characterized as behavioral are probably more numerous today than process-oriented ones, it would be wrong to suggest that the latter are now being superseded altogether.

In general, process-oriented researchers reverse the emphases and concerns of institutionalists. Where the latter typically preoccupied themselves with institutional structure—the framework within which legislative action takes place—and were little interested in that action as such, process-oriented researchers take the institutional character of the legislature for granted and concentrate on the activity transpiring within its framework. Where ''legislation'' for institutionalists refers mainly to the presumed generic function of legislatures, it is for process-oriented researchers the central object of attention. Their aim is, in general, to discover what legislation emerges as the product of legislative activity, and how. Where institutionalists detailed the mechanics of legislative procedures and proceedings, succeeding researchers visualized a sequence of activities, above all decisional activities, constituting a legislative *process*. That process, moreover, is commonly described in terms of which protagonists win and which lose particular contests, and that, in turn, is taken to be a measure of the participants' relative power or influence (also key concepts in this genre of research). Not uncommonly, process-oriented investigators use ''representation'' of the public and its elements to refer to the relative power and influence over legislative decisions of those outside the law-making body.

''Process-oriented'' research is generally less interested in the final product of the legislative process, except perhaps as that serves to index the overall power and influence of participants, than in the sequence of decisions and the application and results of power at various points and stages along the way. It usually seeks above all to observe and describe accurately what transpires throughout the process. The fruits of research, therefore, tend to be detailed and realistic accounts of events and activities, rather than generalizations or theoretical abstractions.

Given this essentially descriptive goal, it is only natural that the prevailing type of process-oriented research design is the case study. Some studies offer overall pictures of the legislative process in particular legislative systems; others follow one decisional strand or a related bundle of them, as particular instances of the working of the legislative process.[5] Surprisingly few, however, extend their view beyond the supposedly archetypal Anglo-American systems; most indeed are exclusively concerned with the American Congress. By comparison with earlier institutional studies, process-oriented research is also characterized by more concern for explanation as well as more realistic description. "Explanation" in this case often takes the form of measuring the relative power or influence of major factors or contenders (party, constituency, etc.) in collective decisions; sometimes it consists of cataloguing various properties and attributes thought to be sources or correlates of those contenders' power and influence.[6]

Documents are an important source of data for process-oriented and institutional studies, alike, but they are now searched more for traces of the legislative process than for descriptive evidence about legislative structure. Aggregative data about legislative decision makers (roll-call votes, legislators' biographies, etc.) and descriptive data about various extralegislative participants (size of membership, socioeconomic and other characteristics of groups, parties, administrators, etc.) are the common raw materials for this type of research. At the same time, process-oriented researchers often go beyond official and semiofficial documents to read the reports of political reporters and other external commentators as data sources. They also look at and listen to the process of legislation, purposefully consulting well-informed participants.

As is true of most case studies, very little process-oriented research starts by devising hypotheses from theories about legislative processes or institutions. As a rule, its generalizations are derived inductively post facto and do not extend beyond the case at hand. That is, the work rarely starts from theory and just as rarely aims at producing theoretical generalizations. Indeed, such investigations seldom even seek to generalize about case studies comparatively.[7]

Although realistic depiction of the day-to-day legislative process is the hallmark of process-oriented legislative research, these studies remain almost as formal and unrealistic as their institutionalist predecessors in the picture of legislators as persons that they implicitly paint. The behavior of legislators is no more the prime concern of process-oriented studies than it was of institutionalist research. Institutionalists found no reason to investigate the actions of legislators presumed to be rationally and individualistically judging the desirability of alternative proposals that seem to appear before them mainly through the operation of formal rules and procedure. On the other hand process-oriented research often appears to assume that legislators' behavior consists mainly of essentially passive, neutral reactions to demands, pressures, and influences put on them by such extrainstitutional actors as pressure groups, political party agencies, administrators, and executive agencies. Although process-oriented studies are concerned with questions about process dynamics that did not interest institutionalists, for one reason or another they generally look outside rather than inside the collective body of legislators for the moving forces, the dynamic elements of the process.

Of course the characteristic that chiefly distinguishes "behavioral" studies from both the other two varieties is that they focus attention on the persons and activities of legislators themselves. As often as not, the individual legislative actor is the unit of analysis; that is, research aims at explaining variations among those individuals' attitudes and behavior. Even when the unit of analysis is the legislative body or a subunit of it (chamber, committee, etc.), the individual legislator is the unit of observation, and the collectivity is analyzed in light of the properties emergent from the pattern of component individual actions and behaviors.[8]

Like many process-oriented studies, much behavioral work is concerned with explaining the decision-making activity of the legislature. But behavioral research into such questions focuses more on the individual choice-making behavior, the decisional premises of legislators and others, tending to view external pressures and influences through the perceptions of the legislative actors subjected to them. For example, whereas a common central question for process-oriented studies is the relative aggregate influence of party as compared with constituency pressures over the legislative product, behavioral research is more likely to investigate the factors that might make individual legislators respond differently to the influence of party, constituency, or pressure groups. Process-oriented studies provide demographic and socioeconomic background profiles of the legislature as a collective body, suggesting that these might operate as intervening variables affecting the influence of party, constituency, or pressure group; but behavioral studies are more likely to investigate the conditions under which these profiles might operate as described, and why. Behaviorists are also concerned with how such actions vary among individual legislators. How, for example, do legislators' individual ideological views and biases, as related to party, constituency, or group pressure affect their voting behavior?[9] How much, and how, does the relative safeness or competitiveness of legislators' districts affect their responsiveness to party and other voting cues?[10] These are only the most common of a widening variety of questions addressed by behavioral research in pursuit of essentially the same knowledge sought by process-oriented research.

Another distinguishing characteristic of behavioral research, however, is its attention to questions that transcend matters directly affecting legislation, legislative decisions, or power and influence within the legislative process. For example, an early subject of behavioral research was the "institutional behavior" already mentioned. Quite apart from their voting decisions and directly related actions, legislators' behavior comprises varying degrees and modes of awareness of and conformity to both the formal prescriptions of legislative and, equally important, various informal norms and rules-of-the-game that supplement and sometimes modify them.[11] Likewise, underlying and helping to shape most legislative activities are members' role conceptions relative to legislative and subject-matter expertise, leadership office, and other positions and statuses, not to mention their interpersonal relationships with colleagues and other participants in the legislative process.[12] The term "legislative behavior" thus comes to cover perceptions, attitudes, beliefs, habit patterns, and actions of a variety far greater than was originally suggested by the term. Increasingly "legislative behavior" is used to refer not just to intracameral activities of legislators and the ideas and attitudes relating thereto, but to extracameral behavioral phenomena—being recruited and campaigning for legislative office, errand running for constituents, and many others.

In effect this expansion of meaning of the term "legislative behavior" reflects an important conceptual shift. It is the *representative* character and function of the representative body, not primarily its legislative function, which is increasingly the principal theoretical focus of investigation. This of course is evident in the formulation of research questions about the relationship between legislators' voting behavior (policy decisions), their ideological and other personal views and biases on the issues they handle, the cues and clues from their party or from interest groups, and the policy views and demands of constituents and public.[13] In addition, however, there is increasing recognition of the possibility that the response and reaction of public and constituents to legislative events might be quite independent of legislative policy output simply conceived.[14] In short, legislative research begins to recognize the importance of *legitimizing* government and governmental policies, and to investigate what part the legislature and legislators play in that process and function, as well as how they play it.

The behavioral approach has been credited by competent observers with relative epistemological and methodological sophistication, both with respect to its desire to follow rigorous, logicoempirical methods of thought in formulating its research designs and its utilization of complex and advanced methods of quantitative analysis of data.[15] Behavioral legislative research does exhibit the latter characteristic in good measure. But behavioral research has not made a substantial theoretical leap forward over the conceptualization and design of nonbehavioral research. As the foregoing summary suggests, the conceptual span of behavioral research covers a much wider territory than either institutional or process-oriented conceptions or both of them together, and perhaps it incipiently attacks problems tying them together. But behavioral research is rarely much more theoretical in the proper sense of that word than most other legislative research. Many studies, it is true, use the language of "political systems analysis"—the "inputs" of demands and support, the "outputs" of policies and other "authoritative allocations of value," the "feedback" of output to the input side of the system.[16] But these terms serve more often as labels for filing and systematizing research findings than as basic concepts in theoretical generalizations from which research-able hypotheses are (or could be) deduced. One often encounters borrowings from middle-range psychological "theories" about cognitive dissonance (balance), role, reference group, and so on. But these, too, rarely serve as genuine sources of hypotheses to be tested; still more rarely do they benefit from the results of legislative behavior research.

Systematically collected survey data from samples or whole memberships of legislatures is perhaps the characteristic raw material for behavioral legislative research, which also sometimes utilizes legislative electoral data rarely exploited before. But there is still heavy reliance on roll-call, biographical, and other aggregative data long familiar in legislative research. Although the focused, cross-sectional study is increasingly more common than the more holistic depiction of legislative institutions and processes, the study of the single-case or the single-system research site still overwhelmingly outnumbers comparative investigations of even two systems or sites. And although more and more studies (institutional and process oriented, as well as behavioral) of European, non-European, and non-Western legislative systems are now appearing, it remains true that the favorite research sites for legislative study are American (both state and national) and, to a lesser extent, British and Western European.[17]

LEGISLATIVE RESEARCH AND POLITICAL KNOWLEDGE

More directly germane to present purposes than the characteristics most commonly exhibited in legislative studies individually is the collective product they constitute. It would be egregiously presumptuous to attempt to synthesize or even systematically summarize here the substantive results of the four-score-or-so years of legislative research so rudely characterized in the previous section. But several observations can be offered without venturing quite that far.

First, the knowledge we have is exceedingly incremental. What we know has grown by accretion of numerous bits and pieces; we can point to no striking "breakthroughs" or major discoveries that have increased or changed our understanding in dramatic or revolutionary fashion. Although there are obvious differences of quality and value among the many studies extant, few represent critical turning points or major landmarks.

Some observers have viewed the changes in prevailing mood and conception from institutional to process-oriented and behavioral research as constituting something like significant landmarks. Insofar as that view implies an evolutionary progress from "lower" to "higher" forms of research, it is clearly wrong. At best that sequence of development is the simple reflection of the incremental process whereby today's research of necessity builds on whatever has gone before. To be sure, the terms "institutional," "process oriented," and "behavioral" describe bodies of research that differ in their objectives and their methods, as described. And up to a point there is a certain logical order of priority among the bodies of knowledge yielded by each one. That is, understanding of legislative processes rests on a fundamental grasp of the institutional framework—the stable political structures—that surround and organize the variable, dynamic activities of goal-pursuing legislators, enabling them to deal predictably with one another. Likewise, there is (for students of government and politics) no special reason to be interested in the behavior patterns of legislators in particular, and no basis for knowing which of their behavior patterns are interesting, except as curiosity is guided by more general concerns about political and social consequences of legislative institutions and processes. But more important than this kind of logical relationship among the three principal emphases historically represented in legislative study, we must stress that they are essentially different emphases, and not wholly alternative, contradictory approaches. They are complementary pieces of a larger whole. Their results are not competitive with one another but additive in the overall incremental body of knowledge.

A second observation, not really as critical or unkind as it may at first glance appear, is that the increments so far amassed tend mainly to answer questions about what, where, and how. That is, we have produced mostly descriptive information about legislative institutions, processes, and behavior, in particular times and places. Even the "explanations" offered by many process-oriented and most behavioral studies are essentially factual statements about observed correlations between one or another dependent variables in, again, particular cases. Insofar as we have similar information or correlations about several or many different political or legislative systems, it might appear that we have comparative analysis pushing beyond mere description. But such cross-system data and findings seldom constitute synthesis or genuine comparative analysis but only the additive presentation of descriptive statements about the various individual systems and cases described. Above all, we rarely have answers to the question, why do the institutions and processes look and work the way they do in system A but not in systems B, C, and D? Why do legislators feel and think as they do and go about their business one way in system E, but another way in systems F and G?

At the same time it must be recognized that even our descriptive knowledge is far from comprehensive or complete. On the one hand, even in purely descriptive terms, our information about some political and legislative systems is meager or at best fragmentary and uncertain. This is most obviously the case with respect to representative bodies in newer nations and so-called developing societies. But it is also true of a number of American states, and the statement is still more applicable to our knowledge about city councils and other local representative bodies in the United States and elsewhere. Nor do we have a very clear picture, in a purely descriptive sense, of institutions, processes, or legislators' behavior in historic systems of the past.

By the same token, for any system about which we do have substantial descriptive information, there are always important categories of information missing, not just about legislators' attitudes and behavior as revealed by survey data, which is in some respects more difficult to amass on a broad front, but also about legislative institutions and processes that might be thought to be more readily susceptible to descriptive scrutiny. An obvious example is roll-call data, which are only now becoming truly abundant for that most studied legislative body, the Congress of the United States. Similarly, surprisingly little is known about the social backgrounds and demographic characteristics of legislators in more than a few sessions of any given legislature. Thus whatever research site a modern researcher chooses, and however abstract and theoretical his research objectives, he will probably feel the need for more complete descriptive characterization of the legislative situation—in institution, process, and behavioral respects—than is immediately available to him. Correlatively, legislative research that is purely descriptive in its objectives, so long as it provides "old-fashioned" information about systems for which such data were hitherto lacking or increases the dimensions of our information about even well-studied systems, is likely to contribute just as significantly to our knowledge as more ambitious and more sophisticated efforts.

A third observation relates to the other side of the theory-data or explanation-description coin, that is to the character of conceptual and theoretical problems in the field. To admit the necessity and value of further descriptive research is not to belie the importance of these problems. Obviously, some theoretical notions or conceptual orientations, however implicit or inchoate, are inevitably governing researchers' choices about what data to collect and how to organize and classify them. Just as obviously, therefore, an important task of legislative research is to make these guiding notions explicit and clear, and to explain their theoretical justification. It also seems obvious, at least in the abstract, that the results of even the most purely descriptive data collection and analysis can be interpreted and evaluated only in the light of a more general conception, a "theory," that identifies the logical relationship among the various topics and subjects of research and maps out other areas of knowledge and ignorance in relation to them. Bits and pieces of information do not "cumulate" into knowledge autonomously and automatically by simple accretion; they must be organized into logically ordered sets and hierarchies of generalizations by analytic and synthetic intelligence. There is perhaps nothing more characteristic of the field of legislative research as a whole than the absence of such theoretical integration.[18]

This lack is sometimes taken to imply the need for high-priority efforts to formulate an overarching ideational structure, a "theory of legislatures," that would logically interrelate all the presently disparate pieces of our information and at the same time provide the stimulus, the organizing principles, and the theoretical objectives for future research.

The course and the fruits of past research, however, suggest that conceptual and theoretical problems might more profitably be tackled in somewhat different fashion. One most troublesome problem is the commonly ambiguous relation of legislative study to broader political study; indeed, some commentators have cited lack of clear relevance to more general concerns. The questions that most call for answering are not theoretical questions about why the facts of legislative life are what they are found to be, but questions about why it matters that we know what they are, and what difference it makes to anyone "politically" (using the term in its most generic sense) that they are that way. What is called for is not a "theory of legislatures" but a slightly more simple notion no less difficult to formulate: a coherent conception of the generic character of government as a basic social process in human society, surely including an idea of the place that legislative institutions and processes do, could, or might occupy in it, and of how variations in that state would affect social and political life.

LEGISLATURES, REPRESENTATION, AND SUPPORT

A number of recent legislative studies, including the one reported in this book, move in the direction just described. Current work puts less emphasis on explicit, self-conscious attempts at formal model following or theory building. It also differs from earlier efforts because the problems attacked have broader political science implications. Moreover, the newer studies design their research and report its results with more careful attention to what the data say about the bearing of the legislative institutions, processes, and behavior examined on the wider processes of government in the societies under investigation.

The changing research role and meanings of the concept of "representation" not only offer an excellent example of movement in the direction of more broadly based studies but bring us directly to the work at hand. Inasmuch as the terms "legislature" and "representative body" have long been used almost synonymously, one would think that this concept constituted a crucial, if not the most central theoretical focus of legislative research from the beginning. But as our discussion of changing research emphases may already have suggested, that is not quite the case. As a theoretical concept, the term ''representation'' clearly has reference to the linkage between the apparatus and activity of government on the one hand, and the general body of citizens—the public and its individual and various group components—on the other.[19] Until very recently, however, legislative research—whether institutional, process oriented, or behavioral—generally has not asked questions and gathered data about that linkage itself but has simply made unquestioned assumptions about it and looked at some presumed part of it, usually on the legislative side. At the same time, political research in other fields that might have been seized on as shedding light on the problem likewise tended to take for granted the character of the linkage per se, proceeding to examine one or another facet of public and citizen attitudes and behavior through opinion surveys, voting studies, and so on. In both cases, the linkage was conceived of not primarily as a *process*, an actual connection to be empirically examined, but as a static comparative relationship between the two elements linked. And in both cases, both public and legislative side were conceived of fairly simply in terms of the conscious will and intent of the individual actors involved respecting the legislative (policy) decisions that the representative body might or might not make. Thus without ever being formally defined or even much discussed, ''representation'' for most legislative research was long unthinkingly viewed as having to do with how closely the results of actions by legislators (representatives) matched the wishes or desires (interests) of citizens.

From institutional studies we can learn something about the formal electoral relationship between legislators and the constitutents who elect them, but not very much in actual fact about the correspondence between legislators' action and voters' thoughts, whose variations in consequence of varying electoral arrangements would seem to be the justification for studying the institutions in the first place. We can learn something, too, about the variations in the decision-making structure within the legislature. For example, Woodrow Wilson, the first professional scholar to study a legislature, described how the tyrannical powers of Congressional committees constitute a structure of decisional power different from and contradictory to what was constitutionally intended.[20] The clear implication, which Wilson and later students well recognized, is that decisions reached by committees and imposed on the whole Congress might well differ from decisions that would have been reached by the whole body working differently. But it was many years before either Wilson or his successors investigated empirically the character of those putative differences or compared the policy decisions made by

Congress' "little legislatures" with any observed desires, feelings, or thoughts of the public. Similarly, studies of legislative procedure, organization, staffing, and other institutional features as such, were seldom concerned with examining the effects of variations in such features on legislative performance in general, let alone their effects on anything more immediately touching the representative relationship.

One variety of process-oriented study narrowed its focus as just mentioned and suggested some possible connections between legislative performance and institutional structure. This is the set of studies tabulating and examining the number of bills, resolutions, and statutes in various subject-matter categories that are introduced, considered, and acted on in a given legislative time and place, exploring the amount of time spent on these instruments in various procedural activities (committee hearings, floor debates, etc.) and the kinds of final decision reached.[21] Such works add substantially to our picture of the overall shape and character of the legislative process, and the allocation of legislators' time, attention, and energy, yet they rarely compare or facilitate comparison of the product of legislative activity with anything outside the legislature, on the public side of the representational relationship. They mainly suggest how one or another variation in the institutional framework and the established ways of operating in a given legislative body might affect the overall efficiency or productivity of the legislative operation.

More directly pertinent to the subject of representational linkage are process-oriented case studies of particular policy decisions, since most of these not only describe the substantive policy content of particular legislative acts but usually point out explicitly how that product compares with the wishes of extralegislative interests and forces active in promoting and inhibiting enactment. We have already noted that such studies come close to defining representation in terms of the power and influence over the decisions of the beneficiaries and victims most immediately concerned. The studies do not, however, push actual observation beyond that kind of description. They offer no empirical data about how parts of the public other than the winners and losers in a given struggle might feel about the decisions, or what either they or the actors do about such feelings. Nor do they tell us much about how legislators are guided in making their decisions, and how the guidance received might affect legislators' relationships with active elements in the public.

Process-oriented studies, therefore, contain some useful and important information about the collective decision-making patterns of some legislatures, and even more about the connection observed in some particular cases between very specific legislative objectives of certain types of political actors, namely, organized political interest groups, and those legislative outputs of direct interest to the groups specified. Each kind of knowledge is valuable in itself, but none takes us very far toward understanding representation in its broader, more interesting connotations.

Many behavioral studies go considerably further in this direction. Most deal with the choice-making behavior of the individual legislator. Earlier behavioral studies especially approach this problem indirectly, by compiling profiles of the occupational and other socioeconomic and personal background characteristics of the memberships of various legislative bodies. The common conclusion of such investigations is that the legislature is highly "unrepresentative" of the people it is supposed to serve. Comparing the individual legislator with the average for people in his district, or comparing the average of a whole legislature with the averages of their total public, we find almost invariably that legislators are older, more often male than female, better educated, wealthier, of higher occupational status, and so on. The tacit assumption is that the choices made by a legislator or a legislature of one kind of background would differ from those made by another, but the character of the differences to be expected and the mechanism underlying the choices are rarely made precise or explicit. The conceptual inadequacy of merely comparing demographic characteristics of legislators and their publics without relating observed differences to expected or observed attitudes, actions, or behavior of either the public or the representatives is by now quite familiar.[22]

Many more recent behavioral studies expressly recognize this shortcoming and examine the relationship between representatives and represented more directly, not just to discover the effects of their respective socioeconomic and personal characteristics, but with a somewhat broader perspective. Current investigations tend to be conceived in terms of a Burkean typology of possible representational relationships. That is, they seek to learn whether, how far, and under what circumstances legislators know what their electors want, do what they think their electors want, or pursue their individual notions in the face of, at the expense of, or to the neglect of electors' desires.[23] These studies not only widen the angle of vision that legislative research can take in both legislative and public sides of the representational relationship, they also begin to look into the character of some of the bonds and some of the mechanisms linking the two together—the role of political parties, legislators' actual contacts with constituents, and so on. Thus we are beginining to see genuine studies of representation, unlike most earlier projects of research.

Besides offering valuable knowledge of the previously enumerated aspects of the representational relationship, the findings of the more recent studies reveal some of the limitations of the prevailing conceptions of the problem of representation and suggest ways of correcting and improving it. For example, the prevailing concern has been with relationships between specific public-policy wishes and will of public, individuals, and groups, on the one hand, and legislators on the other. There is little doubt that a substantial portion of legislators' attitudes and activity can be realistically described in terms relating to such policy concerns, but recent research leaves even less doubt that they are applicable to only a fraction of the political behavior of only a part of the public. Similarly, the representational relationship is generally conceived of primarily as linking legislators with "constituents," rather than with "citizens" or "public," in more general terms. Again, research findings show that legislators are acutely aware of the special relationship between themselves and the voters who elect them, and that they are intensely concerned with what kind of judgment, primarily but not solely electoral, their constituents (not some general public) will pass on them and their actions. But again, research also clearly reveals that most people who constitute the public only occasionally see themselves as and act like "constituents," although more often and in other ways they may well be concerned with and react to government in general and legislative activity in particular.

In thinking about the linkage between legislators and citizens, therefore, it seems clearly desirable and necessary to look beyond the formal legislative policy decisions and the related choice-making activities of individual legislators, beyond voters' policy preferences (if any) and their electoral decisions for or against legislative candidates, and beyond the person-to-person relationships between representatives and their constituents (both face to face in capitol and constituency, and further removed) through the various media of mass communications. All these, to be sure, are important elements of the representative relationship, by no means to be overlooked or ignored. It is particularly worth investigating the extent to which and the conditions under which different legislators and different citizens entertain attitudes and engage in behavior appropriately described in terms of this instrumental, constituency-to-policy conception of representation. Equally useful would be a measure of what proportion of actual legislature-public relationships in a given case can be appropriately described in that fashion, and how far different political systems differ from one another with respect to that proportion.

To deal with such questions requires preliminary notions about what aspects of representative relationships exist other than the instrumental one. It is here that the concept of "support," originally introduced to political research in David Easton's conceptualization of "the political system," comes into play.[24] The concept of support has reference, in the first instance, to the *effects* of citizens' attitudes and behavior on governmental officials, processes, and institutions. Anything people do or do not do, think or do not think, believe or do not believe, that has the consequence of promoting the continued existence and activity of a government, an institution or process, or an official career, is by definition supportive of that object; actions, ideas, and beliefs that work against it are by definition nonsupportive.

Easton's distinction between "specific" and "diffuse" support is particularly relevant to moving the conceptualization of representation beyond the long-prevalent instrumental version of it. In these terms, instrumental conceptions of representation logically lead to studies of "specific support" only—more often than not to specific support by constituents of their own representatives, not of legislative products or government more generally. Recognition of phenomena suggested by the term "diffuse support" and continuing efforts to distinguish that concept theoretically and empirically from "specific" support rapidly introduced a wide variety of new topics and problems into the domain of research on representation. For example, once this line of thinking is begun, it becomes apparent that people's preceptions of the response to the collective legislative body, the legislature as an institution, in terms of vaguely perceived and often casually evaluated general performance are as vital an element in the representational relationship between public and legislature as more self-conscious and specific judgments about particular policy actions of individual legislators or the legislature as a whole. And from that it becomes equally plain that people are as often responding to symbols and symbolized characteristics as to matter-of-fact observations of legislative activity or observable material consequences of legislative actions or overall performance.

What governs such symbolic and global responses by public and constituents? How much do the day-to-day decisions and actions of legislators individually, or of the legislature collectively, have to do with the mechanism(s) of control? How do such attitudes and actions on the part of public and constituents affect the attitudes and behavior of legislators? To such questions, legislative research to date provides no answers and few clues to where such answers may be sought, since they stem from conceptions of representation more complex than those of the investigators.

CONCLUSION

The research reported in the chapters to follow reflects concern for representation in the wider sense and offer at least tentative answers to some of the questions posed. The findings reported here thus help to broaden our conception of representation and present important additions to our knowledge about that relationship as more broadly conceived.

In the process, they also demonstrate that other quality described previously as conspicuously needed in modern legislative research—namely, relevance to more fundamental problems and questions of government in human affairs. For better understanding of the dynamics of support for legislators and legislatures will clearly add to our understanding of the working of representative democracy. Better knowledge of the distribution of support among a population, and about the participation of various segments in granting, withholding, or being unconcerned about such support, adds an important dimension to our knowledge about the behavior of citizens in democracies. Still more generally, if more indirectly, findings about the symbolic bases of legislative support will relate directly to our efforts to answer broader questions about politics as symbolic behavior. And knowledge about differences in goals, perspectives, and modes of behavior between legislators and public, and between different categories and groups of each, will have relevance to more general questions about the character, causes, and consequences of different relationships between "elite" and "mass" in politics everywhere, not just in representative democracies.

The general conclusion from this survey of the course of legislative research preceding studies such as the one presented here, then, is reasonably optimistic: researchers today are generally better aware than were their predecessors of where they are going and what steps are appropriate to arrive at the destination. It would no doubt be a wild-eyed exaggeration to use that basis to say of legislative research what Condorcet said of mankind and society—that the Golden Age lies ahead of us, not behind us. But then, the aim of scientific research is less utopian than rapid entry into the Golden Age. No more than other known research, the work reported below does not answer or even directly recognize all the "big questions" described earlier. Still, it is no faint praise, nor any exaggeration, to suggest (returning to Harry Eckstein's characterization quoted at the outset) that it is not "merely" a case study, but one that constitutes "a small step toward a remote destination, the union of comparative generalizations and configurative data in well-formulated theories resting on a sound empirical base."[25]

NOTES

1.   Harry Eckstein, *Division and Cohesion in a Democracy* (Princeton, 1966), p. vii.

2.   David Easton, "The New Revolution in Political Science," *American Political Science Review*, Vol. 63 (1969), 1051–1061.

3.   The table and accompanying discussion obviously do not offer a comprehensive account of legislative research. There are no doubt important studies that fit poorly into the framework, and there are few that are fully described by any one category. The schema is offered as a set of "ideal types," a heuristic device to aid thinking about future research, not as a comprehensive classification of past studies. For more general and descriptive surveys see Heinz Eulau and Katherine Hinckley, "Legislative Institutions and Processes," in James A. Robinson, ed., *Political Science Annual 1*

(Indianapolis, Ind., 1966), pp. 85–189; Norman Meller, "Legislative Behavior Research," *Western Political Quarterly,* Vol. 13 (1960), 131–153, and " 'Legislative Behavior Research' Revisited: A Review of Five Years' Publication," *Western Political Quarterly,* Vol. 18 (1965), 776–793; and John C. Wahlke, "Behavioral Analyses of Representative Bodies," in Austin Ranney, ed., *Essays on the Behavioral Study of Politics* (Urbana, Ill., 1962), pp. 173–190.

4. For example, Robert Luce, *Legislative Assemblies* (Boston, 1924), Notable congressional studies include, for example, George B. Galloway, *The Legislative Process in Congress* (New York, 1953), Roland Young, *This is Congress* (New York, 1943). For British examples, see Sir Ivor Jennings, *Parliament,* 2nd ed. (Cambridge, 1957), and *Cabinet Government* (Cambridge, 1936).

5. For examples of such case studies, see Dayton D. McKean, *Pressures on the Legislature of New Jersey* (New York, 1938); Belle Zeller, *Pressure Politics in New York* (New York, 1937); Bertram D. Gross, *The Legislative Struggle* (New York, 1953); E. E. Schattschneider, *Politics, Pressures, and the Tariff* (New York, 1935); and Stephen K. Bailey and Howard D. Samuel, *Congress Makes a Law* (New York, 1952).

6. One of the earliest systematic, comprehensive studies going beyond formalities neatly fits this description: Abbott Lawrence Lowell, "The Influence of Party upon Legislation in England and America," *Annual Report of the American Historical Association for 1901,* 2 vols. (Washington, D.C., 1902) Vol. 1, pp. 321–544. Better known and equally illustrative is Julius Turner, *Party and Constituency: Pressures on Congress* (Baltimore, 1951).

7. A noteworthy exception is the pioneering work of Lowell cited in note 6.

8. The distinction is best illustrated by Heinz Eulau and Kenneth Prewitt, *Labyrinths of Democracy* (Indianapolis, Ind., 1973), which utilizes survey data about city councilmen's perceptions to investigate the decisional structures of city councils in the San Francisco Bay Area.

9. Recent examples from congressional research are: John W. Kingdon, *Congressmen's Voting Decisions* (New York, 1973); and John E. Jackson, *Constituencies and Leaders in Congress* (Cambridge, Mass., 1974).

10. For a good recent summary, see Morris P. Fiorina, *Representatives, Roll Calls, and Constituencies* (Lexington, Mass., 1974).

11. Donald R. Matthews, *U.S. Senators and Their World* (Chapel Hill, N.C., 1960); John C. Wahlke, Heinz Eulau, William Buchanan, and LeRoy C. Ferguson, *The Legislative System* (New York, 1962); and James D. Barber, *The Lawmakers* (New Haven, Conn., 1965).

12. Wahlke, Eulau, Buchanan, and Ferguson, *The Legislative System,* Chapters 7, 11, 12, 13, 14, and 15.

13. Warren E. Miller and Donald E. Stokes, "Constituency Influence in Congress," *American Political Science Review,* Vol. 57 (1963), 45–56.

14. John C. Wahlke, "Policy Demands and System Support," *British Journal of Political Science,* Vol. 1 (1971), 271–290.

15. David Easton, "The Current Meaning of 'Behavioralism,' " in James C. Charlesworth, ed., *Contemporary Political Analysis* (New York, 1967), pp. 11–31; and Heinz Eulau, *The Behavioral Persuasion in Politics* (New York, 1963).

16. Easton, *A Systems Analysis of Political Life* (New York, 1965).

17. Allan Kornberg, ed., *Legislatures in Comparative Perspective* (New York, 1972); Allan Kornberg and Lloyd D. Musolf, eds., *Legislatures in Developmental Perspective* (Durham, N.C., 1970).

18. Gerhard Loewenberg, "Comparative Legislative Research," in Samuel C. Patterson and John C. Wahlke, eds., *Comparative Legislative Behavior: Frontiers of Research* (New York, 1972), pp. 3–21.

19.   Hanna F. Pitkin, *The Concept of Representation* (Berkeley, Calif., 1967) provides an excellent summary and survey of the various meanings of the concept of representation.

20.   Woodrow Wilson, *Congressional Government* (New York, 1956; first published in 1885).

21.   Lawrence H. Chamberlain, *The President, Congress and Legislation* (New York, 1946) is a good example.

22.   In an early study, still one of the most thorough of its kind, Charles S. Hyneman explicitly pointed out that there is no reason to examine such characteristics or make such profiles without looking for the behavioral consequences of the differences found. See "Who Makes Our Laws?" *Political Science Quarterly,* Vol. 55 (1940), 556–51.

23.   Two classic studies setting the style for most subsequent research are Heinz Eulau et al., "The Role of the Representative: Some Empirical Observations on the Theory of Edmund Burke," *American Political Science Review,* Vol. 53 (1959), 742–756, and Miller and Stokes, "Constituency Influence in Congress."

24.   David Easton, *The Political System* (New York, 1953). See also *A Systems Analysis of Political Life.* op. cit.

25.   Eckstein, *Division and Cohesion in a Democracy,* p. vii.

1 THE LEGISLATURE AS A TARGET

Walter Bagehot once depicted the legislative institution as a "standing wonder."[1] His wonderment about the House of Commons in the nineteenth century led him to analyze what kinds of functions Parliament performed that contributed to the civility and stability of British government. He apparently thought that the House of Commons survived as a part of the English constitution of representative government largely because of the genius of its formal structure and internal mechanics. And many who have sought to explain the development and persistence of representative legislatures in democratic societies have focused their attention on the legislature itself, as if its peculiar form and the perfection of its modus operandi could alone guarantee its endurance. Wonderment probably is not a very good characterization of the reaction of most Americans to their legislative institutions, yet it is very commonplace to find Americans who think that the maintenance and persistence of representative legislatures can best be secured through the strategy of internal reform of the bodies' organization and procedure.

Without denying for one moment the importance of legislatures as viable political organizations in themselves, capable of effectively converting meaningful public demands into public policy, we would like to suggest the significance of public support for legislative institutions as a vital element contributing to their durability. It is not at all a new idea that public support for a political institution like a legislature is a condition for its survival in a democratic political system. John Stuart Mill suggested as much more than a hundred years ago.[2] In his classic essay on representative government, Mill argued that a representative system could not last if the people were not committed to its institutions and compliant with its laws. A representative institution may fail if a people "are unequal to the exertions necessary for preserving it; if they will not fight for it when it is directly attacked . . ." or if they "will not cooperate actively with the law and the public authorities. . . ." A legislature, the centerpiece of representative government, must, among other things, have substantial support in the mass public if it is to survive as a representative institution or if it is to perform the functions of representation effectively.

The American legislature is a target of a great deal of public criticism—more in 1974 and 1975 than was the case when this study was originally conceived and the data collected. The publicly articulated criticisms reflect a waning public confidence in legislative institutions. For example, Louis Harris has asked a sample of the American public about their confidence in Congress on four occasions: 1966, 1972, 1973, and 1974. In the first poll, 44 percent of the respondents expressed a great deal of confidence in Congress, but in each of the succeeding surveys the percentage of the population expressing great confidence in Congress was less than it had been in 1966. By 1974 only 18 percent of the respondents said that they had great confidence in Congress.

Although we know that confidence in Congress, and possibly support, have fallen during the past decade, many questions remain. Where in the mass public is support for the legislature greatest, and where is it least exhibited? How is support, or lack of it, in the general public linked to the legislative elites themselves? What kinds of attitudes do citizens actually have about legislators and about the political processes in legislative systems? Finally, what kinds of attitudes about the political system in general are associated with support or hostility toward the legislative institution? The research reported here answers these questions during a period when support was relatively high. It thus can serve as a basis of comparison for research that seeks to understand and explain the apparent decline in support that has been reported since 1966.

In this book we have singled out one state legislature for careful scrutiny and detailed analysis. The Iowa General Assembly, as the legislature is officially called, is not necessarily a typical American legislature, but it serves our purposes reasonably well. We asked a very large number of Iowans about their attitudes toward the state legislature, attempting to answer for one legislature the kinds of questions we think are of very great general importance. If we can begin to understand the nature and structure of public support or hostility toward the legislature in one state, we shall have a basis for building on the knowledge acquired in that one case by inquiry elsewhere, to create a body of comparative generalizations about representatives and represented. One American state, Iowa, becomes for practical purposes our laboratory. It is a political system with clear boundaries, and it is sufficiently autonomous to permit us to test our ideas within it. It has a legislative institution that is similar to many others in America. And, for research purposes, gathering the necessary data there was convenient for us. Some of the important facts of life about politics in Iowa are necessary for an adequate interpretation of the findings elaborated in this book, but the purpose of the book is to describe and explain attitudes toward the legislature, not to exemplify or expound on politics in Iowa.

THE LEGISLATURE

The legislature in Iowa functions in an environment that is socially and economically very homogeneous.[3] The state essentially has a white, Protestant, middle-class population, and political conflict rarely crystallizes along class, racial, ethnic, or religious lines. Although ethnic and nationality diversity is considerable within the state's population—there are concentrations of Germans, Norwegians, Czechs, Irishmen, and some Indians—these differences do not tend to be reflected in political terms. Yet Iowa has, especially in the post-World War II era, undergone important social and political changes. Considerable population mobility has occurred, and a large number of Iowans have moved from the farms, transforming a traditionally rural and agricultural state into a mixed economy with a substantial urban-industrial component. Public demands on the state and local governments have become more complex, reflecting the increasing needs for services and the liberalization of traditional practices felt by an ever-growing urban population. The political interest group structure of the state has shifted from dominance by the Iowa Farm Bureau Federation to a more pluralistic pattern in which no one organized group can exert overwhelming influence on political affairs. The traditional Republicanism of the state has given way to a more politically competitive environment.

The internal organization and procedure of Iowa's bicameral legislature is not at all unusual. At the time of this study it met for a period of about 6 months out of every 2 years. It had a workable number of committees in both House and Senate, and a fairly effective leadership structure. A small research bureau assisted legislators during sessions, and interim legislative committees worked between sessions. The most visible and prevailing characteristic of the legislature was its partisan makeup. As Figure 1.1 dramatizes, the legislature has been predominantly Republican in the last half-century, with two periods of Democratic control—one in the mid-1930s and another in the mid-1960s.[4] That there has been some decline in the proportion of Republicans in the legislature since the early 1950s indicates the impact on the legislature of reapportionment and increased political party competitiveness among the electorate.

Shifting party dominance in the legislature since World War II has not systematically affected the irregular but steady increase in party competition within the legislature itself. Sessions of the legislature since 1945 have exhibited greater and

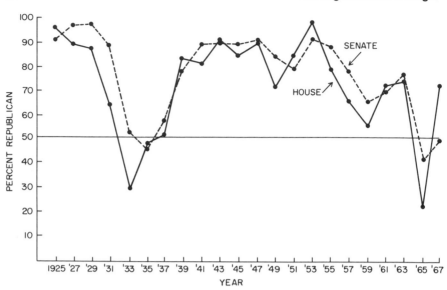

Figure 1.1 Proportion of Republicans in the Iowa legislature, 1925–1967.

greater levels of voting along party lines. That is, there has been an increasing tendency for a larger proportion of roll-call votes taken in the legislature to reflect interparty conflict. In the 1945 session, only about one-fifth of the votes in the House and Senate involved a majority of the Democrats voting together against a majority of Republicans (see Figure 1.2). Party voting peaked at very high levels in 1965, and in the 1967 session about half the roll-call votes in both houses were party votes.

Similarly, although fluctuating a great deal, the internal voting cohesion of Republican and Democratic legislators has increased (see Figures 1.3 and 1.4). In both houses, the proportion of party votes in which 90 percent or more of the Republican legislators voted with their fellow partisans—where the cohesion index was 80 or higher—tended to increase spasmodically in the postwar years. Republican party cohesion in the legislature was very low in the 1940s and 1950s, but by the mid-1960s more than one-third of all party votes reflected very high party cohesion. Democratic party cohesion, which has been much more irregular, skyrocketed in the 1953 session when there were very few Democrats in either house, but the general picture is one of some increase in cohesion.

Increasing levels of interparty conflict in the legislature, and increasing levels of intraparty cohesiveness, are indicative of the developmental pattern of the Iowa legislature, which is one of growing partisan politization. The legislature has increasingly become a party-political institution, where legislative decisions as

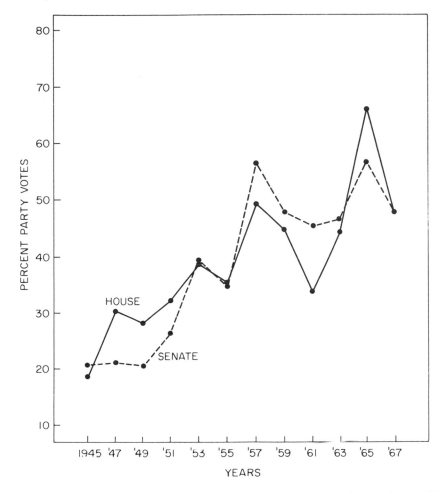

Figure 1.2 Party voting in the Iowa General Assembly, 1945–1967. Source: Charles W. Wiggins, "Party Voting in the Sixty-Second Iowa General Assembly," *Iowa Business Digest*, Vol. 39 (December 1967), 3–11.

well as the image of the legislature to outsiders, tend to be defined in terms of political party differentiation.

THE REPRESENTATIVES

Most Iowa legislators are under 55 years old, they are Protestants, and they have gone to college. Although more than half have grown up in homes where the father's occupation was that of farmer, most legislators now are business or

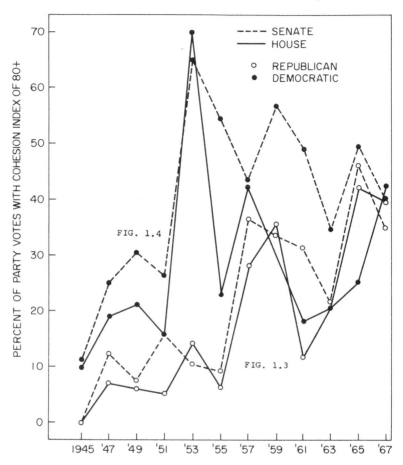

Figures 1.3 and 1.4 Republican and Democratic party cohesion in the Iowa General Assembly, 1945–1967. Source: Charles W. Wiggins, "Party Voting in the Sixty-Second Iowa General Assembly," *Iowa Business Digest,* Vol. 39 (December 1967), 3–11.

professional men. Although Iowa ordinarily is thought of as an agricultural state, very few legislators are farmers who actually live on the farm (only 2 percent in 1967). A more detailed profile of legislators who were interviewed in 1965 and in 1967 indicates the nature of the target for public and legislator attitudes toward the legislature as such. Table 1.1 shows the occupational composition of these two legislative sessions, along with the occupations of legislators' fathers. In both sessions, more than half the legislators' fathers were farmers, although a sizable proportion of legislators came from business and professional families. A preponderance of members of the 1967 session were themselves business or professional

Table 1.1 Occupations of Iowa Legislators and Their Fathers

Occupation	1967 Legislature		1965 Legislature	
	Legislators	Fathers	Legislators	Fathers
Professional or managerial	58.0	30.4	32.8	25.2
Farmer	33.1	51.4	27.7	53.8
Foreman, operative, service	3.3	9.9	8.4	3.4
Skilled or unskilled worker	2.2	7.2	15.1	14.3
Other	3.3	1.1	16.0	3.4
Total	99.9	100.0	100.0	100.1
No. of cases	181	181	119	119

men, compared with a higher percentage of working men in the 1965 session. The occupational difference between these two sessions occurs because the 1965 session was overwhelmingly Democratic, whereas the 1967 session was largely made up of Republicans. There were also more retired men in the 1965 session. But clearly the Iowa legislature, like most American state legislatures, has been recruited largely from the professional and managerial occupations. In contrast to the national Congress and the legislatures of a number of other states, a rather small proportion of Iowa legislators have been lawyers. In 1967, 14 percent of the members of the House were lawyers, and the proportion of lawyers has never been much higher than that since 1945. More lawyers have served in the Senate, but even there the number of lawyers has declined from more than one-third in the first postwar session to 18 percent in 1967.

As Table 1.2 illustrates, Iowa legislators have a fairly high level of formal education. In 1967 nearly 88 percent had some college experience, and about 55 percent were college graduates. The high Democratic and working-class component in the 1965 legislature made that group somewhat lower in the levels of education of its members. Again, Table 1.2 shows that Iowa legislators are preponderantly Protestant, although because of the large Democratic majority in the 1965 session, nearly one-third of these legislators were Catholics. Finally, only about one-third of the legislators in either of the sessions in the mid-1960s

Table 1.2   Education, Religion, and Age of Iowa Legislators

Characteristic	1967 Legislators	1965 Legislators
Education		
High school or less	22.1	33.6
Some college	33.1	25.2
College degree	17.1	17.6
Post-graduate education	12.7	11.8
Law degree	14.9	11.8
Total	99.9	100.0
Religion		
Protestant	76.8	61.3
Catholic	14.9	31.9
Jewish	.6	.8
None, other, no response	7.7	5.9
Total	100.0	99.9
Age		
35 and under	13.3	21.0
36 - 45	26.0	23.5
46 - 55	26.5	22.7
56 - 70	30.4	28.6
Over 70	3.9	4.2
Total	100.1	100.0
No. of cases	181	119

were older than 55 years of age, although the 1965 members were, on the average, somewhat younger than those in 1967.

Since a preponderance of legislators are middle-class Protestants with a fairly high level of education, and all are serving in an institutionalized political body, these lawmakers could be expected to be a very politicized group. We can draw from interviews with both 1967 and 1965 legislators to indicate in some detail the extent to which legislators are involved in political life (see Table 1.3). For instance, far more than half the legislators in both sessions reported political interests antecedent to their adulthood, and two-fifths of the 1967 members indicated that politics was discussed in their homes a great deal when they were growing up. Again, two-fifths of the 1967 legislators and 55 percent of the 1965 members came from politically active families, and one-third of the 1967 members came from families in which an immediate member was a public or party

Table 1.3 Politization of Legislators, 1965 and 1967

	1967 Legislators	1965 Legislators
Pre-adult recollections of interest in politics	55.8	61.3
Politics discussed a great deal at home when legislators were growing up	39.2	**
Parents or other members of legislators immediate family were active in politics	39.2	55.4
Members of legislators immediate family held governmental or party office	32.0	**
Legislator held public office prior to election as state legislator	49.2	48.7
Willing to serve three terms or more in future sessions	54.7	**
Willing to serve as legislative party leader*	45.2	**
Considered seeking full-time public office	44.2	**
No. of cases	181	119

*N=157 members not in leadership positions.
**Not asked in 1965.

officeholder. Just short of half the members of both sessions had held some public office prior to their election as legislators, and 44 percent of the 1967 legislators had considered seeking a full-time public office. Finally, a substantial proportion of the 1967 members were willing to serve in future legislatures and were willing to serve in some leadership position. Thus the legislature is a relatively highly politicized human group, and it can be said to be a quasi-professional political body in which a substantial proportion of the members are highly committed to active political life.

We have stressed the partisan composition of the legislature, as well as increasing levels of party voting and cohesion, and our interviews with 1965 and 1967 legislators can suggest in some detail their attitudes toward political parties and party commitment. On the whole, Iowa legislators are committed to the hybrid American brand of party government. They regard legislative partisanship as important, and they think voter choice and public participation in political affairs should be channeled along partisan lines (see Table 1.4). But the characteristic American ambivalence about political parties and their role in the political process is also reflected in legislators' attitudes. About 45 percent of the 1965 legislators and 56 percent of the 1967 members did not endorse party responsibility with regard to important state policy issues, in the strictest sense. And most members agreed that a member's own partisans may not be more reliable than the party opposition.

Table 1.4   Legislators' Attitudes Toward Partisanship and Parties

	% Who Disagree	
Item	1967 Legislators	1965 Legislators
Partisanship and party loyalty are necessary for campaigns, but after the election a legislator should not think about legislation in terms of party or party loyalty.	69.1	**
The interests of all the people would be better served if all legislators were elected without party labels.	82.3	71.4
Under our form of government, people in general should take a direct interest in government rather than through a political party.	75.7	61.3
If a bill's passage or defeat is important for a member's party, he should vote with a party even if it costs him support in his district.	55.8	44.5
The two parties should take clearcut opposing stands on more of the important state issues in order to encourage party responsibility.	*	62.2
It's just as important for a member to be on guard against the ideas put out by the members of his own party as against those of the opposition.	19.3	13.4
No. of cases	181	119

*Not asked in 1967.
**Not asked in 1965.

We have said enough to suggest in rough form what the legislature is like as it presents itself as a target for public attitudes and evaluations. We are going to probe in detail what a wide variety of people think about the operation and influence of parties in the legislature, legislators' motivations for candidacy, the attributes people think legislators have or should have, and citizens' perceptions of their own and others' legislative influence. We also examine citizens' evaluations of the legislature in general and their support for it as an institution.

THE REPRESENTED

Much of our analysis focuses on the attitudes of citizens about the legislature. Since later in the book we discuss evidence based on samples from the Iowa population, here we need to comment on the general shape of the population in the 1960s when our investigation took place. First, the population of the state had declined gradually relative to the total national population. As Figure 1.5 indicates, Iowans constituted slightly more than 2 percent of the United States population in 1929, but only about 1.5 percent in 1961. The state's population was slightly under 3 million in the 1960s. Iowa had the smallest population in its

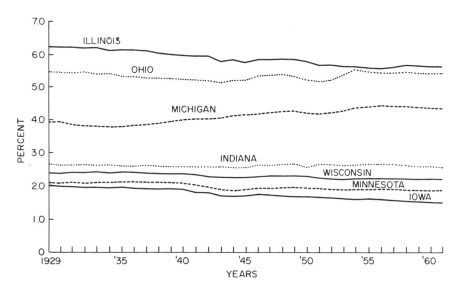

Figure 1.5 Population of Iowa and other states in its region as a percentage of the population of the United States, 1929–1960. Source: Robert C. Turner, "Recent Economic Growth in Seven States: Ohio, Indiana, Illinois, Michigan, Wisconsin, Minnesota, and Iowa," *Iowa Business Digest,* Vol. 34 (November 1963), 13.

region, although all seven states in the region have exhibited a downward drift in population, especially after World War II. But the decline of the state's population was accompanied by another fundamental population trend—increasing urbanization. Figure 1.6 graphically reveals the internal shifts in the Iowa population. The rural farm population has declined rapidly since the 1930s because of movement both out of the state and to the cities. The urban population has grown quite rapidly, reaching about 1½ million by the time of the 1960 census. Since 1940, the rural nonfarm population has increased gradually, giving the state more than 600,000 such residents by 1960.

The growth of the urban population of Iowa is reflected in substantial climbs in nonagricultural employment, and this tendency is depicted for the period of the 1950s and 1960s in Figure 1.7. Industrialization of eastern Iowa, especially after

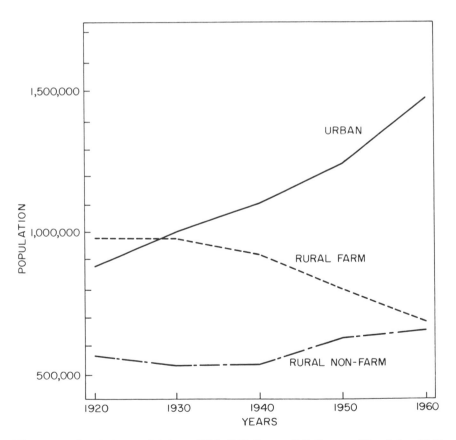

Figure 1.6   Population trends in Iowa, 1920–1960. Source: U.S. Census of Population: 1940, 1950, and 1960.

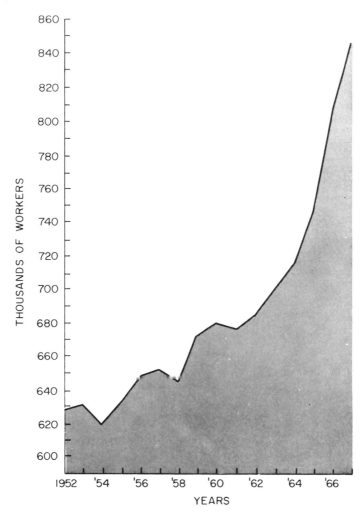

Figure 1.7 Nonagricultural employment in Iowa, 1952–1967. Source: *Des Moines Sunday Register,* January 7, 1968, p. 16-A.

1961, has brought about very considerable increases in nonagricultural employment. There were about 630,000 nonagricultural workers in Iowa in 1952, and this part of the population had grown by more than 200,000 by 1967, in a state with a population of less than 3 million over a period during which the total population declined somewhat. It is of interest to note further that the increasingly nonagricultural working population is not heavily unionized. In 1964 union membership in Iowa constituted only 21 percent of the work force. This proportion was considerably lower than in the surrounding states of Minnesota, Wisconsin, Illinois, and Missouri, although somewhat higher than in Nebraska.

The economic welfare of the population compared with that of other states in the region, is suggested by Figure 1.8, which shows the per capita personal incomes in Iowa and six other states as a proportion of total national per capita personal income. The data in Figure 1.8 indicate the very deep impact of the 1929–1932 depression in Iowa and reflect as well the rapid postwar prosperity of the state's agriculture. Farmers prospered handsomely in 1948, but since then Iowa's percentage has fluctuated irregularly, closely reflecting agricultural prices.

Although the state is not a particularly affluent one in economic terms, in its culture it is very much a white middle-class society. Only about 1 percent of the population is nonwhite. And Iowans are more likely than the national population to identify themselves as middle class. In 1966, 47 percent of a sample of Iowans identified themselves as middle class, compared with only 39 percent of a national sample interviewed in 1964. At the same time, politics in Iowa has been a middle-class politics traditionally, witnessed by the rock-ribbed Republicanism of

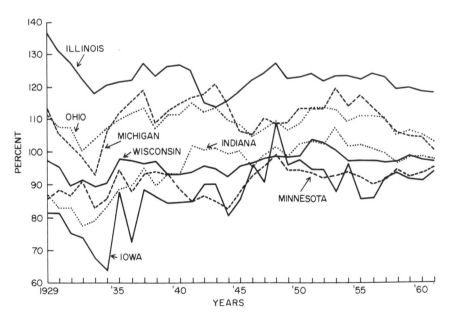

Figure 1.8 Per capita personal income in Iowa and other states in its region as a percentage of per capita income in the United States, 1929–1961. Source: Robert C. Turner, "Recent Economic Growth in Seven States: Ohio, Indiana, Illinois, Michigan, Wisconsin, Minnesota, and Iowa," *Iowa Business Digest,* Vol. 34 (November 1963), 17.

Iowa small towns and cities. Main Street is the source of Republican strength in the state.

Iowa farmers; although they have been politically volatile like farmers in other parts of the land, have had fairly strong Democratic attitudes. In the 1960s Iowa farmers clearly thought the Democratic Party could do a better job of dealing with farm problems. For example, the Wallace's Farmer Poll, conducted regularly among Iowa farmers by *Wallace's Farmer Magazine,* asked their sample of farmers from 1960 to 1964 which party could help raise farm prices or handle farm problems (see Table 1.5). In every survey, farmers preferred the Democratic Party by margins of more than 2-to-1.

Furthermore, with urbanization Iowa has become a reasonably competitive state politically, at least in terms of the partisan identifications of its people. Between 1964 and 1966, more Iowans identified themselves as Democrats than as Republicans, although before 1964 there were considerably more Republican party identifiers. Figure 1.9 shows the trend in party identification in Iowa from 1956 to 1966. By the post-1965 statewide election period, about the same proportion of Iowans identified themselves as Republicans and Democrats, and about 20 percent described themselves as Independents. This distribution of party identification, of course, indicates that Iowa is considerably more Republican in

Table 1.5   Iowa Farmers' Attitudes Toward Best Political Party to Handle Farm Problems, 1960–1964*

Date	Democrats Better	Republicans Better	No Difference	Undecided Don't Know	Total	No. of Cases
February 1960	47.0	11.3	31.5	10.3	100.1	400
August 1960	46.2	16.3	24.5	13.1	100.1	650
October 1960	46.8	15.7	22.0	15.5	100.0	650
June 1962	42.7	18.5	38.8		100.0	534
October 1962	37.3	13.6	31.5	17.6	100.0	689
August 1964	36.9	14.9	32.0	16.2	100.0	531

*The 1960 polls asked about "helping to raise farm income," while the 1962 and 1964 polls asked about "handling farm problems."

SOURCE: Wallace's Farmer Poll; data deposited in the Laboratory for Political Research, Department of Political Science, University of Iowa.

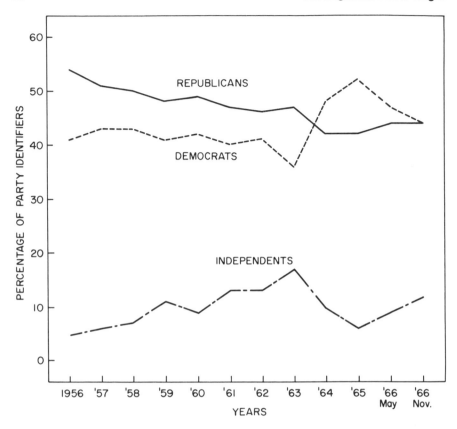

Figure 1.9 Political party identification in the Iowa population, 1956–1966. Source: *Des Moines Register and Tribune,* Iowa Poll; data deposited in the Laboratory for Political Research, Department of Political Science, University of Iowa, Iowa City.

party identification than is the country as a whole (see Table 1.6). In 1966 about 38 percent of Iowans identified themselves as Democrats, whereas more than 45 percent of the Michigan Survey Research Center's national sample identified themselves as Democrats. Similarly, somewhat more than 38 percent of Iowans identified themselves as Republicans, compared with less than one-quarter of the national adult population.

As Table 1.6 indicates, in terms of party identification Iowans in 1966 were as highly politicized as the national population as a whole. The proportion of Iowans who were party identified equaled, and the percentage who were strong identifiers exceeded, those segments of the national population. In other respects, Iowans, if anything, constituted a more highly politized population than the national one. This should be true because the educational level in Iowa exceeds the national

Table 1.6   Party Identification in Iowa and in the United States *

Party Identification	Iowa 1966	United States 1966
Strong Democrat	18.7	17.8
Weak Democrat	19.0	27.4
Independent	20.0	28.0
Weak Republican	17.9	15.0
Strong Republican	20.7	9.5
Other, Don't Know	3.8	2.2
Total	100.1	99.9
No. of cases	1,001	1,291

*The question was "Generally speaking, do you usually think of yourself as a Republican, a Democrat, an Independent, or what?"

SOURCE: The Iowa data came from interviews in November 1966; the data for the United States are from the 1966 post-election study by the Survey Research Center, University of Michigan.

average, and we know that education and political involvement are highly correlated. We can draw from Iowa and national surveys to show the relative political involvement of Iowans and Americans generally; some particularly interesting comparisons appear in Table 1.7. Iowans were somewhat less attentive to governmental or political affairs in 1966 than people in the country as a whole, but they were more likely to talk politics with others and try to persuade them to vote for a party or candidate. Like Americans generally, more Iowans expressed interest in the statewide and Congressional election of 1966. Seventy percent of Iowans reported voting in the 1966 election, compared with only 62 percent of the national sample.

THE DATA FOR ANALYSIS

Within the environment of legislature, representatives, and represented, we have selected sets of data generated by interviewing people (see Table 1.8). Our intent was to compare and explain attitudes toward the legislature held in the general adult public and within political elite groups including the legislators themselves.

Table 1.7   Political Involvement in Iowa and in the United States

Political Activity	Iowa 1966	United States 1966
Follow reports of political and governmental affairs:		
Regularly	44.4	34.7
Often	12.2	30.2
From time-to-time	32.9	17.7
Rarely, never	10.6	17.1
Don't know	--	.3
Total	100.1	100.0
Interested in recent election campaign:		
Very interested	32.8	29.7
Somewhat interested	42.8	39.8
Not much interested	24.1	29.0
Don't know	.4	1.5
Total	100.1	100.0
Talk to people about voting for parties or candidates:		
Yes	33.6	22.2
No	65.7	77.4
Don't know	.8	.4
Total	100.1	100.0
Voted in recent election:		
Yes	70.1	62.1
No, did not vote	29.9	37.6
Don't know	.1	.2
Total	100.1	99.9
Number of cases	1,001	1,291

SOURCE: same as Table 1.6.

To accomplish this, we interviewed a random household probability sample of the adult population of Iowa in November 1966, after the midterm elections. The number of respondents in our population survey came to the convenient total of 1001. These respondents were interviewed in their homes by professional interviewers, and the interviews lasted about an hour. Then during the spring of 1967 we interviewed 181 of the 185 members of the Iowa legislature—including 123 House members and 58 Senators. These legislators were interviewed in the capitol

Table 1.8 Sources of Data for Analysis

Respondents	Number
General public	1,001
Attentive constituents	484
Legislators	181
Lobbyists	99
County party chairmen	90

during the legislative session. In identifying attentive constituents, we proceeded on the assumption that such individuals should, by and large, be salient to legislators themselves; thus it should be possible for legislators to identify at least the major attentive constituents in their own districts. Accordingly, when we interviewed Iowa legislators in 1967, we asked them to nominate persons in their own counties whom they regarded as politically knowledgeable and aware and whose advice they might seek out about legislative issues or problems. From the more than 600 names given us by legislators, we selected and interviewed 484 nominated constituents who matched the communities in which our general population respondents resided. In the same communities, we also interviewed county party chairmen in both major parties if they had not been nominated by legislators as attentive constituents. This strategy gave us interview materials from 90 out of 198 possible Iowa county party chairmen. Finally, we drew a sample of 100 lobbyists from the lobbyist registration lists prepared by the Chief Clerk of the House of Representatives for the 1967 legislative session, and were able to interview 99 of these lobbyists. Since the survey schedule for each of these five groups of respondents contained a common core of comparable interview items, a host of direct comparisons can be made across these five samples.

NOTES

1. Walter Bagehot, *The English Constitution and Other Political Essays* (New York, 1898), p. 207.

2. John Stuart Mill, *Utilitarianism, Liberty, and Representative Government* (Everyman's Library edition, New York, 1950), pp. 238–242.

3. See Ronald D. Hedlund and Charles W. Wiggins, "Legislative Politics in Iowa," in Samuel C. Patterson, ed., *Midwest Legislative Politics* (Iowa City, 1967), pp. 7–36.

4. Democrats again captured control of both houses as a result of the 1974 election.

2 SUPPORT FOR THE LEGISLATURE

Political systems or subsystems, like institutions of all kinds, require public support to survive, to achieve their goals, or to perform effectively. Schools, churches, community chests, and social clubs all require, and ordinarily seek, support among their own members, among potential members, and in the community at large. Large-scale withdrawal of support from such organized groups or institutions usually signals their demise. In a somewhat similar way, legislatures require support to persist, to deal effectively with public and organized group demands, and to make necessary political decisions. In this respect, legislatures probably do not differ from a wide variety of organized groups and institutions. But since legislatures, more than most public and private groups and more than the bureaucratic or judicial branches of the government, are representative political institutions, the generation of public support is an important prerequisite for successful decision making on public policy. Furthermore, by conferring legitimacy and authority on most other governmental acts, the legislature becomes a source of support for the system as a whole. Thus the crucial representative role of legislatures is such that support for the entire political system may well hinge on support for this most representative agency.

THE NATURE OF SUPPORT

Support is a flexible concept because it is incomplete; that is, support is always support for something. Support always takes an object; it makes little sense to talk about support in general. Political scientists have studied the evolution and importance of support for a large number of objects. Support for political parties and candidates is a major focus in political science. The growth of support for particular policies has also been an important part of what political scientists study.

Because support is important in understanding so many aspects of politics, David Easton treats support as one of two major inputs to the political system. He argues that in addition to demands, support provides a "summary variable" with which to examine linkages between the political system and its environment.

Along with support for political candidates, parties, specific policies, and other aspects of politics, Easton insists that one must attempt to understand support for the basic structures of the political system. He has said that

> . . . if demands are to be processed into binding decisions, regardless of whose demands they are, it is not enough that support be collected behind them so as to impress the authorities with the need to adopt them as a basis for decisions. Basically, a large proportion of political research has been devoted to just this matter. Studies of voting behavior, interest groups, parties, and legislative analysis have all sought to reveal the way in which support is distributed, shifted, and mobilized behind varying demands (issues) or behind personalities and leadership groups seeking positions of authority. But if the authorities are to be able to make decisions, to get them accepted as binding, and to put them into effect without extensive use of coercion, solidarity must be developed not only around some set of authorities themselves, but around the major aspects of the system within which the authorities operate.[1]

Easton argues at some length for the necessity of support for the basic structures of the political system. He believes that without such support, government would be possible only through the use of coercion. In the research reported here we have chosen to study support for one of the basic institutions of government in Western democracies—the legislature. It is one of "the major aspects of the system within which the authorities operate," and we sought to understand the basis of public support for this institution.

"Support for a candidate" rather obviously refers to attitudes and behaviors, such as favoring the candidate's election, voting for the candidate, and working in the election campaign. The list is not exhaustive, but there is little question that each item could be classified as support for the candidate. "Support for the legislature" is harder to identify, but the statement of John Stuart Mill, quoted in Chapter 1, provides a beginning frame of reference for conceptualizing legislative support.

Mill suggested that a legislature could not last if the people were not committed to it and compliant with its laws. One component, or dimension, of support for legislatures is the extent to which members of the political system are committed to that system as a political institution. At the extreme, the committed person is willing to preserve and maintain the legislature no matter what it does, and the uncommitted person is willing for it to be abolished. Another dimension of legislative support is compliance—willingness to be obedient, to act in accordance with the programs and enactments authorized by the institution.

It is possible to imagine political leaders seeking to mobilize support in a way that stresses one or the other of the dimensions of support. Leaders may emphasize institutional commitment. They may engage in behaviors and pursue programs designed to engender positive enthusiasm for the system; they may try to mobilize the mass population in a commitment to loyalty and involvement in the system. Or, leaders may stress compliance. They may deliberately attempt to maintain mass political apathy, to distract mass participation, and to foster unquestioning subservience in political circuses and symbols. The point is that although we would expect them to be related, *institutional commitment* and *compliance* are discernible dimensions of legislative support.

The phenomenon we want to explain in this book is legislative support. This is our dependent variable. After we have examined this variable to assess its shape and form, we test the adequacy of a number of independent variables which we think will help to explain why some kinds of people are more supportive of the legislature than others.

MEASUREMENT OF SUPPORT

We have attempted to measure support for the legislature as an institution by recording the degree of agreement or disagreement of respondents to seven attitudinal statements; we expected four of the statements to tap predispositions to comply with the legislative programs and other enactments, and we thought three would tap commitment to the legislature itself. The seven statements are spelled out in full in Table 2.1, which also shows the most intensively supportive proportions for each group of respondents. The category "most intensively supportive" refers to those who *strongly* agreed or disagreed, depending on the direction of the item as given in Table 2.1.

Although the percentages arrayed in Table 2.1 make it clear that large proportions of the Iowa samples expressed attitudes of compliance with the laws passed by the legislature, preference for legislative lawmaking, and commitment to the existence of the legislature as an institution, some notable variations are evident. In the mass public sample, the least legislative support was evinced by the question of the governor taking the law into his own hands rather than waiting for the legislature to act: more than one-fourth of the sample agreed that there were times when the governor should do this, and only 12 percent strongly disagreed. Nearly one-sixth agreed that sometimes citizens should take the law into their own hands without waiting for the legislature to take action, although more than half disagreed and more than one-fourth disagreed strongly. In contrast, very marked legislative support was indicated by the high proportions in the public sample

Table 2.1   Attitudes of Support for the Legislature

Legislative Support Items	Direction of Support	Percent Intensely Supportive					
		Public	Party Leaders	Attentive Constituents	Lobbyists	Legislators
If you don't particularly agree with a state law, it is all right to break it if you are careful not to get caught.	Disagree	42.1	58.9	63.2	64.6	71.3
There are times when it almost seems better for the citizens of the state to take the law into their own hands rather than wait for the state legislature to act.	Disagree	28.0	62.2	67.8	73.7	64.6
Even though one might strongly disagree with a state law, after it has been passed by the state legislature one ought to obey it.	Agree	21.6	38.9	41.9	36.4	51.9
If the Iowa legislature continually passed laws that the people disagreed with, it might be better to do away with the legislature altogether.	Disagree	16.4	32.2	37.8	45.5	57.5
There are times when it would almost seem better for the Governor to take the law into his own hands rather than wait for the state legislature to act.	Disagree	11.8	32.2	43.8	52.5	52.5
One should be willing to do everything that he could to make sure that any proposal to abolish the state legislature were defeated.	Agree	9.8	35.6	38.2	32.3	48.6
It would not make much difference if the constitution of Iowa were rewritten so as to reduce the powers of the state legislature.	Disagree	6.9	14.4	16.3	20.2	31.5
No. of cases		1,001	90	484	99	181

whose responses indicated a belief that citizens ought to comply with laws passed by the legislature regardless of whether a person agreed with them. Less than 3 percent were willing to agree that it was all right to disobey the law. These data suggest that for some, extraordinary action by the governor or by citizens can sometimes be acceptable substitutes for the legislative process, but outright failure to comply when legislative authority has been exercised rarely is acceptable.

Again, in the public sample the items involving retention of the legislature and reduction of its powers produced greater difficulty in responding—there were more "don't know" responses here—but the pattern for the three items is quite similar for those who did respond. Across these items, about 12 percent were willing to consider abolishing the legislature or reducing its constitutional powers. More than two-thirds did not wish to reduce legislative power, 72 percent agreed that proposals to abolish the legislature should be defeated, and more than 78 percent disagreed that the legislature should be abolished if it persistently passed disagreeable laws.

In the elite groups, highly supportive responses were expressed by large proportions of the respondents, compared with the public sample. Thus from nearly two-thirds up to about three-quarters of the party leaders, attentive constituents, lobbyists, and legislators strongly disagreed that it was all right to break state laws or for citizens to take the law into their own hands. From nearly one-third to about half the respondents in the elite groups took the intensively supportive position on questions of obeying disagreeable state laws, abolishing the legislature, or the governor taking matters out of legislative hands.

These seven attitudinal items provided a workable basis for indices of legislative support. For purposes of careful analysis of support, it is desirable to reduce responses for the seven support items to a single score for each respondent. To perform this task, we chose the method of factor analysis which made it feasible to take a close look at the phenomenon of legislative support. We had two hypotheses about the interrelationships of these seven items. We first expected that support for the legislature would form a general dimension. In statistical terms, we expected that all the individual attitudinal items would have high factor loadings on the first factor when subjected to a principal component analysis, and that this factor would account for most of the explained variance. We also thought that this general dimension of support could be divided into two more specific dimensions, which we have already suggested—those of compliance and institutional commitment.

The results of the factor analysis appear in Table 2.2, and they are reasonably in accord with our expectations. The table presents each support item, the principal component factor loadings, the loadings for the two-factor rotated solution, and the variance accounted for. By looking at the bottom of Table 2.2, one can see that

Table 2.2 Dimensions of Legislative Support

Legislative Support Items	Mass Public			Party Leaders			Attentive Constituents			Lobbyists			Legislators		
	PC*	I	II	PC	I	II	PC	I	II	PC	I	II	PC	I	II
1 Times when citizens take law into own hands	.591	.745	.033	.678	.800	-.039	.681	.664	.296	.682	.673	-.263	.685	.791	.038
2 All right to break law if you disagree with it	.594	.679	.116	.474	.607	.042	.584	.823	-.002	.631	.169	-.773	.665	.587	.316
3 Times when the Governor should take law into his own hands	.575	.552	.237	.627	.554	-.316	.524	.310	.433	.571	.731	-.025	.696	.798	.047
4 Ought to obey laws even if one disagrees	-.502	-.505	-.180	-.711	-.664	.290	-.621	-.658	-.218	-.576	-.075	.798	-.624	-.531	-.328
5 Ought to do everything to prevent abolishing the legislature	-.482	.015	-.766	-.463	-.019	.782	-.613	-.155	-.716	-.511	-.520	.179	-.611	-.529	-.306
6 If passed laws people disagreed with do away with legislature	.645	.305	.638	.569	.046	-.578	.583	.256	.571	.676	.742	-.174	.650	.309	.719
7 Wouldn't make much difference if legislative powers were reduced	.580	.226	.632	.508	.249	-.530	.525	.001	.745	.554	.253	-.556	.477	.032	.830
% of total variance	70.5		45.9	67.9		46.1	71.1		49.3	71.1		51.2	74.3		54.0
% of explained variance															

*PC = Principal Component

our first expectation—that the principal component would produce high loadings for all items—was generally borne out. And the principal component accounts for more than 70 percent of the explained variance in every case.

Two factors accounted for about half the total variance in the interrelationships of the seven support items and generally ordered these items in an adequately satisfying way. The analysis for the mass public plainly confirms the bidimensional character of our support items. The first factor is related to the willingness to comply with decisions reached in the legislative system. Four items have high loadings on this factor. (1) There are times when citizens should take the law into their own hands. (2) It is all right to break the law if you disagree with it. (3) There are times when the governor should take the law into his own hands. (4) One ought to obey laws even if one disagrees. For the mass public, these four items all had the highest factor loadings on factor I. Since these four items directly reflect compliance with legislative decisions, we call them together the "compliance factor."

The second factor is related to institutional maintenance. Three items have high loadings on this factor. (1) One ought to do everything possible to prevent abolition of the legislature. (2) If it passes laws people disagree with, better do away with the legislature. (3) It would not make much difference if legislative powers were reduced. Supportive responses to these items indicate a willingness to maintain the legislative system in the face of generally unsatisfactory performance, and we can name it the "institutional commitment factor." As Table 2.2 reveals, the compliance and institutional commitment factors are very clearly distinguishable for the mass public. Only one item has a secondary loading as high as .305, whereas all the primary loadings are substantially higher.

The factor-analytic results with the data from the mass public are replicated for the party leaders sample and, with one deviation in each case, for both attentive constituents and legislators. Only the lobbyists deviate substantially from the dominant factor pattern. Although we cannot fully account for the erratic pattern of factor loadings for the 99 lobbyists in our analysis, the evidence is sufficient to conclude that there are indeed two definable subdimensions of diffuse legislative support in our attitudinal data which deserve some separate consideration. In practice, however, we are mainly concerned with the principal component for the purpose of giving respondents a support score. We used the factor analysis in Table 2.2 to generate standardized factor scores for all respondents, and these scores become our exact measurement of diffuse legislative support, for further analysis.

For the sake of simplicity of presentation, we have divided all respondents into one of three categories—those whose legislative support scores are high, those whose scores are medium, and those whose scores are low. In the High category are those whose support scores fall more than one-half a standard deviation above the mean; Medium scorers are from one-half a standard deviation above the mean to one-half a standard deviation below the mean; Low supporters were more than one-half a standard deviation below the mean. This division of the support scores into three groups makes possible the straightforward comparison of our five groups in terms of their relative levels of legislative support (see Table 2.3). Examination of the percentages for each group makes the sizable differences among them fairly clear. High support shifts from 15 percent in the mass public, to nearly half among lobbyists and attentive constituents, to about two-thirds among legislators. Low support moves in the opposite direction.

Analysis of variance is used to assess intergroup differences in support; we find evidence of very substantial differences in support among the five groups of respondents [$F = 124.36$, degrees of freedom (df) = 4, 1831, $p < .001$]. When the separate factors of compliance and institutional commitment are utilized to compare these groups, group differences hold. For example, when we plot the mean support scores for each group, showing the principal component means and the means for each of the separate factors, group differences in level of support are clear. Figure 2.1 displays these comparisons and shows graphically the extent to which legislative support climbs from the mass public to legislators. Insofar as the principal factor is concerned, the largest difference between groups of respondents occurs between the mass public and the elite groups (*t*-test differences for both dimensions are significant at the .05 level or higher). At the same time, legislators differ significantly in support from the other three elite groups—they are more supportive of the legislature than lobbyists, party leaders, or attentive constituents. The figure indicates that the significantly higher legislative support exhibited by legislators is mainly due to their much higher level of

Table 2.3 Legislative Support by the Mass Public and by Political Elites

Legislative Support (Principal Component)	Mass Public	Party Leaders	Attentive Consti- tuents	Lobbyists	Legis- lators
High	15.2	39.6	49.8	45.5	63.5
Medium	32.0	31.9	29.8	38.4	23.8
Low	52.8	28.6	20.5	16.2	12.7
Total	100.0	100.1	100.1	100.1	100.0
No. of cases	1,001	90	484	99	181

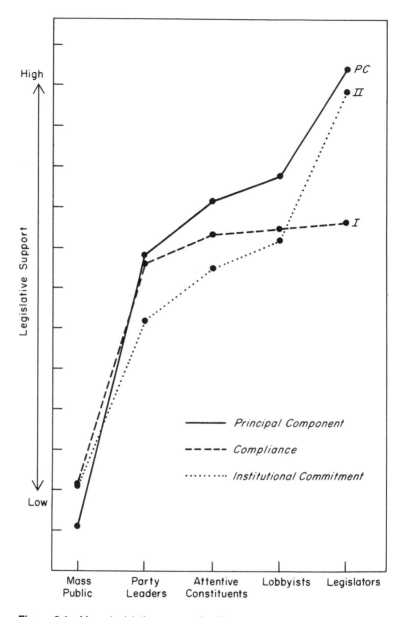

Figure 2.1 Mean legislative support levels.

institutional commitment (factor II). All the elite groups differ significantly from the mass public on the compliance factor (factor I), but they do not differ from one another. However, in the case of institutional commitment, all the elite groups are significantly more supportive than the mass public, and legislators are significantly more supportive than other elite groups. These results are as they should be—we would have no particular reason to expect legislators to be more compliant than other groups of political leaders, but it is quite plausible that as members of the institution, they would be more committed to it than members of elite groups outside the institution.

It should be pointed out that legislative support in the mass public is quite high. In Table 2.3 and Figure 2.1, support in the mass public is shown to be low in relation to political elite groups. But this should not imply in any sense that the mass of citizens do not support the legislature and political elites do support it. In fact, we would expect analyses in other political systems to demonstrate that relative to the appropriate mass publics, support for the legislature in Iowa is high. In general, Iowa is a supportive political environment for the legislature. But we have shown that legislative support grows very dramatically as one goes from the mass public, to county party leaders, to attentive constituents, to lobbyists, to legislators.

EXPLAINING DIFFERENCES IN LEGISLATIVE SUPPORT

The variables we assess in their relative capacity to explain variations in legislative support are portrayed in Figure 2.2. As the figure indicates, the independent variables for this analysis can be grouped into three general categories: political predispositional factors, structural factors, and phenomenal factors. In the predispositional category, we have measured our subjects' ideological orientations, their sense of interpersonal trust, the salience of politics to them, and their sense of political potency. With respect to structural factors, we have gathered data for variations in socioeconomic status and for differences in locations in the political strata. Finally, the factors labeled phenomenal are those which we think affect in an immediate way people's supportive feelings—their views about who influences legislators, who the decisional referents of legislators are, differences between people's expectations about the legislature and how they think it actually is, pride in the system, and a set of perceptions about the role of representation, compromise, experience, and opportunism in the Iowa legislature.

The specific variables included within each factor serve as operational indicators of that factor. Initially the simple relationship of each of these variables to

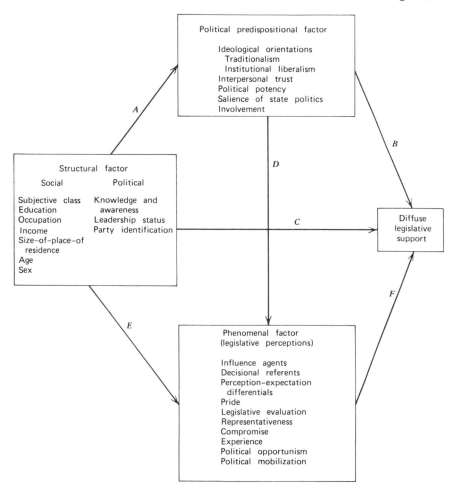

Figure 2.2 Explanatory model for diffuse legislative support in Iowa.

legislative support is examined, to reduce the number of explanatory variables to a more manageable size. In Chapter 9 a more complex analysis is undertaken, aimed at refining further the germaneness of this model.

SUPPORT FOR THE LEGISLATURE AND EVALUATION OF ITS PERFORMANCE

In our 1966 and 1967 interviews we asked respondents to rate the legislature by indicating whether the last session's performance had been excellent, good, fair, or poor. These evaluations provide a rough measure of our respondents' impressions of the adequacy of legislative output. The results of asking for such evaluations from the general adult population sample and the sample of attentive constituents are given in Table 2.4. It is evident that in all groups, evaluations bulge very heavily in the good and fair categories. Rather few rate the legislature as excellent. Differences among groups are not extraordinary, although attentive constituents give the legislature a notably higher rating than do other groups. Interestingly, lobbyists are most critical in their evaluations, with 10 percent of them saying the legislature does a poor job, and a smaller percentage of lobbyists indicated the legislature does an excellent job than was the case for other groups.

Theoretically, support for the legislature and evaluations of its performance should be related in two ways. First, those who are most supportive of the legislature would be likely to have more positive evaluations of the performance of the legislature. Second, we would expect that over time, evaluations of the performance of the legislature would affect the level of support for the legislature. Direct comparisons between the two are presented in Table 2.5, which in effect combines the data in Tables 2.3 and 2.4. To make the presentation more readable, and without doing injustice to the results, we have combined those who rated the legislature as doing an excellent job or a good job into the category "high," and we have labeled as "low" those who rated the legislature as doing a fair job or a poor job. Inspection of Table 2.5 indicates that there is, indeed, some relation between evaluation of legislative performance and legislative support. In every group, a higher proportion of those whose support is high give the legislature a higher rating than do low diffuse supporters. For instance, in the mass public 60

Table 2.4   Evaluation of the Legislature by the Mass Public and by Political Elites

Performance Evaluation	Mass Public	Party Leaders	Lobbyists	Attentive Constituents
Excellent job	4.8	5.0	2.2	7.3
Good job	49.9	53.2	54.4	61.5
Fair job	41.2	33.4	33.3	25.0
Poor job	4.0	8.4	10.0	6.3
Total	99.9	100.0	100.0	100.1
No. of cases	931	90	96	479

Table 2.5   Comparisons of Legislative Support and Performance Evaluation

Group	Performance Evaluation	Legislative Support		
		High	Medium	Low
Mass	High	60.1	55.9	52.7
Public	Low	39.9	44.1	47.4
	Total	100.0	100.0	100.0
Party	High	65.7	48.2	53.8
Leaders	Low	34.3	.51.7	46.2
	Total	100.0	99.9	100.0
Attentive	High	62.6	58.4	47.5
Constituents	Low	37.4	41.6	52.5
	Total	100.0	100.0	100.0
Lobbyists	High	76.7	63.6	50.0
	Low	23.3	32.4	50.0
	Total	100.0	100.0	100.0

percent of the high supporters evaluated the legislature as doing an excellent or good job, whereas only 53 percent of the low supporters gave the legislature those ratings, and this pattern is consistent for the other groups as well. (We cannot include legislators in this comparison because we did not ask them to evaluate themselves; thus we do not have performance evaluation data from them.)

At the same time, it is clear from Table 2.5 that the relationship between evaluation and support is not strong. Except for lobbyists, more than one-third of the high supporters in each group give the legislature a low evaluation; and, roughly half the low supporters in every category are high in their evaluations. To make the case another way, we could compare those who are high or low in evaluations to see if support varied. Doing this produces the same conclusion. There is not a very significant difference between those who evaluate the legislature positively or poorly in terms of variations in support. We conclude that the relation between evaluations of performance and support was positive but fairly weak in Iowa in 1966 and 1967.

Another way to study differences between the two variables is to examine the effect of party identification on them. We would expect party identification to have some effect on evaluation of the performance of a particular session of the legislature. If the legislature were controlled by the Democrats, as was the case in Iowa in 1965, we would anticipate that Democratic Party identifiers would give the legislature a higher rating than Republicans. If the legislature were controlled by the Republicans as the lower house was in 1967 in Iowa, we would expect the reverse. But support for the legislature—support for it as an institution—should not be affected by differences in party identification.

Although we have examined this relationship in our Iowa data, we have not probed these possibilities in great depth. (For example, we have not controlled comparisons between party identification and the two variables for a host of potentially relevant variables that may influence these interrelationships.) Nevertheless, we are satisfied that the bivariate comparisons provide sufficient evidence that the effect of party identification on support works the way we have suggested. As Table 2.6 shows, for example, there is a modest relationship between party identification and evaluation of the legislature. This table presents the results only for the mass public, but the elites manifested similar patterns. For the mass public, who were interviewed following the Democratic-controlled 1965 legislative session, Democratic identifiers gave the legislature a higher rating than did Republican identifiers. If we look at similar tables for the elite respondents, especially for party leaders and attentive constituents, we find that because they were interviewed following the 1967 session (in which the Republicans dominated one house and were a very large minority in the other), Republican identifiers tended to rate the legislature more favorably than Democrats.

The effect of party identification on legislative support is a different matter. Here we do not find a significant relationship between the two. Again, Table 2.7 displays these variables for the mass public sample. Inspection of the table suggests relatively small differences among the categories of party identifiers. If anything, Republicans exhibit higher support than Democrats, whereas the reverse was indicated in the case of evaluations: 15 percent of the Strong Democrats

Table 2.6   Evaluations of the Legislature and Party Identification by the Mass Public

Performance Evaluation	Party Identification				
	Strong Democrat	Weak Democrat	Independent	Weak Republican	Strong Republican
High	64.3	58.4	55.5	53.0	45.7
Low	35.8	41.7	44.5	47.1	54.3
Total	100.1	100.1	100.0	100.1	100.0
No. of cases	179	168	191	168	197

Table 2.7   Support for the Legislature and Party Identification by the Mass Public

Legislative Support	Party Identification				
	Strong Democrat	Weak Democrat	Independent	Weak Republican	Strong Republican
High	15.0	11.1	16.5	12.8	20.8
Medium	33.2	26.8	33.5	31.3	32.4
Low	51.9	62.1	50.0	55.9	46.9
Total	100.1	100.0	100.0	100.0	100.1
No. of cases	187	190	200	179	207

were in the high support category, compared to 21 percent of the Strong Republicans. And results essentially the same as those presented in Table 2.7 are observed for the elite respondents. Differences in party identification do affect evaluations measurably more than they affect support.

We can assess these relationships in a more rigorous way by examining the statistical tests for differences as party identification may or may not influence legislative support. For example, the relationship between party identification and evaluations of legislative performance for the mass public produces a chi-square significant at the .01 level, whereas in the same terms the relationship between party identification and legislative support is not statistically significant. Similarly, t-test differences between strong party identifiers show a significant difference between Strong Democrats and Strong Republicans in the mass public ($p < .01$) for evaluations, but in the case of legislative support the difference between strong identifiers is not significant. However, even in the case of the relation between party identification and evaluations, it should be pointed out that the strength of the relationship is not very great for any group (judging from tau-C's or gammas). For evaluations, there is a positive relation with party identification in the mass public and a moderately negative relation in the elite samples, and the relationships between party identification and evaluation of performance are consistently stronger in all groups than is the case for support.

In this chapter we have identified a hierarchy of support for the legislature that goes from the mass public, through subelites, to legislators. We want to delineate this hierarchy more carefully by probing the effects on support levels of differential social and political strata within these groups of respondents, to provide the completest possible map of support in the political system.

NOTES

1. David Easton, *A Systems Analysis of Political Life* (New York, 1965), pp. 157–58.
2. *Ibid.*, p. 273.

3 THE SOCIOPOLITICAL LADDERS OF SUPPORT

We have chosen two sets of structural factors for mapping the terrain of legislative support in our groups of respondents, by estimating their relative effects on variations in support. Our analysis of social stratification makes use of the variables education, occupation, and income. We would expect support to have a distribution in social and political strata consistent with the findings of research on the effects of stratification on other political phenomena. Such factors as political opinion, voting behavior, political activity, and political influence are likely to differ across social strata. Accordingly, we ought to find that legislative support is strongest among those high in levels of education, occupation, and income.

In addition, we examine the influence of differences in the sizes of places respondents live on variations in legislative support. The conventional wisdom advances the hypothesis of decreasing support with increasing size-of-place, extrapolating from the general notion of the greater potential alienation of constituents in large communities compared with those in small ones. In representational terms, people in smaller communities or rural areas may be thought to have greater proximity to their representatives, thus perhaps might be more likely to support the representative institution. Or, it could be contended that in general, compliance with law and commitment to the established institutional order are better maintained in smaller, rather than larger, ecological areas.

Our analysis of political stratification involves the variables political knowledge and participation. As V. O. Key once argued, "the political system is constructed of strata definable in terms of political activity and influence and independent of occupational strata, income levels, and other such readily perceptible indicators beloved of the sociologist and the daily commentator."[1] As indicators of differentiations among political strata, Key used levels of political involvement, political participation, and sense of political efficacy. Political stratification is important for the functioning of political systems because people in different strata have differential influence on the operation of the system, political stratifications are relatively stable over time, and members of different political strata respond to the same situations in quite different ways. Key and others have argued that it is the activity, beliefs, and support provided by the politically active stratum in the United States that makes for a relatively stable and viable political system.[2] In contrast, data analyzed by Converse and Dupeux lead one to suspect that at least in important respects, the instability of the party system in France is the result of the attitudes of the most politically active stratum of French society.[3] In both systems, the analysts either argue or assume that the politically active stratum has more influence than less active segments, but the effects of the influence of each on the systems differ markedly. Using levels of political knowledge and activity as differentia for political stratification, we expected that persons who had a modicum of knowledge about the legislative institution, its members, and how it works, would exhibit greater support than those in the unaware and inactive strata.

SOCIAL AND POLITICAL STRATA

Our data permit displaying differences in education, occupation, income, and size-of-place in the mass public sample and among political elites. These basic distributions are laid out in Table 3.1. The most marked feature of the comparisons in Table 3.1 is that the lower strata—low level of education and income, and low status occupation—diminish greatly as between the mass public and elite groups. The sharp relationship between high socioeconomic status and elite status is illustrated well by these data. For instance, one-fourth of the mass public sample have only a grade school education or less, compared with about 6 percent of the party leaders, 3 percent of the attentive constituents and lobbyists, and 1 percent of the legislators. One-fifth of the mass public have gone beyond high school, contrasted with from two-thirds to three-fourths of the elites. In occupational terms, Table 3.1 indicates how pervasively political elites are composed of persons from the professional and managerial occupations, compared with the mass public. Twenty-two percent of the respondents in the mass public were in the elite occupational group, but 70 percent of the party leaders, three-fourths of the attentive constituents, 81 percent of the lobbyists, and 58 percent of the legislators were. It is worth noting that one-third of the legislators designated themselves as farmers, a higher proportion than for any other group of respondents. In a farm state, this occupational status for a legislative politician has symbolic political value, but recall that less than 2 percent of the legislators actually live on farms. The farmer-legislators might better be thought of as farm managers, since most of them live in a city.

Income levels escalate like levels of education or occupation. The ''high''

Table 3.1 Characteristics of Respondents: Education, Occupation, Income, and Size-of-Place

Characteristic	Mass Public	Party Leaders	Attentive Consti- tuents	Lobby- ists	Legis lators
Education[a]					
High	20.6	61.5	72.7	73.7	76.8
Medium	52.1	31.9	24.2	23.2	21.0
Low	25.9	5.5	2.9	3.0	1.1
Not ascertainable	1.5	1.1	.2	0.0	1.1
Total	100.1	100.0	100.0	99.9	100.0
Occupation					
Professional & managerial	22.4	70.3	74.4	80.8	58.0
Farmer	18.7	16.5	15.9	5.1	33.1
Sales & service worker	9.2	1.1	1.0	5.1	.6
Foremen, operatives, & laborers	22.5	7.7	3.5	4.0	5.0
Housewives, retired, and other	23.9	3.3	5.0	5.1	3.3
Not ascertainable	3.4	1.1	.2	0.0	0.0
Total	100.1	100.0	100.0	100.1	100.0
Income[b]					
High	26.0	79.1	82.9	86.9	*
Medium	33.4	13.2	11.0	7.1	
Low	18.2	1.1	1.0	1.0	
Not ascertainable	22.5	6.6	5.2	5.1	
Total	100.1	100.0	100.1	100.1	
Size-of-Place					
50,000 or more	24.6	13.2	28.3	74.7	23.2
5,000 - 49,999	24.0	33.0	31.0	13.1	28.2
2,500 - 4,999	6.4	14.3	13.2	0.0	11.0
Under 2,500	22.9	22.0	13.6	3.0	35.9
Farm	21.6	16.5	13.4	9.1	1.7
Not ascertainable	.6	1.1	.4	0.0	0.0
Total	100.1	100.1	99.9	99.9	100.0
No. of cases	1001	91	99	484	181

[a]High = 13 or more years of school completed; Medium = 9-12 years of school; Low = 8 years or less of schooling.

[b]High = $8,000 or more; Medium = $4,000-$7,999; Low = $3,999 or less.
*Data for income were not gathered for legislators.

income group is not very high in an absolute sense, but only 26 percent of the respondents in the mass public report incomes above $8000, compared with 80 percent or more of the elite groups. Similarly, 18 percent in the mass public report quite low incomes, whereas this category fits only 1 percent of the elite respondents. The implications of these comparisons are straightforward: political leaders are very definitely recruited from the upper socioeconomic strata of the population.

Differences in the places of residence of mass public and elite groups are less regular. In the general population sample, about one-fourth live in cities of more than 50,000, another fourth live in cities in the size range of 5000 to 50,000, somewhat more than a fourth live in small cities (under 5000 population), and slightly more than one-fifth live on farms. Fewer party leaders live in the largest cities, and more reside in the smaller ones. Compared with the mass public, attentive constituents tend to reside in the larger communities, and this is markedly more true in the case of lobbyists, many of whom, in the nature of their work, live in Des Moines, the state's largest city. The smallest communities are overrepresented among legislators, and people actually living on farms are most underrepresented. There is a regular decline in the proportions of respondents residing on farms from the mass public to the legislators.

We have defined political stratification in our groups of respondents in terms of levels of political knowledge and participation. To classify respondents on political knowledge, we asked them how often the legislature meets and what the term of the representative is. As Table 3.2 shows, in the mass public only 21 percent could surmount both of these hurdles, thus achieving a classification as "high" in political knowledge. Twenty-nine percent could answer neither question correctly. Using the same criteria, we see that compared with the mass public, elite groups are extraordinarily high in their levels of political knowledge. Almost all party leaders, attentive constituents, and lobbyists were in the "high" category. To categorize respondents on political participation, we asked them if they had voted in the 1966 election and if they talked to others about candidates or parties. Again, these modest thresholds were insurmountable for about one-third of the people in the mass public, and only 29 percent of them had both voted and talked about candidates to others. But as with political knowledge, very high proportions of those in the elite groups were in the "high participation" category. As one might expect from their prescribed role, all party leaders reported voting and talking about candidates and parties. Eleven percent of the attentive constituents and 15 percent of the lobbyists reported only voting.

SUPPORT IN SOCIAL AND POLITICAL STRATA

Having looked at the shape of our respondents in terms of their socioeconomic status and their political status, we now can inquire whether either kind of stratification has any effect on support for the legislature. We have every reason to

Table 3.2 Respondents' Levels of Political Knowledge and Participation

Levels	Mass Public	Party Leaders	Attentive Consti- tuents	Lobby- ists	Legis- lators
Political Knowledge[a]					
High	21.4	95.6	96.7	99.0	*
Medium	48.7	3.3	2.1	0.0	
Low	29.0	0.0	0.2	0.0	
Not ascertainable	0.9	1.1	1.0	1.0	
Total	100.1	100.0	100.0	100.0	
Political Participation[b]					
High	28.6	100.0	89.0	80.8	*
Medium	41.5	0.0	10.5	15.2	
Low	30.0	0.0	0.4	4.0	
Total	100.1	100.0	99.9	100.0	
No. of cases	1001	91	99	484	

[a]Respondents were asked, "Do you happen to know how often the state legislature meets in regular session?" and "Do you happen to know for how long a term are Representatives to the state legislature elected?" High = two correct responses; Medium = one correct response; Low = no correct responses.

[b]Respondents were asked, "Did you vote this November 8th or did something keep you from voting?" and "Did you talk to any people and try to show them why they should or should not vote for one of the parties or candidates?" High = voted and talked to people; Medium = voted only; Low = neither voted nor talked to people.

*These data were not gathered for legislators.

believe that it does. In Chapter 2 we mapped the acceleration of support across groups, which indicates that legislative support climbs dramatically from the mass public to the legislators themselves. Tables 3.1 and 3.2 certainly suggest that social and political status moves in the same way.

In making a general comparison of the effect of these variables on legislative support, we can examine mean legislative support scores at each level of education, occupation, income, political knowledge, and participation, for the entire set of our data. In Figure 3.1 we have graphed these means, and the substantial association between each of the social and political variables is amply demonstrated. In every case, increases in social or political status produce considerable increases in legislative support. Those who are low in social status (persons having

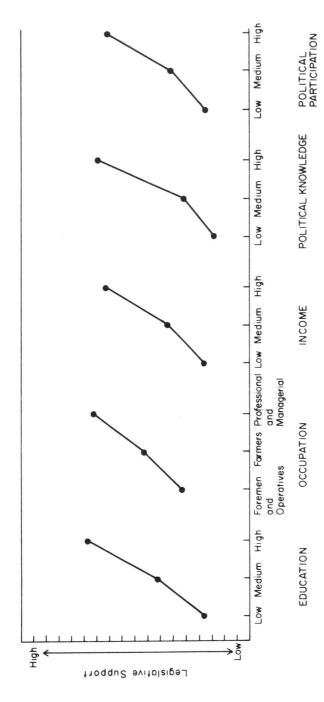

Figure 3.1 Mean legislative support scores by education, occupation, income, and political knowledge and participation (all groups).

only a grade school education or less, who are foremen, operatives or laborers, and who have incomes below $4000 a year) are relatively quite low in legislative support. Those whose social status is high (persons who went beyond secondary school, who are in the professional and managerial occupations, and whose incomes exceed $8000) are relatively higher in legislative support. The same relationship holds for variations in political strata; those high in political knowledge and participation are much more supportive than those in the low strata.

Anticipations about the possible effects of differences in place of residence on legislative support are borne out in none of the Iowa data. In the aggregate, or broken down into individual groups, there is no significant relation between size-of-place and support. Support for the Iowa legislature is spread relatively evenly across the state, from city to small town to farm. This evenness is especially notable for the mass public, where the proportions of respondents in "high," "medium," and "low" legislative support categories are nearly equal in each ecological area from farm to cities of more than 50,000 population. For the elite groups, there is no statistically significant relation—in the sense of significant chi-squares—between systematic variation in size of place and legislative support, but some interesting differences appear. For each elite group except legislators, for example, a higher proportion of the leaders in the largest cities are in the "high" legislative support category than are elite respondents from farm or smallest town communities. Thus to tease a generalization from the data, at least for political elites, we can say that those from the metropolitan areas proportionally exhibit greater support for the legislature than those from the farm. But between farm and metropolis, there are many irregularities in the comparisons of size-of-place and support. In the two largest samples, the mass public and the attentive constituents, legislative support is weakest in the small cities—the ones with populations between 2500 and 5000. The same is true for legislators, but not for party leaders or lobbyists. Although interesting, these differences in support in communities of different sizes should not obscure the main finding—namely, if you systematically increase the size of communities in which respondents live, you do not, in Iowa, systematically increase or decrease the degree of support for the legislature. This condition may be peculiar to areas like Iowa, a very homogeneous state having no very large metropolis, enjoying a high level of rural prosperity, containing almost no major potentially alienated urban population.

SOCIOECONOMIC STATUS AND SUPPORT

In Figure 3.1 we gave the general associations between social and political stratification and legislative support for the mass public and elite samples grouped together. When each group of data is examined separately, these relationships hold up very well. In the case of the socioeconomic status variables, the expected relationship occurs for the mass public and all elite groups except legislators. Levels of education are compared with levels of legislative support in Table 3.3. In the mass public, one-fourth in the high education level are high in legislative support, but only 14 percent in the medium level and 10 percent in the low level are high in support. Party leaders, attentive constituents, and lobbyists exhibit much

Table 3.3   Education and Legislative Support

| Legislative Support | Levels of Education[a] | | |
	High	Medium	Low
Public			
High	25.7	14.0	10.1
Medium	32.0	34.9	27.1
Low	42.2	51.1	62.8
Total	99.9	100.0	100.0
No. of cases	206	521	259
Party Leaders[b]			
High	46.4	26.5	
Medium	28.6	38.2	
Low	25.0	35.3	
Total	100.0	100.0	
No. of cases	56	34	
Attentive Constituents			
High	50.9	46.2	50.0
Medium	30.1	29.9	21.4
Low	19.0	23.9	28.6
Total	100.0	100.0	100.0
No. of cases	352	117	14
Lobbyists[b]			
High	49.3	34.6	
Medium	37.0	42.3	
Low	13.7	23.1	
Total	100.0	100.0	
No. of cases	73	26	
Legislators[b]			
High	63.3	62.5	
Medium	23.0	27.5	
Low	13.7	10.0	
Total	100.0	100.0	
No. of cases	139	40	

[a]High = 13 or more years of school completed; Medium = 9 - 12 years of school; Low = 8 years or less of schooling.

[b]Medium and Low categories are combined because of very small frequencies in the Low education group.

higher levels of legislative support generally, but differences between educational levels remain. Since very few in the elite groups fall into the "low" education category, we have in most cases combined the "medium" and "low" groups. Party leaders of dissimilar educational levels show a substantial difference in legislative support. Nearly a 20 percent difference in high support separates the "high" education level from the others. In the case of attentive constituents, the effect of educational differences is less marked, although the proportion of low legislative supporters grows across educational levels. Again, the effect of education levels remains for lobbyists, since nearly half of them in the "high" education group are high supporters, compared with only one-third in the "medium" and "low" education levels. However, differences in levels of education do not affect legislative support on the part of legislators themselves.

Detailed occupational comparisons are presented in Table 3.4. Because of the small numbers of party leaders, lobbyists, and legislators in some occupational groups, combinations have again been advisable. Support for the legislature increases from mass public to legislators in all occupation groups; and in every set of respondents except for legislators, those in the professional and managerial occupations indicate higher legislative support than in other occupation groups. The difference between professionals' and managers' legislative support and such support in other occupational groups is especially sharp among party leaders. For example, 47 percent of the professional and managerial party leaders exhibit high legislative support, compared with only one-fifth of the farmer party leaders, and slightly less than one-fifth of these in the remaining occupations. As with educational variations, legislators show very high legislative support across occupational groups.

We did not request income data from legislators, but income levels are compared with legislative support for the other groups in Table 3.5. The pattern made familiar from our treatment of educational and occupational levels is repeated in the case of variations in income levels. Generally speaking, legislative support increases from the mass public through the political elites for each category of income level; and in each group, high-income people are more supportive than low-income people. The differences between "high" income respondents and the rest is most marked among party leaders and less notable among lobbyists. Party leaders in the "medium" and "low" income categories are, in fact, proportionately less supportive than similarly classed respondents in the mass public, although there are only a few of them.

The data for education, occupation, and income as they are compared with the general measure of legislative support produce impressive results. As we go from the mass public through each elite group to the legislators themselves, levels of legislative support rise and levels of socioeconomic status rise. But within each

Table 3.4   Occupation and Legislative Support

Legislative Support	Occupational Groups				
	Profes-sional & Mana-gerial	Far-mers	Sales & Service Workers	Foremen, Opera-tives & Laborers	House-Wives Retired & Other
Public					
High	20.1	15.0	17.4	14.2	11.8
Medium	32.6	31.0	31.5	29.8	34.9
Low	47.3	54.0	51.1	56.0	53.4
Total	100.0	100.0	100.0	100.0	100.1
No. of cases	224	187	92	225	238
Party Leaders[a]					
High	46.9	20.0		18.2	
Medium	26.6	40.0		54.5	
Low	26.6	40.0		27.3	
Total	100.1	100.0		100.0	
No. of cases	64	15		11	
Attentive Constituents					
High	51.9	44.2	40.0	41.2	41.7
Medium	28.6	29.9	20.0	35.3	45.8
Low	19.4	26.0	40.0	23.5	12.5
Total	99.9	100.1	100.0	100.0	100.0
No. of cases	360	77	5	17	24
Lobbyists[b]					
High	47.5		36.8		
Medium	37.5		42.1		
Low	15.0		21.0		
Total	100.0		99.9		
No. of cases	80		19		
Legislators[a]					
High	60.0	63.3		87.5	
Medium	27.6	23.3		0.0	
Low	12.4	13.3		12.5	
Total	100.0	99.9		100.0	
No. of cases	105	60		16	

[a]Sales and service workers, foremen, operatives and laborers, and housewives, retired and other are combined because of very small frequencies in individual categories.

[b]Because of the small frequencies in the non-professional/managerial groups, they are combined.

group of respondents, except legislators, there remains a substantial effect of socioeconomic status on legislative support. This analysis emphasizes the pronounced tendency for legislative support to be located in the higher social strata, even among political leaders.

Table 3.5 Income and Legislative Support

Legislative Support	Levels of Income[a]		
	High	Medium	Low
Public			
High	20.8	16.5	12.7
Medium	33.8	35.0	26.5
Low	45.4	48.5	60.8
Total	100.0	100.0	100.0
No. of cases	260	334	182
Party Leaders[b]			
High	44.4	7.7	
Medium	31.9	30.8	
Low	23.6	61.5	
Total	99.9	100.0	
No. of cases	72	13	
Attentive Constituents[b]			
High	51.4	39.7	
Medium	29.4	29.3	
Low	19.2	31.0	
Total	100.0	100.0	
No. of cases	401	58	
Lobbyists[b]			
High	45.3	50.0	
Medium	39.5	25.0	
Low	15.1	25.0	
Total	99.9	100.0	
No. of cases	86	8	

[a]High = $8,000 or more; Medium = $4,000-$7,999; Low = $3,999 or less.

[b]Medium and Low categories are combined because of the very small numbers of elite groups in low income categories.

POLITICAL STRATA AND SUPPORT

In Chapter 2 we demonstrated, in effect, that legislative support varies systematically in terms of different political strata. Our data for political leaders make it very plain that they are substantially more supportive of the legislature than the mass public. And, as expected, political leaders are very high in their levels of political knowledge and participation as we have measured these factors. It remains here to indicate the extent of the effect of political stratification in the mass public, in terms of political knowledge and participation, on legislative support. In addition, we want to see to what extent adding the variables political knowledge and participation to political leadership status may influence the degree of legislative support in leadership groups.

There is a very strong relationship between levels of political knowledge in the mass public and support for the legislature (see Table 3.6). Twenty-eight percent of those who were high in political knowledge were also high in legislative support, in contrast to only 8 percent of those who were low in political knowledge. Low legislative support characterized 40 percent of the high knowledgeables, but 57 percent of the low knowledgeables were low in legislative support. Thus members of the general public who have some minimal knowledge about the legislature are much more likely to support it as an institution than those who do not. Although very few respondents in our political leadership groups were "medium" or "low" in political knowledge by our criteria, and we do not have these data for legislators, the proportions given in Table 3.6 for party leaders and attentive constituents show a relationship consistent with the tendencies displayed by the mass public.

If we take political participation as our desideratum of political stratification, the results are familiar. There is quite a strong association in the mass public between participation and support, with the "high" participation stratum substantially more supportive than the "low" stratum. At the "high" participation level, 21 percent are highly supportive, whereas at the "low" participation level only 10 percent are highly supportive. More concretely, people who participate in political life to the modest extent of voting and talking politics with others are significantly more supportive of the legislative institution than those who do not engage politics to that extent. Since all our party leaders are in the high participation strata, we cannot differentiate among them with respect to support. But attentive constituents and lobbyists are markedly affected by differentiation between "high" participation on the one side and "medium" and "low" participation on the other. The proportion of high supporters drops about 10 percent when "medium" and "low" participators are compared with "high" participators for attentive constituents and lobbyists. And, making the same comparison, there is a 13-percent increase in low support between lower and high participation groups.

We can use the variables political knowledge and political participation as a way of elaborating on our discussion in Chapter 2 of the increase in support across political status groups. Now we are in a position to discriminate within the mass public in terms of involvement levels, thus to more fully set forth the architecture of legislative support in the political system. Figure 3.2 represents the stair-step increase in legislative support across political strata, with the mass public subdivided into three political strata in terms of levels of political knowledge. Trifurcation of the mass public sample by levels of political participation would produce

Table 3.6   Political Knowledge and Legislative Support

Legislative Support	Levels of Political Knowledge[a]		
	High	Medium	Low
Public			
High	27.6	14.4	7.6
Medium	32.7	29.8	35.5
Low	39.7	55.9	56.9
Total	100.0	100.1	100.0
No. of cases	214	287	291
Party Leaders[b]			
High	39.1		33.3
Medium	31.0		66.7
Low	29.9		0.0
Total	100.0		100.0
No. of cases	87		3
Attentive Constituents[b]			
High	50.2		45.5
Medium	30.1		27.3
Low	19.7		27.3
Total	100.0		100.1
No. of cases	468		11
Lobbyists[c]			
High	44.9		
Medium	38.8		
Low	16.3		
Total	100.0		
No. of cases	98		

[a]See Table 3.2 for definition.

[b]Medium and Low categories are combined because of very low frequencies in the Low category.

[c]All lobbyists fell into the High political knowledge category.

essentially the same picture. The three public strata in Figure 3.2 differ significantly from one another in mean legislative support, although the greatest difference is between the "medium" and "high" strata (see Table 3.7). Mass public respondents in the "high" strata provide mean legislative support nearer to that of party leaders than to the lower political strata of the mass public. And, of course, the fairly regular climb of legislative support up the ladder of political strata clearly suggests the importance of linkages between mass publics and elite groups in maintaining the viability of the legislative system. This structure of support for the legislature draws attention to several factors: selective recruitment

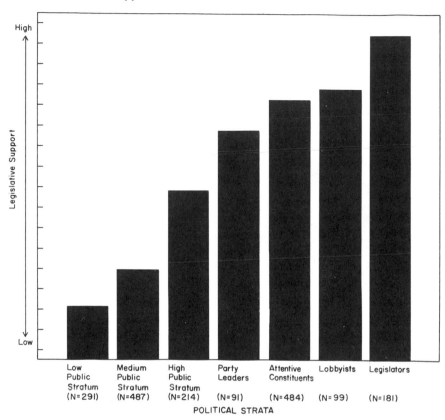

Figure 3.2 Legislative support in political strata.

from the politically active and aware stratum of the mass public, patterns of communication of influence and support up the elite ladder, and institutional positions and roles through which support is held and communicated.

Up to this point, our purpose has been to map support for the legislature in social and political strata of the population; thus we have focused on bivariate relationships. Shortly we assess the influence on legislative support of all these variables taken together. Of course we would expect education, occupation, and income to be highly intercorrelated, and we would not expect an analysis of occupation or income with legislative support to withstand controls for education. As it happens, our expectations are justified. Furthermore, we have indicated that size-of-place is not significantly related to legislative support in Iowa, and this is the case for each level of education. We have argued that social strata and political strata in the Iowa

Table 3.7   Political Participation and Legislative Support

Legislative Support	Levels of Political Participation[a]		
	High	Medium	Low
Public			
High	20.6	14.9	10.4
Medium	32.2	32.3	31.4
Low	47.2	52.8	58.2
Total	100.0	100.0	100.0
No. of cases	300	415	286
Party Leaders[b]			
High	39.6		
Medium	31.9		
Low	28.6		
Total	100.1		
No. of cases	91		
Attentive Constituents[c]			
High	51.0	39.6	
Medium	29.9	28.3	
Low	19.0	32.1	
Total	99.9	100.0	
No. of cases	431	53	
Lobbyists[c]			
High	47.5	36.8	
Medium	38.7	36.8	
Low	13.7	27.4	
Total	99.9	100.0	
No. of cases	80	19	

[a]See Table 3.2 for definition.

[b]All party leaders fell into the High participation category.

[c]Medium and Low categories are combined because of the very small frequencies in the Low category.

population are distinct, and we have mapped legislative support in each dimension. We might suspect the relation between political knowledge and legislative support to be dependent on education levels, but this is not indicated by the data. When controlled for variations in education, political knowledge and support in the mass public are still significantly related. Similarly, when the relation between political participation and legislative support is controlled for education, the two are significantly associated at each education level.

COMPLIANCE AND COMMITMENT

Recall that after defining legislative support in general terms of principal component factor loadings for seven attitudinal items, we showed the bidimensional character of our measure of legislative support, presenting the rotated factor solution calling for two factors. We labeled the factors *compliance* and *institutional commitment*. In this chapter we reported findings on the basis of the general support factor because it displayed our results in the simplest and most direct way. But it is clear that our general measure of legislative support contains two distinguishable subdimensions. However, if we were to make each analysis in a way that presented the results separately for the factors of compliance and commitment, the conclusions to be drawn could not be altered fundamentally. Without recapitulating each comparison in detail, it can be shown that the general pattern of relationships developed with the principal component factor scores for legislative support are not materially disturbed when scores from the two-factor solution are substituted. Table 3.8 is a presentation of the F-ratios for each factor with the six descriptive variables considered earlier. This table includes all respondents for whom measurements were available. With compliance and commitment sepa-

Table 3.8   *F*-Ratios for Factors of Legislative Support and Other Variables

Variables			Rotated Factors			
	Principal Component		Compliance		Institutional Commitment	
	F	P	F	P	F	P
Education	129.42	.01	68.67	.05	52.76	.05
Occupation	45.71	.001	23.43	.01	19.84	.01
Income	72.95	.05	35.56	.05	29.84	.05
Size-of-Place	4.09	*	4.59	*	1.18	*
Political Knowledge	167.41	.01	64.35	.05	78.96	.05
Political Participation	100.94	.01	49.20	.05	40.28	.05

*Not significant

rated, all the variables considered, except for size-of-place, bear a significant relation to support. The same kind of analysis performed on the mass public sample alone provides a pattern of relationships parallel to that depicted in Table 3.8.[4] Again, education, occupation, income, and levels of political knowledge and participation among the mass public are significantly related to legislative support both for the general legislative support factor and for each subdimension taken separately. And in the mass public, once more difference in places of respondents' residence is not significantly related to legislative support. For elite groups, a parallel analysis of variance is not very workable because of the restricted variance of independent variables in these groups. However, inspection of the distributions for the elite groups on the separate factors of compliance and institutional commitment fails to reveal departures from the patterns supplied for the principal factor in Tables 3.3 through 3.7.

Some interesting differences in the effects of education and occupation appear when we examine in detail the relationships between the independent variables in Table 3.8 and the two factors—compliance and commitment—for the mass public sample. The compliance scores for respondents with college and high school educational experience differed strongly from those of subjects with only grade school experience, whereas college and high school groups were less different. In contrast, commitment proved to be much stronger in the college group, and there was a lesser difference between the high school and grade school groups. To put it more succinctly, the break for compliance seems to come between high school and grade school groups, and the break for commitment appears to occur between college and high school groups. We noted earlier that using principal component scores, significant differences occurred between professionals and managers on the one hand, and other occupational groups on the other. Also, professionals and managers in the mass public differed from farmers in general legislative support. Compliance and commitment work somewhat differently between occupational groups. When compliance is taken alone, professionals and managers still differ significantly from workers and housewives, but no longer from farmers. Now, farmers also differ from workers and housewives. When institutional comitment is taken alone, the professional-manager group is significantly different from farmers. And the difference between the professional-manager group, and workers and housewives, although significant, is not nearly as strong as it was with compliance.

MULTIPLE EFFECTS ON LEGISLATIVE SUPPORT

Perhaps the best way to summarize the results of our analysis of legislative support up to this point is to examine the correlations among the major variables we have discussed and assess the relative effects of the independent variables——socioeconomic status, political knowledge, and political participation. As a check on our assessment of the importance of evaluation of legislative performance to support presented in Chapter 2, we have added evaluation of the job of the legislature to the summary.

The critical product-moment correlations (Table 3.9) reveal that legislative performance evaluation bears virtually no correlation with socioeconomic status, political participation, or political knowledge. Here socioeconomic status combines our data for education, occupation, and income in a single scale. Furthermore, evaluation has a very low correlation ($r = .11$) with support. Political participation is quite highly correlated with socioeconomic status and political knowledge, and as we suggested earlier, the correlation between political participation and legislative support is positive and modestly high ($r = .46$). Political knowledge and socioeconomic status also are fairly highly correlated, and socioeconomic status has, again, a modestly high correlation with legislative support ($r = .41$). Finally, as we have already suggested, political knowledge is positively correlated with support ($r = .40$). Thus our major independent variables—socioeconomic status, political knowledge, and political participation—are all correlated in about the same magnitudes with legislative support. They also are highly correlated among themselves: in particular, political knowledge and participation are very highly correlated. The heavy multicollinearity of our independent variables to some extent confounds the net effect of each on legislative support, because each is so substantially affecting the other. Neverthe-

Table 3.9 Intercorrelations of Major Variables

Variables	Performance Evaluation	Political Partici- pation	Socio- economic Status	Political Knowledge
Political participation	.03			
Socio-economic status	.01	.65		
Political knowledge	.01	.74	.57	
Legislative support	.11	.46	.41	.40

less, it is possible to assess the net effects of the independent variables by calculating the multiple regression. If we give legislative support the label X_1, and call performance evaluation X_2, political participation X_3, socioeconomic status X_4, and political knowledge X_5, the multiple regression equation for these data is:

$$X_1 = .09 + .07X_2 + .27X_3 + .18X_4 + .11X_5.$$

The multiple correlation of these independent variables against legislative support is .5, which means that they account for 25 percent of the variance in support. From the regression equation it is plain that in this tentative system of variables, levels of political participation contribute the most to accounting for variations in legislative support (because $\beta = .27$ for X_3), with socioeconomic status making the second most important contribution ($\beta = .18$ for X_4), followed by political knowledge ($\beta = .11$ for X_5). Although there is a small positive correlation between performance evaluation and support ($r = .11$), the regression analysis suggests that the net effect of performance evaluation on support is probably trivial ($\beta = .07$ for X_2).

NOTES

1. V. O. Key, Jr., *Public Opinion and American Democracy* (New York, 1961), pp. 197–198.

2. For instance, see *ibid.*, pp. 536–558; and Robert A. Dahl, *Who Governs?* (New Haven, Conn., 1961), pp. 311–325. Key labeled the highest level of political stratification the "activist subculture"; Dahl uses the term "political stratum."

3. Philip E. Converse and Georges Dupeux, "Politicization of the Electorate in France and the United States," *Public Opinion Quarterly*, Vol. 26 (Spring 1962), 1–23.

4. These data are presented in greater detail in G. R. Boynton, Samuel C. Patterson, and Ronald D. Hedlund, "The Structure of Public Support for Legislative Institutions," *Midwest Journal of Political Science*, Vol. 12 (May 1968), 163–180.

4 LINKAGES BETWEEN CITIZENS AND LEGISLATORS

The ladders of support for the legislature in the social and political structure naturally draw attention to the cementing functions of linkage groups, including party leaders, attentive constituents, and lobbyists, in locking constituents and their representatives together. These political actors are among those whom V. O. Key called the "middlemen" of politics. Whether its members were characterized as middlemen, political activists, or influentials, Key thought that the "thin stratum" lying across the structural path between mass opinion and the upper layer of the political elite was critical to the maintenance and persistence of democratic regimes. He argued that the middlemen could constitute a distinctive political subculture sufficiently independent and diverse to provide the pluralism necessary for the democratic formula, sufficiently active and involved to be able to acquire and exploit access to both the narrower circles of political leadership and the wider circles of political participation, and sufficiently imbued with common motives and norms to maintain and promote public trust, restraint in the exploitation of public opinion, and etiquette in the conduct of opposition politics.[1]

THE ACTIVIST SUBCULTURE

As seen earlier, our samples of party leaders, attentive constituents, and lobbyists appear to constitute a significant slice of the politically active subculture, and as such we can compare them with the public in general and with legislators to make inferences about their capacity to link representatives and represented.[2] We have already showed (in Table 3.1) the extent to which the linkage groups are similar, and akin to legislators, in their locations in the social structure. Like legislators, and distinctly different from the public as a whole, the activists in the linkage groups are characterized by high socioeconomic status; thus access to legislative elites by these middlemen ought *not* to be impeded by social gaps between them. Just as legislators and middlemen rise from roughly the same social milieu, it can be demonstrated that their political life experiences are similar.

We asked our elite respondents about the frequency of political discussion in their homes when they were growing up, whether their parents had been active in politics other than simply voting in elections, whether any family member had held political office, and what their earliest recollections of interest in politics were. Table 4.1 reveals a general pattern of political background similarity between

Table 4.1   Political Leaders' Recollections of Early Political Environment

Political Recollections	Party Leaders	Attentive Constituents	Lobbyists	Legislators
Frequency of political discussion at home while growing up:				
A great deal	42.2	40.1	34.3	39.2
Somewhat	30.0	37.4	43.4	37.0
Not much	23.3	18.4	21.2	19.3
Not at all	4.4	4.1	1.1	4.5
Total	99.9	100.0	100.0	100.0
Other immediate family members active in politics:				
Yes	42.2	39.7	44.4	39.2
No	57.8	60.3	55.6	60.8
Total	100.0	100.0	100.0	100.0
Other immediate family members held political office:				
Yes	46.7	52.9	34.3	32.0
No	53.3	46.9	65.7	68.0
Total	100.0	99.8*	100.0	100.0
Earliest recollection of being interested in politics:				
Pre-teens	27.8	32.9	21.2	22.1
Teens	32.2	34.1	43.4	33.7
Adult	36.7	28.5	31.3	28.7
Late adult	1.1	2.5	0.0	8.8
Undeterminable	2.2	2.1	4.0	6.7
Total	100.0	100.1	99.9	100.0
No. of Cases	90	484	99	181

*This datum was not available for one attentive constituent.

middlemen and legislators. These political leaders come from highly politicized family environments. About two-fifths in each group reported a great deal of political discussion at home while they were growing up, and about the same proportion said that other immediate family members were politically active. Presumably, the highly charged political atmosphere in which these political actors were reared contributed heavily to their early political socialization. Large majorities (more than two-thirds in the cases of attentive constituents and lobbyists) reported their earliest recollections of political interest occurring prior to adulthood.

In the same vein, party leaders, attentive constituents, lobbyists, and legislators have, to a very considerable extent, shared adult political experiences. Roughly half the party leaders and lobbyists had held some public office, as had more than two-thirds of the attentive constituents; and half the legislators had held public office before entering the legislature (see Table 4.2). Vast majorities in all these leadership groups had engaged in ordinary kinds of adult political activities,

Table 4.2   Political Leaders' Adult Political Experiences

Political Experience	Party Leaders	Attentive Constituents	Lobbyists	Legislators
Held public office	53.3	64.9	48.5	49.1
Only elected office	23.3	30.8	15.2	29.8
Only appointed office	12.2	15.9	24.2	13.8
Both	17.8	18.2	9.1	5.5
Never held office	45.6	34.9	51.5	50.3
Make financial contributions	100.0	92.1	80.8	96.7
Attend party meetings	100.0	81.6	75.8	96.1
Served as party convention delegate	100.0	61.8	40.4	82.9
Campaigned for other candidates	97.8	76.7	69.7	86.2
Helped plan campaign strategy	93.3	69.2	45.5	77.3
Held a formal party leadership position	100.0	49.6	34.3	53.6
No. of cases	90	484	99	181

including making financial contributions to parties and candidates, attending party meetings, and participating in campaign activities. Eighty-three percent of the legislators had served as party convention delegates, and 54 percent had held formal positions of leadership in their party. Contrary to some conventional wisdom about the nonpartisan stance of political interest groups, even lobbyists were quite active in party affairs, with 40 percent having served as convention delegates and one-third having occupied party office. Further overlapping among these groups of political actors—in terms of their current status rather than their previous experience—is minimal. Only 7 percent of the attentive constituents had served in the legislature, and only about 7 percent of this group were party leaders, serving as county party chairmen at the same time they were nominated as attentive constituents. Only 1 percent of the attentive constituents were also lobbyists. Since no other overlappings occurred, these activists can be said to be largely independent of one another in terms of their current political status, but they have shared to a considerable extent the same kinds of political experiences.

We indicated in Chapter 3 that party leaders, attentive constituents, and lobbyists share high levels of rudimentary political knowledge about the legislature and that they are highly involved in everyday politics, in contrast to the mass public. Here it is useful to spell out these facets of politization in greater detail than was necessary in the earlier discussion. These details are displayed in Tables 4.3 and 4.4, which reveal the high levels of legislative awareness and political involvement characterizing the leadership groups. It is plain enough that party leaders, attentive constituents, and lobbyists constitute a very homogeneous subculture, illustrated particularly well by their high degree of politization vis-à-vis the mass public. That these middlemen are highly involved in politics is demonstrated by their substantial early political socialization and family political experiences, their political awareness and involvement, and their considerable adult political experience. They share with legislators a highly politicized subculture. Differences between these middlemen of politics and the public at large are very sharp. The middlemen can deal with legislators at their own level and in their own terms. At the same time, there is limited though impressive evidence that the middlemen are in substantial touch with ordinary constituents on a fairly wide basis. Nearly 99 percent of the party leaders, about 90 percent of the attentive constituents, and even 85 percent of the lobbyists, reported talking to citizens about voting for parties or candidates in connection with election campaigns. We think it is fair to assume that most of these contacts were not intramural and that the political middlemen (especially the party leaders and the attentive constituents, who were more widely dispersed geographically) were "opinion leaders" in their communities.

Table 4.3   Legislative Awareness of Public and Elite Groups

Legislative Awareness	Public	Party Leaders	Correct Responses Attentive Constituents	Lobbyists
How many legislators represent county in House and Senate?	22.2	89.0	88.4	87.9
Which party do they belong to?	16.1	84.6	83.1	86.9
How often does the legislature meet in regular session?	24.2	94.5	97.5	99.0
For how long a term are Representatives elected?	67.3	97.8	97.9	99.0
For how long a term are Senators elected?	34.4	92.3	84.3	94.9
Which party controlled the House during the last session?	64.4	97.8	95.7	97.0
Which party controlled the Senate during the last session?	62.5	97.8	95.7	97.0
No. of cases	1,001	90	484	99

We expected contact between party leaders and the mass public to be higher than for other linkage groups, and it was. Political parties are often given prominence in analyses of relations between the mass public and the governing elites. In the American context there are other middlemen in legislative politics, but the important role of party linkages should not be underestimated. A rough indicator of the partisan character of linkage politics in the Iowa context is suggested by comparisons of strength of party identification across the groups we are examining (see Table 4.5). These distributions help to illustrate the extent of Republican Party bias in the Iowa setting. The public is about evenly divided in terms of Democratic and Republican identifiers, and so are the party leaders. (In the latter case, however, county chairmen were deliberately sampled, allowing us to equate the two parties; i.e., both party chairmen were interviewed in sample counties.) Yet

Table 4.4   Political Involvement of Linkage Groups

Political Involvement	Public	Party Leaders	Attentive Constituents	Lobbyists
Interested in politics a great deal	17.9	93.4	85.3	84.8
Very interested in election campaigns	32.8	98.9	91.7	89.9
Follow reports of political and governmental affairs nearly every day	44.4	94.5	93.6	93.9
Read magazines for information about public affairs weekly or more often	27.9	85.7	83.4	78.8
Talk to people about voting for parties or candidates	33.6	98.9	89.6	84.8
Worn campaign button or put sticker on car	21.2	97.8	74.5	53.5
Voted in November 1966 election	70.1	98.9	99.6	96.0
No. of cases	1,001	90	484	99

this equal distribution notwithstanding, legislators, lobbyists, and attentive constituents tended to be strongly identified as Republicans—since attentive constituents were nominated by the preponderantly Republican legislature, we expected them to be overwhelmingly Republican. More interesting are comparisons
among these groups in the strength of party identification. In general, we would
anticipate political activists to reflect greater strength of party identification than
ordinary people, and this expectation is borne out by the data. The proportion of
party leaders who are also strongly identified is significantly larger than the
proportion of those in other leadership groups. Also, the lobbyists, who probably
can least afford strong partisan ties if they are to work with both parties, have the
lowest proportion of strong identifiers of any elite group. Unexpected is the
substantial proportion of the general public indicating a strong party
identification—39 percent.

A second indication of the high politization levels among party leaders and

Table 4.5   Party Identification of Public and Elite Groups

Party Identification	Public	Party Leaders	Attentive Constituents	Lobbyists	Legislators
Strong Democrat	18.7	46.7	18.2	12.1	23.7
Weak Democrat	19.0	2.2	3.3	8.1	11.6
Independent	20.0	0.0	7.9	21.2	0.0
Weak Republican	17.9	0.0	10.3	14.1	14.9
Strong Republican	20.7	51.1	59.1	41.4	49.7
Other, Don't Know	3.8	0.0	1.2	3.0	0.0
Total	100.1	100.0	100.0	99.9	99.9
Strong Identifiers Regardless of Party	39.4	97.8	77.3	53.5	73.4
No. of cases	1,001	90	484	99	181

attentive constituents is their self-reported consistency of party voting in state legislative elections. Only 6 percent of the party leaders indicated that they had voted for candidates of different parties for state legislative office whereas 19 percent of the attentive constituents reported such inconstancy. On the other hand, voting for candidates of different parties was reported much more frequently by lobbyists and the public: 48 percent of those in the public sample said that they crossed party lines in legislative elections, as did 58 percent of the lobbyists. These variations in strength of party identification and voting constancy suggest that linkages between the mass public and legislators through party leaders and attentive constituents occur to a marked extent through partisan channels, whereas lobbyists provide linkages that are relatively less partisan. And of course these findings are in accord with the widely held view of lobbyists—namely, that they constitute a mediate group operating in comparatively less partisan terms than other linkage groups.

We can illuminate the partisan character of linkages between legislators and other political elites in greater detail by considering attentive constituents. These respondents were sampled from among nominees provided by legislators. This nomination process makes it possible to assess the extent to which partisan considerations were salient to legislators in identifying persons with whom they would interact on legislative matters. In Table 4.6 attentive constituents are divided by strength of party identification in terms of the political party affiliation of the nominating legislators. The partisan bias in legislators' awareness and identification of attentives in their constituencies is very pronounced. Attentive

Table 4.6   Partisan Links Between Legislators and Attentive Constituents

Party of Nominating Legislators	Party Identification of Nominated Attentive Constituents				
	Strong Democrats	Weak Democrats	Independents	Weak Republican	Strong Republicans
Democrats	77.3	43.8	23.7	12.0	6.6
Republicans	22.8	56.3	76.4	88.0	93.4
Total	100.1	100.1	100.1	100.0	100.0
No. of cases*	88	16	38	50	286

*Six Attentive Constituents who got multiple nominations are omitted from this table.

constituents who could be classified as Strong Democrats were preponderantly nominated by Democratic legislators, whereas Strong Republican attentives were almost invariably nominated by Republicans in the legislature. At the same time, most Weak Democrats and Independents among attentive constituents were nominated by Republican legislators, indicating the imperfect character of the partisan bias in legislators' perceptions of their most attentive constituents. To avoid the impression that Republican legislators substantially identified Democratic attentives in their districts, however, we must consider the data in Table 4.6 from a different perspective. If we calculate the percentages of Democratic and Republican attentive constituents who were nominated by legislators in both parties, it is clear that Democratic legislators were more inclined than their Republican colleagues to nominate attentive constituents who were identified with the opposite political party. Eighty-three percent of the Republican legislators nominated attentives who identified themselves as Republicans, and only 7 percent named Democratic attentives. On the other hand, 23 percent of the Democratic legislators nominated Republican attentives, whereas 68 percent nominated attentives from their own party. Such interparty differences among legislators might be expected in a political milieu like that of Iowa, where one party has traditionally been dominant. In this context, interestingly enough, Republican constituents were more accessible to Democratic legislators than Democratic constituents were to Republican legislators, although the Republicans were the majority party.

COMMUNICATION LINKAGES

Although we may be satisfied that by showing the existence of a number and variety of affinities among elite groups and legislators we have also demonstrated the existence of a linkage, this assumption may be unwarranted. A sharing of levels of political socialization, political experience, awareness, activity, and partisan commitment is no guarantee that these elites play a brokerage role. What we really need to know is how effectively these elite respondents act as *middlemen* in terms of their contacts with authoritative decision makers and their communication links with the general public. We have already suggested the piece of evidence (reports of talking with citizens about elections) that implies substantial communication linkages between those in the elite groups and the mass public, but our data do not permit us to go beyond this.

On the other side of the ledger, our evidence is rather abundant concerning communication between middlemen and legislators. In our interviews with party leaders, attentive constituents, and lobbyists, we asked about discussion of public problems with local, state, or national governmental officials in general, and then inquired about the extent to which they talked to legislators from their own districts. That almost all our middlemen have extensive contact with public officials is indicated by Table 4.7. Large proportions of party leaders and attentive constituents reported frequent communication with governmental officials and with legislators from their home districts. As could have been anticipated, lobbyists' reports of communications with officials, and particularly with legislators,

Table 4.7   Linkage Contacts

Extent of Linkage	Party Leaders	Attentive Constituents	Lobbyists
Talk about public problems with governmental officials, local, state, or national	98.9	99.4	98.0
Quite often	59.3	58.8	68.7
Often	31.9	26.2	19.2
Not very often	7.7	14.4	10.1
Talk to state legislators from their districts about public problems	95.6	97.6	99.0
Quite often	52.7	57.6	80.8
Often	25.3	26.2	11.1
Not very often	17.6	18.8	7.1
No. of cases	90	484	99

fully indicate their own special location in the linkage structure. These and other items of information about attentive constituents and the other middlemen suggest the likelihood that the middlemen served in overlapping roles between legislators and constituents, forming part of the communicative, active, responsive public for several constituencies.[3] Furthermore, the contacts these middlemen maintained at the state and national levels of government were almost wholly *legislative* in character. For example, very few attentive constituents reported talking regularly to national or state administrative officials (only 5 percent in the case of the national level, and 15 percent at the state level).

The content of communications exchange between middlemen and legislators appears to be largely in the realm of statewide policy. In response to our queries about what matters party leaders, attentive constituents, and lobbyists discussed with state legislators, some mentioned talking about local governmental affairs, but the overwhelming majority reported dealing with statewide issues. The most frequently named topics were state financial problems and education. Again this trend can be illustrated by focusing on the responses of attentive constituents: 59 percent said that they discussed budgetary and tax problems with their legislators, with the most prominent issue being property tax relief, followed by education (reported by 26 percent). Notably missing from the reported content of discussion between all the middlemen—attentive constituents, party leaders, and lobbyists alike—and legislators, is communication that is strictly political. Only fragmentary mention was made by any middlemen respondents of issues like patronage, personnel, reelection problems, party-organizational issues, or political strategy. Thus our data point strongly to the predominance of policy issues in discussions between political middlemen and legislators.

In the mass public, the substantive content of public policy may be of relatively minimal concern, and beliefs about policy issues may tend to be vaguely and inconsistently organized; correlatively, it is possible that communication between political middlemen and ordinary citizens is more likely to concentrate on the attractiveness of various candidates and on a concern about public services.[4] But between middlemen and legislators, communication appears to be overwhelmingly in the realm of substantive policy questions.

Our political middlemen reported not only talking frequently to legislators but also attempting to influence them and thinking that such attempts were efficacious. Comparisons between linkage groups and the mass public are made in Table 4.8, which displays responses to our questions about whether respondents had tried to influence a legislative decision, how successful they thought they could be in changing laws they considered to be bad or unfair, and how likely it was that they would try to do something about such laws. In addition, Table 4.8 includes

Table 4.8   Influence Attempts by Linkage Groups

Influence Attempts	Public	Party Leaders	Attentive Constituents	Lobbyists
Have met state legislators or seen them at a meeting	52.3	97.8	98.0	96.0
Have done something to try to influence a decision by the state legislature				
Often	1.2	25.3	35.5	78.8
Several times	8.3	47.3	50.0	17.2
Once or twice	16.7	18.7	9.5	3.0
Never	71.0	6.6	3.9	0.0
No response	2.9	2.2	1.0	1.0
Likelihood of success of efforts to change a state law considered harmful or unjust				
Very likely	3.9	13.2	10.3	23.2
Moderately likely	7.7	33.0	27.5	30.3
Somewhat likely	20.8	33.0	43.2	32.3
Not at all likely	61.3	18.7	16.1	12.1
No response	6.4	2.2	2.9	2.0
Likelihood of actually doing something to change a legislative enactment considered harmful or unjust				
Very likely	13.0	73.6	71.9	81.8
Moderately likely	13.4	16.5	18.0	11.1
Somewhat likely	28.5	6.6	7.0	6.1
Not at all likely	40.1	1.1	2.1	1.0
No response	5.1	2.2	1.0	0.0
No. of cases	1,001	91	484	99

answers to our general question about the extent to which respondents had met or seen legislators. (Note that in spite of their relatively low level of legislative awareness, more than half the respondents in the general public reported having met a legislator; and almost all the respondents in the linkage groups reported this.)

In terms of influence attempts and their efficacy, fairly dramatic gaps separate the mass public from the elite groups. Seventy-one percent of the public sample said they never had done anything to try to influence a decision by the legislature, compared with 7 percent of the party leaders, 4 percent of the attentive constituents, and none of the lobbyists. Nor surprisingly, more than three out of four lobbyists reported regular influence attempts, but impressively high proportions of party leaders and attentive constituents also reported frequent influence efforts. Attitudes toward the likely success of effort to change state laws are fairly optimistic among the elite groups, whereas pessimism in the general population is very marked. A further indication of differences between the public and the elite in influence activity is apparent from data regarding the likelihood of doing anything at all to change state laws. More than 70 percent of all the elite respondents felt that their efforts to affect state legislation would be successful compared with 61 percent in the mass public who indicated a belief that there was little likelihood of their successfully altering legislation. Correspondingly, proportions ranging above 70 percent of the elites indicated a high probability that they would try to do something to effect legislative change; yet 40 percent of the public sample said it was unlikely that they would attempt any action. In sum, we have convincing evidence that the politically active subculture we have identified in Iowa consists of more than combined sets of persons who share status and political experience. They interact regularly with legislators, largely in public policy terms; they attempt to influence legislators' public policy decisions; and they have a fair amount of confidence that the effort is likely to yield desired results. Because of this interaction and exchange, it seems highly probable that in some sense, support for the legislature is exchanged as well; however, our hard data do not permit us to explore this directly. Presumably compliance with legislative outcomes, and particularly commitment to the institutional life of the legislature, are developed as a result of policy exchanges between middlemen and legislators in the course of their contacts, and the legitimacy of the institutional fabric may be, at least symbolically, passed down from middlemen to mass public.

THE ROLE OF MIDDLEMEN IN LEGISLATIVE RECRUITMENT

Involvement in the recruitment of legislators constitutes a special case of the linkage function of middlemen in politics. The recruitment of legislators cannot be accounted for in terms of their relatively high socioeconomic status simply because, in this regard, they do not differ significantly from members of other elite groups who are not similarly recruited. Nor can legislative recruitment as such be explained in terms of differences attributable to early political socialization or the prelegislative political experiences of legislators. Variables like early recollection of political events and young adult political apprenticeship tend to distinguish elites from mass publics, but they do not distinguish very well among elites, including legislators. (Such experiences probably form the conditions under which the politically active subculture comes to exist.) Thus political recruitment, in general, is a process in which people enter the politically active subculture, but legislative recruitment involves further movement beyond the politicized stratum. Such movement appears to result from a combination of opportunity, availability, and recruitment contact. For example, a finite number of legislative seats will become available in any election year, and a limited number of people will be available to "stand for them" in the sense of desiring and being able to seek legislative office. The number of potential legislators will be further restricted by the desires of the electorate—that is, by the identities of the candidates the public wants. Matching the available people to the available legislative offices is largely a matter of recruiters making contacts within a "pool" of appropriate candidates. [5]

Some legislators are "self-starters" in the pure sense—that is, they recruit themselves for office. [6] These politicians are motivated to seek public office for a variety of personal reasons, which we explore in a future section. Here it is enough to say that self-starters are a rare commodity, especially in Iowa, where extensive contacts by political recruiters make it difficult to isolate pure self-starters. However, if we identify those who feel they were drafted for public service, we are able to test, in part, our notions about self-starters. For example, in our sample of party leaders, 52 percent said they became county chairmen either because they were talked into it or because they were asked to run. Forty-four percent of the 1967 legislators indicated that having been drafted to seek election was a major consideration in their running for office. Our strong impression is that few were pure self-starters, and much of our data pointedly imply the crucial role of recruitment contacts in legislative candidacy.

We expected to find a heavy investment in legislative recruitment activity made by party leaders, attentive constituents, and even lobbyists. A high degree of engagement in legislative recruitment by political middlemen is a rough indicator of the extent to which middlemen serve as potential cue givers to representatives, and the nature of their service; also indicative is the tendency to talk to legislators about policy issues, in attempts to influence them. In a political environment marked by the existence of powerful party organizations with well-established internal party discipline, most recruitment contacts for partisan office should be made by party leaders. [7] But since party organization is generally not very highly developed in Iowa, we expected legislative recruitment contacts to come from other elements of the linkage structure as well. In our surveys, we asked party leaders, attentive constituents, and lobbyists to indicate the approximate number of times they had been sought out by prospective candidates for public office and how many times they had suggested candidacy to others. These contact reports included all public offices, but as we shall illustrate with attentive constituents, responses were given overwhelmingly in terms of state legislative officers.

More recruitment contacts were reported by party leaders than by attentive constituents or lobbyists (see Figure 4.1). Three-fourths of the party leaders said "several" or "many" candidates had talked to them prior to the announcement of their candidacy for political office, compared with 55 percent of the attentive constituents and half the lobbyists. Similarly, two-thirds of the party leaders said they urged candidacy for office on prospects, and 40 percent of the attentive constituents and one-third of the lobbyists reported direct recruiting activity of this

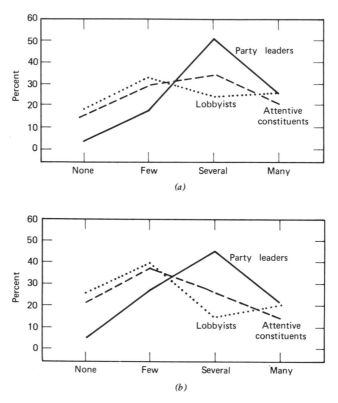

Figure 4.1 Recruitment contacts reported by party leaders, attentive constituents, and lobbyists. *(a)* Candidates talked to person before announcing candidacy; *(b)* Person suggested candidacy for office.

kind. These findings indicate that although party leaders stand at the forefront of political recruitment, substantial recruitment activity is reported by attentive constituents and even by lobbyists. The Iowa findings show that 85 percent of the attentives and 82 percent of the lobbyists did report some incidence of candidate contact, and more than three-fourths in both groups reported that they sought or suggested candidates for public office. The legislative recruitment function in Iowa is by no means the sole domain of party leaders; it is shared with other members of the politically active subculture represented by the leadership groups analyzed here.

The kinds of recruitment contacts reflected in Figure 4.1 were concerned primarily with legislative recruitment, where they had a relatively heavier emphasis on recruitment to the state legislature. For example, when we consider attentive constituents, we find that a significant proportion were involved in the recruitment of candidates for local offices that were heavily legislative in character—about half the attentives reported involvement in the recruitment of county supervisors, city councilmen, and other county and city officers. Furthermore, about one-third of the attentives were recipients of candidacy contacts from prospective members of Congress, and slightly more than one-fifth reported suggesting candidates for Congress. But it is in the scope of state offices that the recruitment role of attentive constituents is most pronounced. Three-fourths of the attentives reported that candidates for state offices discussed their candidacies with the respondents, and two-thirds suggested candidates for state offices. Of these, the overwhelming proportion were candidacies for the state legislature. Forty-two percent of the attentives said that candidates for the Iowa House of Representatives discussed their candidacies with the respondents prior to announcing, and 18 percent said that they had had prior consultations with senatorial candidates. Again, 35 percent of the attentives reported suggesting legislative candidacy to prospective members of the House of Representatives, and 14 percent said that they had been helped recruit prospective senators. Thus it would seem that attentive constituents (as well as party leaders and lobbyists) are not only very much in contact with legislators and communicating to a substantial degree in policy terms, but they are also a recruiting force. We cannot know to what extent the recruitment efforts made by political middlemen in our analysis succeeded in terms of actual legislative candidacies, but it is clear that many of those we interviewed conceived of themselves as important actors in the legislative process.

Legislators also reported a substantial amount of recruitment contact. We asked legislators who had tried to convince them that they should or should not run for the office. Table 4.9 indicates that legislators most frequently reported contacts from businessmen in their districts, county party chairmen, former legislators, and local public officials. Only 12 percent of the legislators said that they had not been contacted at all by one or more of the recruitment agents listed in Table 4.9. From the legislators' view, at least as much recruitment contact appears to come from the kinds of constituents we have identified as attentives as from constituency party leaders. Interestingly, lobbyists are at the bottom of the scale of recruiting agents. The considerable discrepancy between the rather large amount of lobbyist recruitment contacts reported by lobbyists themselves, and the very small incidence of lobbyist recruitment activity reported by legislators, could have occurred because lobbyist contacts were confined to a small proportion of legislators, because legislators tended to underestimate lobbyist recruitment, or because the lobbyists' candidates were unsuccessful.

Since our analysis has focused largely on making comparisons among political

Table 4.9   Recruitment Contacts Reported by Legislators

Recruitment Agent	Percent of Legislators Indicating Contact by Agent About Running and Trying to Convince Legislators That They Should or Should Not Run		
	Total	Democrats	Republicans
Local businessmen	58.0	31.3	71.8
County party chairmen	56.4	60.9	53.0
Former legislators	44.8	45.3	44.4
Local public officials	43.6	39.1	46.2
Members of family	32.6	32.8	32.5
Local newspapers	22.7	6.3	31.6
State public officials	18.2	21.9	16.2
State party officials	16.0	17.2	15.4
Friends	6.6	-	-
Lobbyists	5.5	4.7	3.4
No. of cases	181	64	117

elite groups, we have not stressed party differences. Yet partisan considerations surely are involved in the recruitment process. There is some evidence that recruitment contacts tend more to be targeted to candidates whose partisan identifications are relatively strong. About two-thirds of the weak partisans in both parties (62 percent of the Weak Democrats and 67 percent of the Weak Republicans) said that running for the legislature was largely their own idea, whereas fewer of the strong partisans among legislators (52 percent of the Strong Democrats and 54 percent of the Strong Republicans) made this response. In addition, weak partisans in both parties reported fewer recruitment contacts than did strong identifiers. The mean contacts reported from Strong Democrats and Republicans were 2.8 and 3.5, respectively, whereas comparable means for Weak Democrats and Republicans were 2.5 and 2.6.

Legislators who felt that they were drafted to be candidates reported many more recruitment contacts than did those who felt that running was largely their own idea. If we calculate the mean number of recruitment contacts reported by legislators, separating out legislators who said essentially that they were drafted to legislative service and those who said that running for the legislature was largely their own idea, we find that drafted legislators reported an average of 4 recruitment contacts (4.1 for pure draftees, 3.8 for those who said that their recruitment was partly a draft), whereas self-starters reported only 2.4 recruitment contacts. If we unfold these comparisons by the party affiliation of the legislators, the highest levels of recruitment contacting were reported by drafted Republicans. The mean number of recruitment contacts reported by Republican legislators exceeded those reported by Democrats (3.3 as against 2.7). Self-starting legislators, whether Republican or Democrat, reported the lowest levels of contact for recruitment (2.2 for self-starting Democrats and 2.4 for Republicans). Democratic legislators who said running for office was at least partly a matter of being drafted reported 3.2 recruitment contacts, and drafted Republicans, the most frequently contacted, reported an average of 4.4 contacts. Thus it appears that Democrats were more likely to stand for legislative office on their own, without needing to be recruited. On the other hand, Republicans were more likely to require recruiting by others to service—they were more likely to need an external stimulus.

It is apparent from Table 4.9 that Democratic and Republican legislators differ with respect to some of the recruiting agents from whom they report contacts. The largest differences between parties involve contact from businessmen and local newspapers. The high level of contact reported by legislators from local business-men is mainly attributable to the reports of such contact by nearly three-fourths of the Republican members (compared with less than one-third of the Democratic legislators). Similarly, contact reported from local newspapers (and the daily and weekly press in Iowa is, from all appearances, heavily Republican-oriented) consists largely of contact reported by Republican legislators.

SYSTEMS OF RECRUITMENT

Legislative recruitment probably is not randomly distributed over the political landscape. We now attempt to illuminate two features of the political landscape with regard to recruitment contacts—urban and rural legislative districts, and districts that vary in interparty competitiveness. Our notion is that these desiderata ought to provide the basis for different recruitment systems identifiable in terms of interpersonal recruitment contacts.[8] We have divided legislative districts on an urban-rural basis in terms of the proportions of their populations that are rural-farm. Dividing them by interparty competition shows the districts in which Democrats tend to dominate, those in which Republicans tend to dominate, and those which are relatively competitive. Table 4.10 gives the average recruitment contacts reported by legislators, attentive constituents, and party leaders in the districts of various kinds. Legislators and attentive constituents report more

Table 4.10   Recruitment Contacts Among Different Types of Constituencies

| Report of Contacts From: | Mean of District Mean Contacts | | |
	Republican* Districts	Competitive Districts	Democratic Districts
Legislators**	1.8	3.6	2.5
Attentive Constituents	2.9#	4.4	3.9
Party Leaders	6.8	8.5	9.9
No. of districts	13	27	10

*Republican districts are those where the Democratic vote for governor in 1968 was less than 40%; competitive districts are those where the Democratic gubernatorial vote was 40-49%; Democratic districts are those where the Democratic vote was greater than 50%.

**The legislator means cannot be compared with the means for attentive constituents and party leaders because they derived from a different kind of interview item.

#One very deviant mean has been excluded; if it were included, this entry would be 3.9.

recruitment contacts in the competitive districts than in those which are dominant for either party. Party leaders are clearly quite different from attentive constituents in the concentration of their recruitment efforts; thus they report more contacts on the average than do attentive constituents in all types of districts. Party leader recruitment contact is concentrated in all competitive districts *and* in the predominantly Democratic districts; if anything, it is heavier in the latter.

The distinctiveness of party leaders in the notable clustering of their recruitment contacts in Democratic districts leads us to examine the phenomenon in greater detail. In Table 4.11 differences between Republican party leaders and Democratic party leaders are listed by type of district, and we discover that the least party recruitment effort is expended by Republican Party leaders in relatively safe Republican districts. At the same time, Republican leaders report as much effort in Democratic districts as they do in competitive ones. This is probably because in Iowa in 1967 and 1968 the Republicans felt they had a statewide competitive advantage, which led them to recruit even in Democratic strongholds. Even so, Democratic Party leaders reported a higher level of recruitment contact across the board. Democratic leaders' average number of contacts in Republican districts was 8.7, compared with 4.8 contacts for Republican leaders. And whereas Republican leaders' contacts were 7.1 in Democratic districts, Democratic leaders' contacts reached the high point of 12.6 in districts in which they were most successful. Thus Republican recruitment efforts were about as great in Democratic districts as in competitive ones, and Democratic efforts in their own districts exceeded their effort in competitive ones. This could have occurred as a result of generally favorable prospects for Republican legislative candidates in the 1968 election. However, the evidence here turns out to be quite different, for Democratic party leaders at least, from what was suggested by Seligman for Oregon party recruitment.[9]

Greater recruitment effort might be expected by party leaders in urban districts than in rural ones—our data demonstrate that. Party leader contact in urban districts averaged 9.1, falling to 7.9 in rural districts. But as Table 4.11 indicates, urban Republicans worked harder in all districts divided by interparty competitiveness than did rural Republican Party leaders. Yet, if anything, rural Democratic leaders expended greater recruitment efforts than their urban counterparts, except in the Democratic districts. As a whole, rural Republican Party leaders were the least active in recruitment, by their own reports; their average contacts were 5.6. Rural Democrats reported the highest mean recruitment contacts—10.0; however urban Democrats, with a mean of 9.7, were not much different from rural ones. And as Table 4.11 shows, urban Democrats in Democratic districts were a little more active in recruiting efforts than were rural Democrats in Democratic districts. The average in all districts for urban Republicans was 8.6 contacts. Earlier we indicated that Republican legislators reported somewhat more contact than did Democratic legislators. The contrast between recruitment contact reports by legislators and those of party leaders can occur, of course, because in a climate in which Republicans tended to be elected and more of them were incumbents, Democratic Party leaders may have been in contacting a larger number of potential candidates, more of whom did not get elected.

In this chapter we have shown that increasing levels of support for the legislature through groups of political middlemen accrue in a milieu featuring substantial linkages between citizens and legislatures, as provided by party leaders, attentive constituents, and lobbyists. These middlemen are heavily involved in communication between citizens and legislators, and they are very much embroiled in the recruitment of legislators. Such extensive and intensive interaction, in our opinion, is certainly related to levels of legislative support. We turn now to the legislator himself to see how he envisions his role as a representative, and how the represented citizens perceive him.

Table 4.11   Party and Urban-Rural Differences Among Party Leader Recruitment Contacts

	Mean of District Mean Contacts		
Reported Contacts From Party Leaders	Republican* Districts	Competitive Districts	Democratic Districts
All Republicans	4.8	7.6	7.1
All Democrats	8.7	9.4	12.6
Urban Republicans**	7.0	8.9	8.6
Rural Republicans	4.4	6.9	#
Urban Democrats	#	8.6	13.3
Rural Democrats	9.8	9.9	11.3
No. of districts	13	27	10

*See definitions in Table 4.10.

**Urban districts are those which are less than 30% rural-farm; rural districts are those which are more than 30% rural-farm.

#Too few districts and too few respondents reporting contacts to make a meaningful mean.

NOTES

1. V. O. Key, Jr., *Public Opinion and American Democracy* (New York, 1961), pp. 536–537; see also Dwaine Marvick, "The Middlemen of Politics," in William J. Crotty, ed., *Approaches to the Study of Party Organization* (Boston, 1968), pp. 341–374.

2. For a preliminary analysis of attentive constituents, see G. R. Boynton, Samuel C. Patterson, and Ronald D. Hedlund, "The Missing Links in Legislative Politics: Attentive Constituents," *Journal of Politics,* Vol. 31 (August 1969), 700–721.

3. See Joseph Schlesinger's interesting comments about "enclaved constituencies" in *Ambition and Politics* (Chicago, 1966), pp. 127–133.

4. Philip E. Converse, "The Nature of Belief Systems in Mass Publics," in David Apter, ed., *Ideology and Discontent* (New York, 1964), pp. 206–261.

5. See G. R. Boynton and Samuel C. Patterson, "Legislative Recruitment in a Civic Culture," *Social Science Quarterly,* Vol. 50 (September 1969), 243–263; also Ronald D. Hedlund, "Psychological Predispositions: Political Representatives and the Public," *American Journal of Political Science,* Vol. 17 (August 1973), 489–505.

6. On self-starters in four state legislatures, see John C. Wahlke, Heinz Eulau, William Buchanan, and LeRoy C. Ferguson, *The Legislative System* (New York, 1962), pp. 98–101.

7. See Lewis Bowman and G. R. Boynton, "Recruitment Patterns Among Local Party Officials: A

Model and Some Preliminary Findings in Selected Locale," *American Political Science Review,* Vol. 60 (September 1966), 667–676; Samuel C. Patterson, "Characteristics of Party Leaders," *Western Political Quarterly,* Vol. 16 (June 1963), 332–352; Phillip Althoff and Samuel C. Patterson, "Political Activism in a Rural County," *Midwest Journal of Political Science,* Vol. 10 (February 1966), 39–51.

8. Seligman and Snowiss have particularly endeavored to define variations in recruitment systems. See Lester G. Seligman, "Political Recruitment and Party Structure: A Case Study," *American Political Science Review,* Vol. 55 (March 1961), 77–86; and Leo M. Snowiss, "Congressional Recruitment and Representation," *American Political Science Review,* Vol. 60 (September 1966), 627–639. Also, see Lester G. Seligman, Michael R. King, Chong Lim Kim, and Roland E. Smith, *Patterns of Recruitment: A State Chooses Its Lawmakers* (Chicago, 1974).

9. Seligman found that "in areas safe for the majority party . . . party officials are least active in instigating or supporting candidates." See "Political Recruitment and Party Structure," *American Political Science Review,* Vol. 55 (March 1961), 84.

5 PERSPECTIVES ON LEGISLATORS AND LEGISLATIVE WORK

We now move to an analysis of the perceptions and expectations about the legislature held by the public and elite groups, and their attitudes toward the way in which the legislature works.[1] Specifically, we examine the effects on levels of legislative support of (1) the perceptions and expectations of citizens and leaders with regard to the kinds of people who serve as legislators, (2) the motives citizens and leaders attribute to legislators who have run for public office, and (3) the attitudes of citizens and leaders toward the representativeness of the legislature and the use of compromise in legislative decision making. We expect these factors to bear a positive relationship to legislative support.

PERSPECTIVES ON LEGISLATORS' ATTRIBUTES

What kind of person should a legislator be in the minds of his constituents? What do constituents think legislators are like? To deal with these questions, we asked respondents in our public and elite samples to evaluate a set of 20 attributes that have been suggested as characteristics of legislators (see Table 5.1). All our respondents were asked first to indicate to what extent they thought legislators ought to have each attribute, ranking the qualities on a scale from 1 (very important to have the attribute in question) to 4 (not at all important). Then respondents were asked to make rough judgments about what proportion of the members of the legislature actually had each attribute, gauging their estimates on a scale from 1 (all members) to 5 (none of the members). By giving each response a score, it is possible to see what kinds of priorities the general public and leadership groups assign to different kinds of legislator attributes. (Mean raw scores are listed in Table 5.1 for the general population sample.)

The ordering of legislator attributes by the general public presents some interesting variations between characteristics citizens think legislators ought to have and those they think are actually present in the members of the legislature. As a group,

Table 5.1   Mean Ranks and Scores for Characteristics of Legislators in the Public Sample

Characteristics of Legislators	Important for Legislators to Have the Characteristic		Extent to Which Legislators Actually Have Characteristic	
	Mean	Rank	Mean	Rank
Completely honest	1.08	1	2.50	10
Study problems thoroughly	1.18	2	2.36	8
Know will of people of district	1.27	3	2.31	7
Hard working	1.30	4	2.30	6
Interested in serving others	1.32	5	2.26	5
Special knowledge about state government	1.46	6	2.40	9
Friendly toward others	1.51	7	2.14	2
High prestige in community	1.64	8	2.17	4
Influential in own district	1.64	9	2.16	3
Concerned with small details	1.97	10	3.01	17
Trained in legal work	2.01	11	2.84	15
Just an average citizen	2.09	12	2.51	11
Loyal to his political party	2.14	13	2.06	1
College graduate	2.46	14	2.66	12
Change things slowly if at all	2.51	15	3.10	18
Held previous office	2.55	16	2.69	14
Between ages 45-55	2.78	17	2.68	13
Political beliefs that don't change	2.92	18	2.85	16
Only interested in re-election	3.58	19	3.35	19
Seek personal gain or profit	3.64	20	3.54	20

respondents in the Iowa sample ranked attributes of good character, knowledge and ability, and social status as most desirable, and they ranked attributes of personal gain or manipulation as the least. When the rank orders for attributes legislators should have are compared with ranks for characteristics they actually do have, some rather dramatic shifts occur.[2] Although being completely honest ranks first as a trait legislators should have, it drops to the median rank of attributes legislators are perceived to possess. The highest ranking for perceived attributes is political party loyalty. On the other hand, citizens tend to regard legislators as more friendly, more influential in their districts, and more prestigious than they believe they should be, based on ranked importance of these and other traits. At the same time, the two rank orderings are highly intercorrelated ($r_s = .64$).

It is apparent that the items included in Table 5.1 could be grouped into several distinctive sets, to help reduce the complexity of dealing with 20 different categories. More important, we want to be able to make comparisons among our samples—the public, attentive constituents, party leaders, lobbyists, and legislators—and reducing the number of traits would facilitate this. Since displaying the raw rank orderings for all these groups would be an excessively laborious presentation, we have illustrated the major details only for the general population sample. With the data from that sample, we factor analyzed both the ratings of characteristics respondents felt were important for legislators to have and the attributes respondents felt actually characterized the legislature.[3] The factor analysis of ideal legislator attributes appears in Table 5.2; the factorial structure for actual perceived characteristics is so similar that it is omitted. Six factors accounted for more than half the variance in scores, and the factorial structure is quite unambiguous. We have added to the factor analysis presented in Table 5.2 the mean of the means of items from Table 5.1 included in each factor, as well as the rank order of factors based on these means.

The highest ranking factor in terms of mean scores, factor II, included items having to do with the purposive activity of legislators and is among the top two factors in accounting for variance explained. The second ranking factor, factor IV, including honesty, knowledge of and influence in the legislative district, and community prestige, can be given the summary label the "community status" factor. The factor ranking third, factor V, can be called the "slow and deliberate change" factor from the manifest character of the two items highly loaded on it. The fourth ranking factor in terms of means, factor I, accounts for nearly one-third of the explained variance and deals with the experience or preparation of legislators. The party loyalty factor, factor VI, ranks fifth in mean scores, followed by self-motivation, factor III. The factor analysis and mean scores for the 20 legislator attributes rated by the general public respondents suggest, therefore, the

Table 5.2 Factor Analysis of Characteristics Legislators Ought to Have In the Public Sample

Characteristics of Legislators	Factors*						Mean of Means of Items Included in Factor	Rank of Importance of Factors
	I	II	III	IV	V	VI		
Experience Factor								
Held previous office	.719						2.45	4
Trained in legal work	.686							
College graduate	.583					.336		
Between ages 45-55	.471		.341					
Purposive Activity Factor								
Interested in serving others		.804					1.32	1
Study problems thoroughly		.737						
Special knowledge of state govt.	.345	.713						
Hard working		.436		-.340				
Self-Motivation Factor								
Seek personal gain or profit			.813				3.61	6
Only interested in re-election			.755					
Community Status Factor								
Influential in own district	.333			-.653			1.54	2
Know will of people in district		.323		-.637				
Completely honest				-.552				
High prestige in community				-.513				
Slow and Deliberate Change Factor								
Concerned with details					.804		2.24	3
Change things slowly					.655			
Party Loyalty Factor								
Political beliefs that don't change						.703	2.53	5
Loyal to political party						.691		

*All loadings above .300 are shown.

following hierarchy of expectations about the characteristics of legislators: (1) purposive activity, (2) community status, (3) slow and deliberate change, (4) experience, (5) party loyalty, and (6) self-motivation. A similar analysis was carried out for respondents' ratings of the 20 basic attributes in terms of whether legislators actually exhibited them. The rankings of similar factors for perceived actual attributes were: (1) community status, (2) purposive activity, (3) party loyalty, (4) experience, (5) slow and deliberate change, and (6) self-motivation. This shift in the rankings of factors suggests the nature of differences between Iowans' expectations and perceptions of legislator attributes. The community status and purposive activity factors reverse positions; party loyalty exchanges places with slow and deliberate change; experience remains fourth in rank, and self-motivation is at the bottom of both rankings.

Although these rankings of attribute factors in the general public are of considerable interest in themselves, we were anxious to move to comparisons between the public and elite groups. We do this very simply by calculating means of raw score means for the items in each attribute factor for each subsample. Comparison of these means and the rank order of factors for each sample group makes it possible to see in gross terms the extent of public and elite group differences and to identify the extent to which priorities for perceived and expected characteristics differ. (See Table 5.3 for these means and ranks.) Principally, Table 5.3 points to the overwhelming agreement among elite groups and with the general public regarding the priorities that both thought characterized legislators and both expected of legislators. Political leaders differ in many respects from the public, as we have shown in earlier chapters, but they are very much in agreement on perspectives on the qualities of legislators.

LEGISLATOR ATTRIBUTES AND SUPPORT

Given that one's image of the persons serving as legislators is probably related to one's view of the legislature, we expected that the respondents' perceptions and expectations of the attributes of legislators would be related to their level of legislative support. Respondents with favorable images of legislators should be more likely, we hypothesized, to support the legislature generally. These relationships can be conveniently presented graphically, showing legislative support on one axis and the attribute factor on the other axis. Six pairs of such graphs (Figures 5.1 through 5.6) depict the nexus between attribute factors and support both for respondents' perceptions and expectations. In these exhibits we have combined all the elite groups together, since the picture is not significantly different when each leadership group is plotted separately, and comparisons are more striking in this more simplified form.

As a general observation, we can note that Figures 5.1 through 5.6 illustrate again the hiatus between the general public and elite groups in general levels of legislative support. In every display, the elite groups are substantially higher in support than the public. Another general observation indicated by these figures and registered in a variety of other ways in our evidence is that for the most part, neither public nor elite groups have large numbers of respondents who exhibit great differences between their perceptions of the legislature and their expectations about how it should operate. There are some perception-expectation differences, and as we shall see these differences can be of some importance, but most Iowans are inclined to perceive the state legislature to be nearly what they would prefer it to be.

Table 5.3 Perceptions and Expectations of Attributes of Legislators: Mean of Means of Attribute Factors by Subsamples

Attribute Factors[@]	Perceived Attributes										Expected Attributes									
	Public		Consti-tuents		Party Leaders		Lobbyists		Legis-lators		Public		Consti-tuents		Party Leaders		Lobbyists		Legis-lators	
	$\bar{X}$	Rank	$\bar{X}$	Rank	$\bar{X}$	Rank	$\bar{X}$	Rank	$\bar{X}$	Rank	$\bar{X}$	Rank	$\bar{X}$	Rank	$\bar{X}$	Rank	$\bar{X}$	Rank	$\bar{X}$	Rank
Experience	2.7	4	3.1	5	3.1	5	3.1	4	3.2	5	2.4	4	3.0	5	3.0	5	3.0	5	3.1	5
Purposive Activity	2.3	2	2.6	3	2.6	3	2.6	3	2.4	2	1.3	1	1.3	1	1.3	1	1.4	1	1.5	1
Self-Motivation	3.4	6	3.7	6	3.7	6	3.7	6	3.9	6	3.6	6	3.8	6	3.8	6	3.7	6	3.8	6
Community Status	2.2	1	2.3	1	2.2	1	2.2	1	2.2	1	1.5	2	1.4	2	1.4	2	1.5	2	1.6	2
Slow and Deliberate Change	3.1	5	3.0	4	3.0	4	3.2	5	3.1	4	2.2	3	2.5	3	2.4	3	2.6	3	2.6	3
Party Loyalty	2.5	3	2.4	2	2.4	2	2.6	2	2.7	3	2.5	5	2.8	4	2.5	4	2.8	4	2.8	4

@The items composing each factor are as follows:
Experience = held previous office, trained in legal work, college graduate, and between ages 45-55.
Purposive Activity = interested in serving others, study problems thoroughly, special knowledge of state government, and hard working.

Self-Motivation = seek personal gain or profit and only interested in re-election.
Community Status = influential in own district, know will of district, completely honest, and high prestige in community.

Slow-Deliberate Change = concerned with details and change things slowly.
Party loyalty = political beliefs that don't change and loyal to political party.

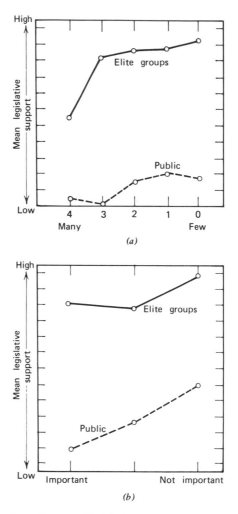

Figure 5.1   The experience factor and legislative support. *(a)* Perceptions, *(b)* expectations.

On the experience factor, higher legislative support comes from those in both the public and elite groups who think that relatively few legislators have the attributes in the experience cluster than from those who perceive that many legislators have these attributes. Similarly, higher support is exhibited by those who think that the experience factors are not important for legislators to have than by those who believe it important for legislators to have the experience characteristics. Basically, perhaps surprisingly, this means that to the extent that citizens perceive or expect legislators to be experienced, they are likely to be less supportive of the legislature. We certainly expected the opposite result, and it is not entirely clear why the present findings should occur. The only explanation we can offer is the seemingly widespread acceptance of the notion of the amateur legislator among Iowans—the part-time legislator, the amateur politician, the Jacksonian democratic man is the folk hero of Iowa politics. These results may be a consequence of this set of generalized attitudes about politicians. Thus those who support the legislature the most may also tend to perceive legislators as amateurs and may expect that this should be the case.

With regard to purposive activity, Figure 5.2 makes it clear that public and leaders tend to show lower legislative support if they perceive and expect the items in this cluster to be unimportant and to characterize few legislators. Legislative support is relatively higher among those who both perceive and expect legislators to be interested in serving others, to study problems thoroughly, to have some special knowledge about state government, and to be hard-working. Conversely, there is a tendency for the self-motivation factor (Figure 5.3) to work in the opposite direction.

Respondents who regard self-seeking as an unimportant legislator characteristic and as an attitude that typifies few legislators, have higher levels of legislative support than do respondents who see many legislators as being self-seeking or believe these to be important attributes. This evidence suggests to us that a morality dimension, widely assumed to be present in Iowa politics, may in fact affect levels of legislative support. In a political culture like that of Iowa, where morality seems to extend to one's expectations and perceptions of the characteristics of politicians, a predisposition toward uprightness is associated with support for the legislature.

Respondent's perceptions and expectations regarding the community status factor (Figure 5.4) demonstrate a generally parallel trend between elite groups and the public for the relationship between one's perceptions of this factor and legislative support. Among all types of Iowans interviewed, those perceiving that many legislators have the community status characteristics—honesty, prestige, empathy, and influence—tend to have higher levels of support than do those perceiving that such traits are displayed by fewer legislators. On the other hand, elite groups reveal only small differences in levels of support for varying expectations on the importance of this factor, whereas among mass public respondents a moderately positive relationship was noted. With respect to the slow and deliberate change factor (Figure 5.5), elite groups tend to exhibit slightly higher support when they both perceive and expect few legislators to change things slowly and be

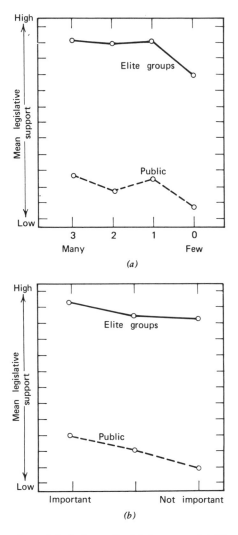

Figure 5.2   The purposive activity factor and legislative support. *(a)* Perceptions, *(b)* expectations.

concerned with small details, but there are no substantial differences among the general citizenry on this count.

The pattern of results for the party loyalty factor (Figure 5.6) is not very easy to interpret. Support is generally higher for those who think many legislators are loyal to their own political party, and support is lower among those who perceive that few legislators are loyal to their party, but the relationship is not very regular.

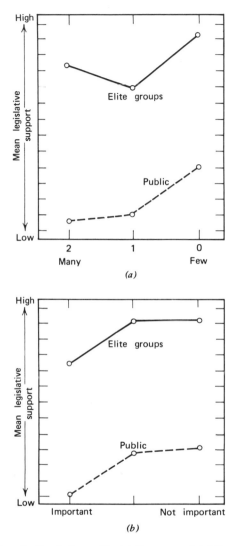

Figure 5.3 The self-motivation factor and legislative support. (a) Perceptions, (b) expectations.

Expectations of party loyalty are less definitive. For the elite groups, it is fairly clear that expectations of party loyalty are associated with high legislative support, but for the public, the reverse seems to hold. These trends are consistent with a good deal of our evidence about public ambiguity regarding party loyalty as opposed to elite group emphasis on the importance of the loyal partisan.

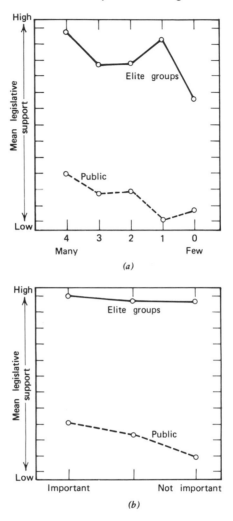

Figure 5.4 The community status factor and legislative support. *(a)* Perceptions, *(b)* expectations.

We have indicated that although perceptions of the attributes of legislators and expectations about them are not greatly different in our Iowa samples, there are some gaps. To the extent that such perceptions and expectations are congruent, we would hypothesize that legislative support is high; to the extent they are incongruent, we would expect legislative support to be low. That is, support should be

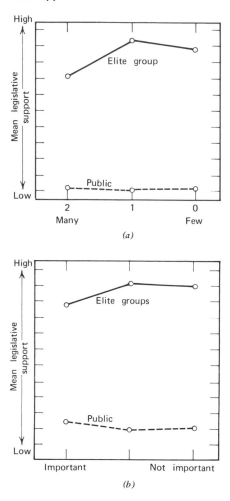

Figure 5.5 The slow and deliberate change factor and legislative support. *(a)* Perceptions, *(b)* expectations.

lower among persons for whom the legislature does not live up to expectations, and higher for those who expect legislators to have certain kinds of characteristics and perceive that they do possess them. We have tested this hypothesis in considerable detail with the data from the general population sample, and for some of the attribute factors there is indeed a significant difference in legislative support in the hypothesized direction. These significant differences occur on the factors

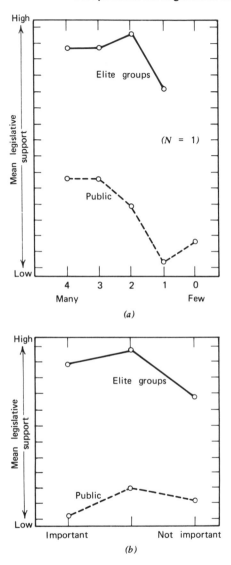

Figure 5.6   The party loyalty factor and legislative support. *(a)* Perceptions, *(b)* expectations.

that show fairly strong correlations with legislative support—namely, community status, experience, and self-motivation. Considering the very high legislative support level in the Iowa sample, and the relatively meager number of respondents for whom there is a significant perception-expectation differential, any finding of statistically significant differences between congruent and incongruent respondents in legislative support is important.

More relevant to the general line of argument in this book is our analysis of the multiple effects of the attribute factors on support. We have performed a multiple regression analysis for each subsample, testing the joint effects of both perceptual and expectational attribute factors. The results of this analysis appear in Table 5.4, where the multiple correlation R and the explained variance R^2, using rotated factor scores for each of the six attribute clusters, are shown for each set of factor analyses and for each subsample. In general, the expectation factors together are more highly correlated with legislative support for all subsamples than are the perception factors. The expectation factors for each sample group involve correlation magnitudes of about .3, and for each group these factors account for about 10 percent of the variance in legislative support. The multiple correlations for the perception factors are very low, accounting for only about 1 percent or less of the variance in support.

ATTITUDES TOWARD LEGISLATORS' MOTIVATIONS FOR CANDIDACY

A second set of perspectives on the legislator was investigated by attempting to ascertain attitudes toward the motivations of individuals who run for legislative office.[4] We expected support for the legislature to be partly a function of positive

Table 5.4   Multiple Correlations Between Legislator Attribute Factors and Legislative Support

Sub-sample	Attributes Legislators Have (Perceptions)		Attributes Legislators Ought to Have (Expectations)	
	R	R^2	R	R^2
Public	.22	.05	.33	.11
Attentive Constituents	.13	.02	.25	.06
Party Leaders	.12	.02	.30	.09
Lobbyists	.24	.06	.31	.09
Legislators	.08	.01	.34	.12

attitudes toward legislative candidacy. By positive attitudes, we mean those which are consistent with general cultural norms about public office—that public office is a public trust, and that persons should seek public office out of a sense of civic duty and a desire to enact policies in the public interest, rather than for personal gain, out of personal ambition, or to promote special interests. To acquire at least rudimentary data on motivations, we submitted a set of 16 propositions about legislators' candidacy motivations to all our respondents, asking them to indicate to what extent they thought each proposition properly characterized legislators as a group (did they think the attributed motive characterized all legislators, most, half, a few, or none?). Table 5.5 presents these propositions, mean scores for the total sample, and ranks of means. In the total sample, which is of course dominated by the mass public sample, recruitment by party leaders was the primary motivating factor mentioned (the mean of 2.3 lies between the categories ''most'' and ''half''). Notice that motives involving personal and private aggrandizement, and motives involving pursuit of a particular issue, proposal, or policy, were attributed to the fewest legislators, and some kind of political or civic obligation was thought to motivate legislative candidacies more often than private gain or special interest. Also apparent is a considerable overlap among some of these attributed motives, and a number logically cluster together.

A standard factor analysis of inter-item correlations from the attributed motives in Table 5.5 produced five very manageable factors: a personal gain factor, a civic duty factor, a sociability factor, a political mobility factor, and a policy orientation factor. The items composing these factors, along with the major factor loadings, are listed in Table 5.6. Two of the 16 items from Table 5.5 are not represented in Table 5.6 (''they are asked to run by party leaders'' and ''they are very interested in politics''), because they did not fit the most readily interpretable factor structure. Recruitment by party leaders is a separate factor, which we consider in a somewhat different way later. Suffice it to say here that except for the legislator group, the groups of respondents had similar perceptions of the extent of party leader recruitment. On the average, the mass public and the nonlegislator elite groups perceived that more than half the legislators were asked to run by party leaders, whereas legislators themselves perceived that fewer than half were recruited by a party. The item ''they are very interested in politics'' appears to hang between the civic duty and sociability factors, and we are not sure why it does not attach itself securely to one or the other.

Having simplified perceptions of the motivational world of legislative recruitment into five major factors, we can make comparisons among subgroups of respondents by factor scoring them and comparing mean factor scores using analysis of variance. Since the raw mean factor scores for each factor by respon-

Table 5.5 Why Legislators Run

Attributed Motive	Mean*	Rank#
They run because they are asked to run by party leaders.	2.3	1
They run because they are politically ambitious.	2.7	2
They run because they are particularly concerned about issues before the legislature.	2.8	3
They run because they feel that they ought to do it as good citizens.	2.8	4
They run because they are very interested in politics.	2.9	5
They run because they feel an obligation to participate.	2.9	6
They run because this is a way to get ahead in politics.	3.0	7
They run because it is a part of their duty as citizens.	3.0	8
They run because this is a stepping stone to higher office.	3.2	9
They run because being in the legislature gives them contacts that are useful in other ways.	3.3	10
They run because they want to campaign for a special policy.	3.3	11
They run because they have some legislative proposals they want to push.	3.4	12
They run because they enjoy campaigning.	3.4	13
They run because they like to meet new people.	3.5	14
They run because it is a good way to make business contacts.	3.6	15
They run for personal gain or profit.	3.6	16

*These means are ordered so that the high ranking ones indicate the motive is attributed to many legislators and the low ranking ones indicate the motive is attributed to a few. Item scoring was as follows: All = 1; Most = 2; Half = 3; Few = 4; and None = 5.

#Ranks are based upon unrounded means, which were not tied.

dent group are not in themselves particularly meaningful, we refrain from presenting the table of their values. It is more meaningful to concentrate on intergroup differences, given in Table 5.7.

Lobbyists, party leaders, and attentive constituents did not differ significantly on any of the five factors. The mass public differed from at least one elite group on all the factors, and from all elite groups on the political mobility and policy

Table 5.6   Factors Motivating Legislative Candidacies

Motivational Items	Factors*				
	I	II	III	IV	V
PERSONAL GAIN FACTOR					
Make contacts useful in other ways	.801				
Good way to make business contacts	.764				
Run for personal gain or profit	.718				
CIVIC DUTY FACTOR					
Part of duty as citizen		.801			
Feel an obligation to participate		.797			
Feel they ought to as good citizens		.779			
Particularly concerned about an issue		.540			.491
SOCIABILITY FACTOR					
Like to meet new people			.916		
Enjoy campaigning	.318	.375	.608		
POLITICAL MOBILITY FACTOR					
Politically ambitious				.863	
Way to get ahead in politics	.378			.703	
Stepping-stone to higher office	.443			.662	
POLICY ORIENTATION FACTOR					
Want to campaign for a special policy					.806
Have legislative proposal to promote					.790

*All factor loadings above .300 are shown.

orientation factors. Across all groups, the greatest differences occurred on the political mobility factor and the least on the civic duty factor. The mass public attributed motivations of personal gain to more legislators than did legislators, party leaders, or attentive constituents. The mass public attributed reasons of civic duty to fewer legislative candidates than did legislators themselves, and so did attentive constituents; but legislators, lobbyists, and party leaders did not differ. The data suggest that citizens in general and attentive constituents thought that significantly more legislators ran for sociability motives than did legislators, although legislators, lobbyists, and party leaders did not differ. In sum, the major

Table 5.7   Differences Among Groups in Perceptions of Why Legislators Run

Factor	F	P	T-test differences where $p < .01$
Personal Gain Factor	15.84	.01	Mass public differs from legislators, party leaders, and attentive constituents
Civic Duty Factor	4.28	N.S.	Legislators differ from mass public and attentive constituents
Sociability Factor	5.75	.05	Mass public differs from legislators and lobbyists; legislators differ from attentive constituents
Political Mobility Factor	99.09	.001	Mass public differs from all elite groups; legislators differ from lobbyists, party leaders, and attentive constituents
Policy Orientation Factor	13.37	.05	Mass public differs from all elite groups

differences in attributed motivations among those who run for legislative office occurred between the mass public and the political elites. Attentive constituents lay closest to the mass public in these data, and lobbyists and party leaders differed from legislators only in their tendency to attribute political mobility motivations to legislators more than did legislators themselves.

The means for each sample group on each of the candidacy motivation factors are given in Table 5.8. The rank orders of factors are also shown, although in some cases differences between factor means are very small and therefore must be interpreted very cautiously. It is interesting, however, that fairly sharp differences materialize between the mass public and the elite groups. The most important reasons for legislative candidacies given by the public are those involving political mobility. Citizens in general tend to think that legislators run for the office mainly to fulfill political ambitions. Although political mobility ranks highly among elite groups, too, the highest ranking factor for them is civic obligation. All groups,

Table 5.8   Attributed Candidacy Motivation Factors: Mean of Factors by Sample

Motivation Factors	Public		Attentive Constituents		Party Leaders		Lobbyists		Legislators	
	$\overline{X}$	Rank	$\overline{X}$	Rank	$\overline{X}$	Rank	$\overline{X}$	Rank	$\overline{X}$	Rank
Personal Gain	3.3	4	3.7	5	3.6	5	3.6	5	3.8	5
Civic Duty	2.9	2	2.9	1	2.8	1	2.9	1	2.7	1
Sociability	3.5	5	3.6	4	3.2	3	3.4	3	3.3	2
Political Mobility	2.6	1	3.3	2	3.1	2	3.3	2	3.5	3
Policy Orientation	3.2	3	3.5	3	3.6	4	3.6	4	3.6	4

mass public and elites, consider personal gain to be the least important motivation for legislative candidacies.

At the same time, small but interesting differences among sample groups not withstanding, the clustering of means near the center of the scale suggests that across all groups a very large range of consensus exists among them about candidacy motivation. It certainly would be stretching the evidence beyond credulity to suggest that the data suggest vast differences between public and elites.

ATTITUDES TOWARD MOTIVATION FOR CANDIDACY AND LEGISLATIVE SUPPORT

We expected attitudes about the motivations for legislative candidacies to be somewhat related to supportive predispositions toward the legislative institution. We thought, for example, that the most supportive respondents would be those who believed the following:

1.   Few legislators seek office purely for personal gain.
2.   Most candidates do not run to make business or political contacts.
3.   Many legislators run out of a sense of civic duty or to further specific policies.

Our analysis into these relationships involved computing a mean legislative support score from factor scores generated from a factor analysis of the seven items discussed in Chapter 2 for the sets of respondents "high" or "low" on our motivation factors. Since these mean legislative support scores, displayed in Table

Table 5.9   Candidacy Motivation Factors and Legislative Support

	Mean Legislative Support Scores		
Factor by Sub-Sample	Low on Motivation Factor	Intermediate on Motivation Factor	High on Motivation Factor
PERSONAL GAIN	Many run for Personal Gain		Few run for Personal Gain
Public	-.42	-.43	-.22
Attentive Constituents	.36	.36	.49
Party Leaders	.29	.19	.32
Lobbyists	.48	.37	.54
Legislators	1.05	.70	.75
CIVIC DUTY	Few run for Civic Duty		Many run for Civic Duty
Public	-.34	-.42	-.39
Attentive Constituents	.37	.40	.49
Party Leaders	.23	.56	.01
Lobbyists	.51	.40	.54
Legislators	.57	.66	.89
SOCIABILITY	Many run for Sociability		Few run for Sociability
Public	-.37	-.39	-.41
Attentive Constituents	.48	.46	.28
Party Leaders	.50	.25	.26
Lobbyists	.81	.37	.39
Legislators	.90	.78	.60
POLITICAL MOBILITY	Few run for Political Mobility		Many run for Political Mobility
Public	-.23	-.33	-.58
Attentive Constituents	.47	.49	.13
Party Leaders	.40	.24	.04
Lobbyists	.36	.64	.28
Legislators	.75	.74	.72
POLICY ORIENTATION	Many run for Policy		Few run for Policy
Public	-.47	-.37	-.31
Attentive Constituents	.52	.32	.47
Party Leaders	.83	.22	.11
Lobbyists	.06	.51	.65
Legislators	.58	.96	.65

5.9, were constructed from factor scores, they have no inherent interpretable meaning beyond a high score indicating a high level of legislative support; however, these scores make it possible to see the relative effects of perceived motivation factors on legislative support.

The results of the analysis do not conform entirely to our expectations. Indeed, for most sample groups, those who were high on the personal gain factor (i.e., those who generally thought few legislators ran for personal gain) were relatively more supportive of the legislature than those who were low on this factor, although the relationship is not entirely regular for all elite groups, and in fact is slightly reversed for legislators themselves. The product-moment correlation between the personal gain factor and legislative support is $+.21$. The civic duty and sociability factors did not correlate with legislative support for all samples combined, although for legislators, support was substantially higher among those who felt that many legislators ran because of a sense of civic duty than for those who believed that few members were so motivated. Additionally, although in the mass public legislative support did not vary in terms of the sociability factor, elite group support for the legislature was generally higher among those who felt that many legislators ran for sociability reasons than for other reasons.

Our expectations about the effects of the political mobility factor on legislative support did not materialize very well. In fact, although we thought respondents would be more supportive if they believed that relatively few legislators were motivated by political ambition, the reverse turned out to be true for the mass public, attentive constituents, and party leaders. The results for lobbyists are inconclusive, and legislators did not differ in support levels across variations in the political mobility factor. The product-moment correlation for the entire data set proved to be positive $(r = +.25)$.

Similarly, sample groups differed in terms of their legislative support along the policy orientation factor. In the general public, our expectations again were not borne out; legislative support was, in fact, slightly higher (less negative) among those who believed that few legislators ran because of a desire to promote public policies. Interestingly enough, an even stronger relationship of this kind occurred among lobbyists. Lobbyists who thought that a few legislators ran for office for policy promotion reasons were much more supportive than those who felt that many legislators ran for this reason. Equally interesting are the results for party leaders, who presumably are very concerned that legislators should be policy-oriented: our original expectations about the relationship between policy orientation and support were fulfilled only for party leaders. The relationship between these variables is such that legislative support increases to the extent that party leaders believed that legislators were motivated to be candidates for office to promote policies. For the entire company of respondents, however, the correlation between the policy orientation factor and legislative support was a very modest $+.11$.

The combined effects of candidacy motivation factors on legislative support for each of our samples are not striking, although a small portion of the variance in legislative support is explained by these combined factors for lobbyists ($R^2 = .12$), who presumably are more sensitive in their daily work to the career motivations of legislators. The multiple correlations appear in Table 5.10, along with the variance in legislative support explained by the combined candidacy motivation factors. The multiple correlations are in the vicinity of .2 for the general public, attentive constituents and legislators; .3 for party leaders; and .4 for lobbyists.

LEGISLATIVE REPRESENTATIVENESS AND COMPROMISE

We wanted our analysis of legislative support to include an additional feature of the phenomenal perspectives on the represented: their attitudes toward the representativeness of the legislature and toward legislative compromise. We asked all our respondents questions through which we hoped to assess their sense of representative efficacy—to what extent they thought that the legislature acted on behalf of the represented, and to what extent they believed that the legislature was run by an oligarchy unconcerned with the public good. We thought that respondents who perceived the legislature to be very efficacious on the representativeness factor would exhibit considerably higher support for the institution as such than those who believed the legislature to be unrepresentative of the citizenry. We also wanted a notion of respondents' views about legislative compromise, the *sine qua non* of legislative life. We thought that support for the legislature would be higher

Table 5.10 Attributed Candidacy Motivation Factors and Legislative Support: Multiple Regression

Sample	Multiple Correlation and Variance Explained	
	R	R^2
Public	.23	.05
Attentive Constituents	.22	.05
Party Leaders	.29	.08
Lobbyists	.35	.12
Legislators	.15	.02

among those who appeared to believe in legislative compromise than among those who seemed to scorn the accommodator's role of the legislature.

To gather evidence on these matters, we asked all our Iowa respondents a number of questions about their attitudes toward the representativeness of the legislature and the virtue of compromise. These items are listed in Table 5.11, along with the percentages of each sample group who agreed with each attitude statement. Between 25 and 29 percent of all sample groups except legislators indicated that they felt the legislature did not represent citizens very well; only 15 percent of the legislators themselves took this view. One-fourth of the respondents in the mass public indicated a belief that the legislature was controlled by a clique impervious to public demands, but less than one-fifth of the attentive constituents, party leaders, and lobbyists took this view, and only 8 percent of the legislators espoused it. Overwhelming majorities of all sample groups, however, indicated that the legislature usually acted in the public interest, and only a small proportion in each group suggested that the legislature need not pay attention to small opposition groups. Similarly, very high proportions in every sample appeared to endorse compromise and the accommodation of conflicting interests in the legislative arena.

In keeping with our practice, we factor analysed these items, and the results

Table 5.11   Attitudes Toward Representation and Compromise

Item		Percent Who Agree			
	Public	Attentive Consti-tuents	Party Leaders	Lobbyists	Legislators
The Iowa state legislature does not represent the citizens of Iowa very well.	28.5	27.1	25.6	25.3	15.4
The legislature is controlled by a small handful of men who run it pretty much to suit themselves, no matter what the people want.	24.6	19.8	13.3	15.2	8.3
Most of the things the legislature does are in the interest of the general public, rather than in the interests of special groups.	68.0	75.9	75.6	73.7	85.0
The legislature need not pay attention to opposition to legislation if it comes from a rather small group.	8.5	5.6	3.3	4.0	4.9
The state legislature is important because it is here that differences of opinion about what the state ought to do can be re-solved by compromise for the good of all.	86.5	95.7	95.6	95.9	94.4
When there is a sharp division of opinion in the legislature, both sides should try to go along with the interests of the other group as much as possible rather than insisting that their proposal is the only correct one.	69.2	72.1	74.4	66.7	64.1

were as expected. Table 5.12 plainly shows two quite unambiguous factors: representativeness and compromise. These factor loadings were used to score respondents on the two dimensions named, to create summary variables that could be easily related to legislative support.

REPRESENTATIVENESS, COMPROMISE, AND LEGISLATIVE SUPPORT

Again in accord with our standard procedure, we divided respondents in each sample into high, intermediate, and low clusters along the representativeness and compromise dimensions, and calculated mean legislative support scores for each of the clusters. For each factor, we expected legislative support to be much higher among those whose feelings of representative efficacy and favorableness toward

Table 5.12   Factor Analysis of Representation and Compromise for the Public

Items	Factors*	
	I	II
REPRESENTATIVENESS		
State legislature does not represent citizens	.642	
Legislature controlled by handful	.707	
Legislature works for special interest	-.620	
Legislature can ignore small opposition	.412	
COMPROMISE		
Legislature compromises on differences for the good of all		-.754
Both sides should go along with other groups as much as possible		.589

*All loadings above .300 are shown.

compromise were high, and we anticipated that the reverse would be true for low levels of each variable. From the mean support scores (Table 5.13), we see that the expected relationship materializes for each sample group. For the mass public, the highly efficacious group with respect to representativeness had a slightly positive mean legislative support score, whereas the low group was very low in legislative support. The same pattern, with varying degrees of strength, holds for each elite group, somewhat more strongly for party leaders and lobbyists than for attentive constituents and legislators. When all respondents are taken together, the correlation between representativeness and legislative support is + .33

We performed a similar kind of analysis for the conjunction between variation in respondent scores on the compromise factor and legislative support. The relationship between attitudes toward compromise and support for the legislature is as we expected; there is a positive association, in general, between acceptance of compromise and legislative support. The mean legislative support scores by compromise factor groups and sample groups are presented in Table 5.14. The relationship is quite marked for the public, lobbyists, and legislators, where legislative support systematically falls from the "high compromise" to the "low compromise" groups. For attentive constituents and party leaders, the relationship is less regular but still visible. Considering all respondents together in one large data set, the correlation between variation in the compromise factor and variation in legislative support is +.27.

Once again we combined factorial dimensions to assess their joint impact on legislative support. We did this for each sample group, calculating the multiple correlation coefficients (Table 5.15) and the variance explained by the combined

Table 5.13   Legislative Representativeness and Legislative Support

| | Mean Legislative Support Scores | | |
Sample	High Representativeness	Intermediate Representativeness	Low Representativeness
Public	.011	-.379	-.658
Attentive Constituents	.963	.259	.206
Party Leaders	.518	.207	.063
Lobbyists	.984	.287	.073
Legislators	.935	.474	.436

Table 5.14 Legislative Compromise and Legislative Support

Sample	Mean Legislative Support Scores		
	High Compromise	Intermediate Compromise	Low Compromise
Public	.231	-.436	-.564
Attentive Constituents	.724	.303	.329
Party Leaders	.596	.132	.206
Lobbyists	.873	.371	.101
Legislators	1.135	.653	.432

Table 5.15 Multiple Correlations Between Representation-Compromise and Legislative Support

Sample	R	R^2
Public	.39	.16
Attentive Constituents	.34	.11
Party Leaders	.25	.06
Lobbyists	.54	.30
Legislators	.42	.17

dimensions. It is clear that for each sample except that of party leaders, the combined influences of representativeness and compromise are at least somewhat more useful in accounting for variance in legislative support than either factor individually. In fact, we have no ready explanation for the detailed differences in the explanatory power of the combined dimensions among sample groups. We cannot advance an argument that helps to account for the following conditions: (1) very little variance in legislative support is explained by the representation and compromise factors for party leaders, and (2) a relatively extraordinary proportion of the variance in legislative support is accounted for by these two dimensions for lobbyists. We can only suggest the possibility that the role of the party leader may serve to debase the connection between representativeness-compromise and support for the legislature. There may be a tendency for party leaders to think of a supportable legislative institution as one in which party oppositions are maximized over interparty accommodation, or they may believe that the legislature ought to be run by a small group—the party leadership—in its own interest. We also suggest that thinking of the legislature as a representative body in accord with politicocultural norms, and as a compromising institution, may also be built into the lobbyists' role. Unlike the party militant, the lobbyist presumably is more likely to have a vested interest in legislative compromise and an occupational proclivity to think of the legislative body as a relatively adequate vehicle for the representation of the people.

MULTIPLE EFFECTS ON LEGISLATIVE SUPPORT

In Chapter 3 we dealt with the structural factors of socioeconomic and political status, demonstrating that about one-fourth of the variance in legislative support could be accounted for by considering these dimensions (along with the minor importance of performance evaluation). How much of the variation in legislative support can be accounted for by the variables we have introduced in this chapter? We have considered some 23 phenomenal variables here—an unseemly number to include in a multiple regression analysis.[5] We have tried to reduce the number of variables to be included in an analysis of their multiple effects by making additive combinations of some of them. We combined the two experience attribute factors into one variable measuring both the importance respondents attribute to the set of legislator characteristics and the extent to which respondents think legislators ought to have these traits. We combined the two self-motivation attribute factors and the personal gain motivation factor into a composite variable we call "political opportunism." This variable measures the extent to which respondents both perceived and expected legislators to seek personal gain and to be interested only in reelection, and the extent to which making contacts for personal or business contacts was thought to be important to legislators as a reason for seeking office. Finally, we combined the purposive activity and community status attribute factors with the civic duty motivation factor to create a variable we call "good guys," since it arrays respondents in terms of the extent to which they think legislators are or should be more or less well-informed, hard-working, interested in public service, honest, in tune with sentiments in their districts, and prestigious and influential in their districts, along with the extent to which they think legislators are motivated to run for office because of a sense of civic duty. These operations reduced the total number of variables to 18, which we used to conduct a step-wise multiple regression analysis against legislative support. This analysis makes it very clear that 5 of the 18 variables provide the bulk of the explanatory power: the experience factors, the representativeness factor, the compromise factor, the political opportunism factors, and the political mobility factor. These five variables for the total sample moderately correlate with legislative support individually (for the zero-order correlations, see Table 5.16). All together, they produce a multiple correlation coefficient of .56, accounting for 31 percent of the variance in legislative support. Adding more variables contributes very little to the multiple correlation or the variance explained. We can explain about one-third of the variation in legislative support by taking into account the experience factors, the representativeness factor, the compromise factor, the political opportunism factors, and the political mobility factor. Three variables—experience, representativeness, and compromise—are the most important, judging from the standardized regression coefficients (Table 5.16). When the regression analysis is put into the form of an expression indicating the character of the regression slopes, the best equation for these data is

$$X_1 = .36 + .13X_2 + .28X_3 + .23X_4 + .10X_5 - .13X_6$$

where X_1 = Legislative support
X_2 = Experience factors
X_3 = Representativeness factor
X_4 = Compromise factor
X_5 = Political opportunism factors
X_6 = Political mobility factor

This equation indicates the preeminence in accounting for level of legislative support of expectations about the maturity, educational experience, and experience in public offices of legislators, attitudes toward the representativeness of the legislative institution, and attitudes toward making political compromises in the legislature. Notably missing from this explanatory system is the party loyalty attribute factor. Just as we found earlier that the partisan attachments of our respondents were not significantly associated with their degree of support for the legislature, we now see that expectations about the party loyalty of legislators do not make an important contribution to legislative support. Thus we have demonstrated that how citizens view the legislator, how citizens conceive of their relationship to the legislature, and how citizens perceive the way in which the legislature carries on its work are factors that in our specific ways of delineation, account for a substantial part of the degree of support citizens accord to the legislative institution

Table 5.16   Perspectives on the Legislature and Legislative Support: Multiple Effects

Variables in the Regression Analysis	Zero-order Correlation with Legislative Support	Standardized Regression Coefficients (beta's)
Experience factors	.35	.26
Representativeness factor	.33	.27
Compromise factor	.27	.24
Political Opportunism factors	.21	.14
Political Mobility factor	-.25	-.14

NOTES

1. A different version of this chapter has appeared in Samuel C. Patterson and G. R. Boynton, *Citizens, Leaders, and Legislators: Perspectives on Support for the American Legislature* (Beverly Hills, Calif., 1974), a publication of the Sage Comparative Legislative Research Series.

2. For a different treatment of these data, see Samuel C. Patterson, G. R. Boynton, and Ronald D. Hedlund, ''Perceptions and Expectations of the Legislature and Support for It,'' *American Journal of Sociology,* Vol. 75 (July 1969), 62–76.

3. Because two of the items in Table 5.1 did not produce unambiguous factor loadings (''friendly toward others'' and ''just an average citizen''), they were omitted from further analysis.

4. Part of this analysis was been presented in Samuel C. Patterson and G. R. Boynton, ''Legislative Recruitment in a Civic Culture,'' *Social Science Quarterly,* Vol. 50 (September 1969), 243–263.

5. Four of the variables included in the regression analysis have not been discussed in this chapter. They were omitted because the results of their analysis did not turn out to be particularly interesting intrinsically; they bore only very trivial zero-order correlations with legislative support, and they contributed almost nothing to the overall multiple regression analysis. The four variables referred to respondents' general impressions of the job the legislature does (whether they thought of it largely as a law-making machine, whether they conceived of it mainly in terms of representation, whether they were able to see it as a place where specific kinds of policies are made, or whether they thought of it largely as a place where people are ''in motion''—working hard, taking care of problems, etc.). We have presented some of this evidence in G. R. Boynton, Samuel C. Patterson, and Ronald D. Hedlund, ''The Missing Links in Legislative Politics: Attentive Constituents,'' *Journal of Politics,* Vol. 31 (August 1969), 700–721.

6 INFLUENCE AGENTS AND LEGISLATIVE DECISION MAKING

Having explored public and elite attitudes toward legislatures and their work, we now shift attention to popular perceptions of influence agents and their effect on legislatures. What perceptions do those in the mass public and in political elites have of the relative political influence of legislators' constituents, governmental leaders, party leaders, and political interest groups? Do their expectations of the influence these agencies ought to have differ distinctively from their perceptions of the influence these agencies actually wield? Do members of political elite groups differ substantially from the general public in these respects? Are there clear connections between perspectives on legislative influence and support for the legislature as an institution? In this chapter we map the hierarchy of expected and perceived influence on the legislature and, on a wide canvas, attempt to specify the principal directions of legislative choice as they are viewed in the mass public and in elite groups.

Support for the legislature should accrue in terms of people's conceptions of the structure of influence in the legislature. Presumably, if it were generally believed that the legislature is under the influence of evil groups, vested interests, or illegitimate political bosses, support for the legislature would be extremely low. Similarly, if it were thought that legislators are consistently making public policy choices that run contrary to the interests they were elected to represent, we could assume that support for the legislature would be low. On the other hand, if legislators in the main are seen to be influenced by their own constituents, or if legislators are perceived to make decisions largely in terms of the interests of their constituent, we could expect support for the legislature to be relatively high. Also, if there is a very large gap between the hierarchy of influence in the legislature which people believe ought to exist, and the structure of influence which they believe actually exists, we would expect support for the legislature to be low. Conversely, if there is a high degree of consistency between the perceived and the expected structures of influence on the legislature, we would expect support for the legislature to be very high. Differences in patterns of perceived and expected influence may exist between the mass public and political elite groups, if so, we can explore the extent to which such differences contribute to the linkage by political leaders of people in the mass population to their political institutions.

PUBLIC ATTITUDES TOWARD LEGISLATIVE INFLUENCE

To tap our respondents' perceptions and expectations of legislative influence, we asked in our interviews for ratings of the 13 agencies of legislative influence listed in Table 6.1. First, respondents indicated on a 10 point scale the agencies they thought ought to be influential in the legislature; then they rated them again in terms of the degree of influence they thought the agencies actually had. The metric for each item looked like this:[1]

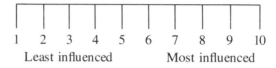

In portraying and assessing these data and their effects on legislative support, we present four separate analyses of the responses from the two ratings of the influence agencies: (a) congruency between perceptions and expectations of influence agents among respondents in the public sample; (b) comparison of the public sample with elite groups on their perceptions, their expectations, and the resultant differentials; (c) a factor analysis of the "should" and of the "do in fact" perceptions of influence agents; and (d) the effects of one's perceptions of influence agents on support for the legislature.

Table 6.1 provides two types of information about the perceptions of the mass public. The first shows the distribution into three categories. The "congruent" group consists of respondents who, within a latitude of 3 points on the rating scale, felt that the agency in question had about as much influence as it ought to have. On either side of this "congruent" group we show the proportions of the sample who felt that the particular agency had more or less influence than it should. The second analysis in Table 6.1 gives the sample means for each rating, the rank orders, and the differences between means.

It is clear from Table 6.1 that there are discontinuities among agencies of legislative influence in terms of the general public's perceptions and expectations. Of the agencies rated, constituents are thought to be the most underrepresented in terms of influence in the legislature. Forty-four percent of the Iowa sample felt that constituents have less influence in the legislature than they should have, whereas

Table 6.1 Congruencies in the Mass Public Between Influence Agencies Ought To Have and Influence They Do Have

Legislative Influence Agencies	% Who Say Agency Has Less Influence Than it Should	% Who Are Congruent	% Who Say Agency Has More Influence Than it Should	Influence Agency Ought to Have		Influence Agency Does Have		Mean Difference
				Mean	Rank	Mean	Rank	
Constituents	43.7	48.2	8.2	8.2	1	6.8	1	-1.36
Statewide opinion polls	34.2	50.3	15.6	6.7	2	6.1	4.5	- .59
Experts in legislature	29.3	52.2	18.6	6.6	3	6.3	2	- .40
Experts in state government	25.1	53.9	16.0	6.4	4	6.2	3	- .23
Governor	13.8	47.9	38.4	4.9	5	6.0	6	+1.07
Labor	18.0	43.6	31.2	4.6	6	5.6	7.5	+1.06
Party leaders in the legislature	8.6	36.3	40.3	4.5	7	6.1	4.5	+1.62
Chamber of Commerce	20.2	57.6	22.3	4.2	8	4.4	10	+ .22
Farm Bureau	15.8	44.2	34.7	4.1	9	5.0	9	+ .87
Chairmen of state parties	9.4	45.0	45.7	3.8	10	5.6	7.5	+1.78
National Farmers Organization	14.6	55.7	27.7	3.6	11	4.2	11.5	+ .56
Banks	10.9	40.0	29.3	3.2	12	4.2	11.5	+1.03
Insurance Companies	7.9	53.6	38.6	2.6	13	4.1	13	+1.53

"constituents" ranked first as the group that ought to have such influence. Although ratings of constituent influence produced a large negative mean difference between expectations and perceptions of influence, constituents were still rated by respondents as the agency having the most influence in the legislature. In general, the order of expected and perceived influence is: (1) constituents and polls reflecting public opinion, (2) experts, (3) party leaders, and (4) interest groups. The proportion of respondents who believe that constituents, polls, and experts have less influence than they should is larger than the proportion believing that these agents have more influence than they should. However, a higher proportion of respondents felt that all the other agencies of influence had more influence than they should, rather than less. The rank order correlation between perceived and expected influence agencies in the general public is very high ($r_s = .91$).

The largest differences in mean ratings are for legislative and extralegislative party leaders. Legislative party leaders fall at the median rank in expected influence but are ranked fourth by respondents in perceived actual influence (tied with statewide public opinion polls). But relatively high proportions of the mass public respondents, 40 and 46 percent, felt that party leaders (in the legislature and as chairmen of state parties) have more influence in the legislature than they should. Also the difference of mean scores for each type of party leader is very high and positive (leaders score higher in perceived than in expected influence). All this evidence shows that in Iowa, party leaders are seen by the mass public to be the most overtly influential of all agents.

Interest groups generally fall at the bottom of the rank orders of perceived and expected influence. Unlike constituents and experts, who show a negative difference between expected and perceived influence, but like party leaders (including the governor), interest groups are thought to have more influence than they should. Labor, banks, and insurance companies display the highest differences in means; farm organizations and the chamber of commerce give the least differences between expected and perceived influence.

We indicated in Chapter 2 that support for the legislature in Iowa appears to be very high. In the general Iowa population, perspectives on influence in the legislature appear to provide a basis for the high level of legislative support in the population. Iowans do not appear to have the view that their legislative body is controlled by special interests. Furthermore, there is a very high degree of consistency between perceptions of actual influence in the legislature and expectations of agencies that ought to have legislative influence. Since the hiatus between these two is not very substantial, high public support for the legislature seems quite understandable.

Table 6.2   Public and Elite Expectations of Legislative Influence Agencies

Legislative Influence Agencies	Public Mean	Rank	Attentive Constituents Mean	Rank	Party Leaders Mean	Rank	Lobbyists Mean	Rank	Legislators Mean	Rank
Constituents	8.2	1	8.4	1	8.4	1	8.3	1	7.8	1
Statewide opinion polls	6.7	2	5.4	5	5.4	5	5.2	5	5.0	5
Experts in legislature	6.6	3	6.9	2	6.7	2	7.0	2	6.9	2
Experts in state government	6.4	4	6.2	3	6.2	3.5	5.9	3.5	5.9	3
Governor	4.9	5	4.5	7	4.8	7	4.8	6	4.1	7
Labor	4.6	6	3.5	10	3.5	9	4.0	9	3.2	10
Party Leaders in Legislature	4.5	7	5.6	4	6.2	3.5	5.9	3.5	5.8	4
Chamber of Commerce	4.2	8	4.1	8	4.1	8	4.2	8	3.6	8
Farm Bureau	4.1	9	3.8	9	3.0	10.5	3.8	11.5	3.3	9
Chairmen of State Parties	3.8	10	4.6	6	5.2	6	4.7	7	4.5	6
National Farmers' Organization	3.6	11	2.9	13	2.8	12	3.0	13	2.7	13
Banks	3.2	12	3.4	11	3.0	10.5	3.8	11.5	3.0	11
Insurance Companies	2.6	13	3.0	12	2.6	13	3.9	10	2.9	12

ELITE ATTITUDES TOWARD LEGISLATIVE INFLUENCE

In Tables 6.2 and 6.3, attentive constituents, party leaders, lobbyists, and legislators are compared with the general public. In terms of expectations of influence by these agencies (Table 6.2), the hierarchy of the expected influence among elite groups is very nearly the same. Differences between the elite groups and the general public are very small. The principal difference comes in the somewhat greater degree of influence expected of party leaders inside and outside the legislative body. In addition, political leaders do not expect statewide opinion polls to carry the weight of influence that is accorded them by the general population. However, it is clear that the similarities among leadership groups, and between leadership echelons and the general public, are much more pronounced than the differences.

Table 6.3   Public and Elite Perceptions of Legislative Influence Agencies

Legislative Influence Agencies	Public Mean	Rank	Attentive Constituents Mean	Rank	Party Leaders Mean	Rank	Lobbyists Mean	Rank	Legislators Mean	Rank
Constituents	6.8	1	7.0	1	6.9	1	6.9	2.5	7.3	1
Statewide opinion polls	6.1	4.5	5.7	4.5	5.6	5	5.0	9.5	5.1	5
Experts in legislature	6.3	2	6.7	3	6.7	2	6.9	2.5	6.3	2
Experts in state government	6.2	3	5.6	6.5	5.4	6	5.6	7	5.7	4
Governor	6.0	6	5.5	8	5.2	7.5	5.9	5.5	4.3	8
Labor	5.6	7.5	5.0	9	4.7	9	4.4	12	3.3	12
Party Leaders in Legislature	6.1	4.5	6.8	2	6.6	3	7.1	1	6.2	3
Chamber of Commerce	4.4	10	4.5	10	4.5	10	4.7	11	4.1	9
Farm Bureau	5.0	9	5.7	4.5	6.1	4	6.1	4	4.6	7
Chairmen of State Parties	5.6	7.5	5.6	6.5	5.2	7.5	5.9	5.5	4.8	6
NFO	4.2	11.5	3.0	13	2.9	13	2.7	13	2.5	13
Banks	4.2	11.5	4.3	11	4.4	11.5	5.5	8	3.8	10.5
Insurance Companies	4.1	13	4.2	12	4.4	11.5	5.0	9.5	3.8	10.5

A very similar pattern occurs when we turn to perceptions of actual influence in the legislature (Table 6.3). As with the expectations of influence, elite groups and general public tend to feel that constituents are more influential in the legislature than other potential agencies. Insofar as perceptions of legislative influence are concerned, the political leadership groups exhibit some interesting differences. For example, lobbyists view statewide opinion polls as being much less influential with the legislature than do other of the leadership groups, and they perceive the legislative party leadership as the most influential agency. Legislators perceive the farm bureau and labor unions as somewhat less influential than do the other leadership groups, although the low rating of labor by legislators is made by lobbyists as well.

Also, there are some interesting differences between the leadership groups in general and the mass public. For example, for legislators themselves, experts in the state government are regarded as less influential by the leadership groups than by the general public. More influence in the legislature is attributed to party leaders by respondents in the elite groups than by respondents in the mass public. But in spite of these small differences, one is again struck by the very substantial degree of similarity in the perceptions of the influence structure around the state legislature given by both political leaders and citizens in general.

Therefore, as we suggested earlier, two kinds of empirical statement appear to be justified in the light of the generally high public support accorded the Iowa legislature. First, legislative support is high because people do not regard the legislature as dominated by vested interests; rather, they think that citizens in general constitute the most influential agency with the legislature. Second, support for the legislature is high because there are no significant gaps between attributed and expected legislative influence. Those who are thought to deserve to have most influence in the legislature actually are believed to have it. And leaders' hierarchies of perceived and expected influence are not greatly different from those reported by the general public.

One possible caveat, however, appears if we look at overall data on the perception-expectation differentials (see Table 6.4). The most obvious feature is the comparatively small absolute difference in values for every measure across public and elite groups; however, a one-way analysis of variance across type of respondent shows that four of these six differences have statistically significant F-ratios of explained to unexplained variance. Most striking are legislators who have scores that differ the most from the other groups. (This is confirmed by an examination of t-scores comparing groups.) These legislators have either the highest or the lowest score for each of the six measures, suggesting their comparatively greater deviance. For example, legislators have the highest instance of *no difference in rankings* between expectation and perception of agent influence (4.4); the largest number of instances of an agent expected to have more influence than it was perceived he should (3.9); the lowest number of instances of an agent seen as having more influence than he should (4.6); and lowest average of difference in rating for all three measures—absolute (2.0), positive (1.7), and negative (1.9). Thus of the five groups studied, legislators, who have the best insider perspective on legislative operations and also probably have the greatest sensitivity to the Iowa legislature's image, have the lowest differential level between the perceived and expected influence of these 13 agents. On the other hand, the largest average perception-expectation differential score for all questions, as well as for positive and negative directions, is always observed for mass public respondents. To the extent that there is a greater expectation-perception differential among the public, and to the extent that such a differential *is* linked to support, we might have partial evidence in Table 6.4 to explain why levels of support are lower within the mass public. Conversely, the greater convergence of perceptions with expectations among legislators may also contribute to the law-

Table 6.4   Differential Propensity to Name Influence Agents

Type of Differential[a]	Type of Respondent					One-Way Anova		
	Mass Public	Party Leaders	Attentive Constituents	Lobby- ists	Legis- lators	df	F-ratio	Signi- ficance
Average Number of Agent Pairs Where No Differential was Detected	3.6	3.4	3.6	3.2	4.4	4,1854	4.30	$p < .005$
Average Difference in Rating Scores	2.7	2.4	2.4	2.3	2.0	4,1854	6.39	$p < .0001$
Average Number of Agent Pairs Where Respondent Reported that the Agent SHOULD HAVE more Influence Than was Perceived (Positive Direction)	3.4	3.6	3.5	3.5	3.9	4,1854	1.22	$p > .05$
Average Difference in Positive Direction	2.3	1.9	2.1	2.0	1.7	4,1854	3.86	$p < .005$
Average Number of Agent Pairs Where Respondent Reported That the Agent DID IN FACT Have more Influence than it Should (Negative Direction)	5.0	5.3	5.5	5.0	4.6	4,1854	0.38	$p > .05$
Average Difference In Negative Direction	2.6	2.4	2.4	2.3	1.9	4,1854	5.71	$p < .0005$

[a]In this context a "differential" is defined as a numerical rating on the SHOULD question that differs from the numerical rating on the DO IN FACT question.

makers' higher levels of legislative support. On the other hand, other factors probably are also related to high and low differential patterns and may affect any relationship between support and the existence of a perception-expectation differential. A more conclusive resolution of this possibility must therefore await later multivariate analysis.

FACTOR ANALYSES OF PERCEPTIONS AND EXPECTATIONS REGARDING INFLUENCE AGENTS

To assess more precisely the effect of variations in perspectives of legislative influence on diffuse support for the legislature and to continue comparing perceptions with expectations, we again use factor analysis. Because the 13 influence agencies to which we have referred constitute an unwieldy set of variables taken individually, we have factor analyzed them, condensing them into a logically meaningful and parsimonious set. The analysis was repeated for each set of questions—perceptions and expectations. The 13 influence agencies fall neatly into four distinct groups for both the perception and the expectation analyses, and the subsequent analysis with four factors is therefore quite straightforward. Table 6.5 shows the results of the factor analysis when all groups were combined. The first factor identifies pressure group influence; the second, the influence of legislative and state governmental experts and citizen opinion; the third, statewide and legislative party leadership; and the fourth, the results of statewide public opinion polls. (We have conducted a similar kind of analysis with each sample, and the results produced by this extended analysis are essentially the same as that given when all respondents were combined.)

When a similar factor analysis was completed for the perceived influence ratings

Table 6.5 Factor Analysis of Agencies that Ought To Be Influential in the Legislature

Legislative Influence Agencies	I Pressure Groups	II Experts	III Partisanism	IV Populism
Farm Bureau	.770			
National Farmers Organization	.754			
Insurance Companies	.722			
Banks	.719		.346	
Labor	.665			
Chamber of Commerce	.648			
Legislative Experts		.818		
Experts in State Government		.739		
Citizen Opinions		.518		.330
Party Leaders in the Legislature			.809	
Chairmen of the State Parties			.775	
Governor			.544	.472
Public Opinion Polls				.828
Cumulative % of Total Variance	33.8	45.4	55.0	62.5
Cumulative % of Explained Variance	54.0	72.7	88.0	100.0

Factors[a]

[a]All loadings above .300 are shown.

(Table 6.6), some interesting shifts are noted. For example, pressure groups normally identified with the Republican Party—insurance companies, the banks, the farm bureau, and the chamber of commerce—load highly on factor I, whereas the Democratic-oriented ones—labor and the NFO—load on factor III. In addition, the governor, Democrat Harold Hughes, loads highly with labor and the NFO on factor III. Thus when the arena shifts from expectations to perceptions, a quite different factor structure emerges. This structure seems to differentiate between political parties—factor I being Republican and factor III being Democratic, to blend citizen opinions with public opinion polls—factor IV constituents, and to blur partially the distinction between experts and party leaders—factor II.

INFLUENCE AGENTS AND LEGISLATIVE SUPPORT

We have adopted three strategies to assess the relative effects of perspectives of legislative influence on legislative support. First we analyzed the proposition that

Table 6.6   Factor Analysis of Agencies that Are in Fact Influential in the Legislature

Legislative Influence Agencies[a]	Factors[a]			
	I Republicans	II Experts	III Democratic	IV Constituents
Insurance Companies	.803			
Banks	.796			
Farm Bureau	.714			
Chamber of Commerce	.693	.323		
Legislative Experts		.812		
Experts in State Government		.750		
Party Leaders in the Legislature		.557	-.323	
Chairmen of the State Parties	.314	.489	-.459	
Governor			-.738	
Labor			-.648	
NFO			-.604	
Citizen Opinions				.847
Public Opinion Polls			-.358	.753
Cumulative % of Total Variance	35.3	47.6	55.5	62.6
Cumulative % of Explained Variance	56.5	76.1	88.8	100.0

[a]All loadings above .300 are shown.

there would be a substantial correlation between perceived legislative influence and support for the legislature. We expected increases in perceived influence by experts and constituents to be associated with high legislative support, and increases in interest group or party leadership influences to be associated with relatively lower legislative support. The actual correlations are very low, but they develop in the expected direction. When all four factors are combined in a multiple regression analysis, a somewhat more impressive set of correlations is produced. Table 6.7 lists the multiple correlation coefficients and the variance explained by the four attributed influence factors for each of the sample groups. For the general public, attentive constituents, and legislators, the multiple correlation is on the order of .2, which means that only a relatively small proportion of the variance in the legislative support can be accounted for in terms of influence attribution. For party leaders and lobbyists, the multiple correlation is on the order of .4; thus in these samples, influence attributions account for about 16 or 17 percent of the variation in legislative support.

Another strategy for assessing the effects of perceived and expected legislative influence on support for the legislature was to test the hypothesis that if there is a wide differential between the legislative influence citizens perceive to be wielded by interest groups, constituents, experts, and party leaders, and the influence citizens expect these groups ought to have, then legislative support will tend to be low. Conversely, if perceived and expected influences are roughly congruent, legislative support will tend to be high. Given both the high general support of the legislature and the rather high degree of congruency between expectations about legislative influence and perceptions of it, the Iowa data were far from ideal for rigorous testing of this hypothesis. For each set of factors for expectations and perceptions, we selected the most congruent and the most incongruent respondents

Table 6.7   Attributed Legislative Influence and Support for the Legislature

Samples	Regression	Analysis
	R	R^2
Public	.22	.05
Attentive Constituents	.24	.06
Party Leaders	.40	.16
Lobbyists	.41	.17
Legislators	.24	.06

from the mass public, on the basis of two criteria: consistency of responses and level of expectations. The application of these criteria led to a selection of respondents that would juxtapose the most congruent and the most incongruent perception-expectation responses for each factor. Utilizing mean legislative support scores for both groups, it was possible to test the differences between these sets of means.[2] For the influence agency factors, significant differences (*t*-tests) materialize only for the influence of constituents and interest groups. It can be said that if constituency opinion is seen to be less influential in legislative decision making than it should, or if interest groups are seen to be more influential than they should be, support for the legislature will be relatively low. Differences between perceptions and expectations about the influence of party leaders or experts appear to have little effect on legislative support. Of course the evidence is not powerful, but it does provide some support for the hypothesis that certain perception-expectation differentials in the mass public influence support, or lack of support, for a legislature.

A third test of these data involved using multiple regression for infleunce agent variables that were significantly related to the dependent variable. From a total of 14 variables discussed in this chapter, 7 had sufficient zero-order correlations with legislative support to justify including them in the regression analysis. Table 6.8 provides the product-moment correlations, the beta values, and the regression equation. This analysis indicates that the multiple R for these seven variables with legislative support is .33, thus explaining about 11 percent of the total variance in the dependent variable. Given the probable effects of background variables on perceptions and expectations of influence agents and on legislative support, it seems unlikely that respondents' images of legislative influence agencies have much independent effect on level of legislative support.

Table 6.8   Perspectives on the Legislature and Legislative Support: Multiple Effects

Variables in the Regression Analysis	Zero-order Correlation with Legislative Support	Standardized Regression Coefficients (beta's)
Populism Should Factor	-.23	-.18
Net Expectation/Perception Difference	-.14	-.09
Democratic Do Factor	.22	.12
Experts Should Factor	.11	.11
Pressure Groups Should Factor	-.11	-.10
Partisanism Should Factor	.07	.06

$$X_1 = .18 - .17X_2 - .07X_3 + .12X_4 + .11X_5 - .09X_6 + .05X_7$$

where X_1 = legislative support

X_2 = populism should factor

X_3 = net expectation-perception difference

X_4 = Democratic do factor

X_5 = experts should factor

X_6 = pressure groups should factor

X_7 = partisanism should factor

multiple R = .33

multiple R^2 = .11

NOTES

1 Each respondent scored a series of items such as "legislators should be influenced by the opinions of the citizens of their districts." Later in the interview schedule, respondents scored the same kinds of item in the form, "legislators are influenced by the opinions of citizens in their districts."

2 A more elaborate presentation of this analysis is available in Samuel C. Patterson, G. R. Boynton, and Ronald D. Hedlund, "Perceptions and Expectations of the Legislature and Support for It," *American Journal of Sociology*, Vol. 75 (July 1969), 62–76.

7 DECISIONAL REFERENTS

One of the primary activities associated with legislatures is decision making. Whether a legislature is viewed as an autonomous branch of government independently charting its own course on matters of public policy, or as a subordinate institution that acts in response to external pressures, some type of decisional process is inherent, even if it involves a decision to acquiesce.

Decision making has been described as the selection of goals that are consistent with one's values, followed by the use of appropriate means to achieve these goals.[1] As goals are translated to the operational level, they become referents or criteria for decision making.[2] However, the making of decisions in a legislature is a relative matter in that public policy choices often are made under conflicting pressures. We could not encompass all the possible conflicting pressures on legislative choice in any single study, but in this study of Iowa we tried to identify the major referents for legislative decision making and to assess their relative effects across the range of decisions made during a legislative session. The priorities assigned to these referents when they were juxtaposed against one another were also considered.

Recent political science research into individual-level choice making by legislators suggests six general decisional referents: system constituents, district constituents, legislator predispositions, the chief executive, political parties, and pressure groups.[3] We wanted to know how our Iowa respondents perceived these six referents, to determine how persons order these criteria and to assess the effects of variation in this ordering on support for the legislature. Data ascertaining the comparative judgments of respondents for the referents were collected using the paired comparison scaling technique. Paired comparisons are a psychological scaling technique based upon Louis L. Thurstone's law of comparative judgment, which is especially useful for determining scale values and the ordering of stimuli along some underlying continuum.

> The essence of the method is that sets of pairs of stimuli, or items of different values on a single continuum . . . are presented to the subject with instructions to choose one

member of each pair on the basis of some stated criterion. The criterion much be: which one better characterizes the subject, or which does the subject prefer . . . it is assumed that he will choose the one item that fits his own needs. A unique feature of the scale is that the social desirability values of the paired members were determined empirically. . . .[4]

Paired comparison analysis thus produces information about the stimuli (stimulus-centered), provides a scale score and ranking of stimuli along the continuum under study, and treats the rankings given by additional respondents as verifications of the judgmental processes.[5] In our Iowa study the six decisional referents were the stimuli being tested.

Since the research design assumed that a respondent's preferential ordering of referents might differ from his perceptions of which referents were actually being favored in decision making, two separate paired comparisons were included. With the first we tried to determine the respondent's expectations regarding which referents ought to be highly valued—"which one *should* the legislator choose? The second was designed to help us learn his perceptions of the referents actually used in decision making—which one *would in fact* the legislator choose?[6] The overall rankings of the six referents, the consistency of preference individuals demonstrated among the referents, and the effects of the differences between one's preferential and actual ordering of referents on one's level of legislative support are the major topic of this chapter.

PERSPECTIVES ON LEGISLATORS' DECISIONAL REFERENTS

A basic analysis of the paired comparison data for all the respondents combined reveals that 45 percent of them thought legislators ought to choose district interests over statewide concerns. (See Table 7.1, which should be read by column.) At the same time, 33 percent said that the concerns of the district ought to have priority over one's own conscience, and about 86 percent believed that the district should take precedence over the party's interests. The second part of Table 7.1 lists priorities in terms of legislators' actual choices. Thus, for example, 70 percent of the respondents felt that legislators choose district over state interest, 54 percent believed that legislators consider district interests over their own conscience, and 51 percent believed that legislators place district over party interests.

These paired comparisons give a rough idea of the hierarchy of perceived and expected referents for legislative choices. It is overwhelmingly clear from Table 7.1 that respondents generally felt that legislators ought to give their highest decision-making priority to the dictates of their own judgment or conscience. The

Table 7.1 Perceived and Expected Choices for Legislators Among Decisional Referents: All Respondents

Decisional Referents	Decisional Referents					
	District	State	Conscience	Party	Group	Governor
			Legislator Ought to Choose			
District	–	54.3	66.3	13.8	5.3	14.5
State	45.1	–	67.5	17.4	6.9	10.0
Conscience	33.5	32.2	–	17.5	12.6	14.4
Party	85.7	82.4	82.4	–	24.5	26.1
Group	94.5	92.9	87.2	74.7	–	62.2
Governor	85.2	89.8	85.5	72.9	36.2	–
Ranking	2.5	2.5	1	4	6	5
			Legislators Actually Do Choose			
District	–	29.8	45.8	48.6	17.2	22.4
State	70.0	–	55.4	60.9	25.9	23.6
Conscience	54.0	44.5	–	51.2	30.8	31.8
Party	51.2	38.8	48.6	–	13.7	18.0
Group	82.5	73.9	68.9	85.9	–	55.9
Governor	77.3	75.9	68.0	81.7	43.4	–
Ranking	1	4	3	2	6	5

second most important priority was attached with about equal weight to the interests of the legislators' district and the state as a whole. Party influences ranked next, then the influence of the governor, and finally, pressures from interest groups. This hierarchy of priorities is roughly consistent with the pattern exhibited in Chapter 6 concerning the perceptions and expectations about influence agencies in the legislature. The analysis underscores again the low esteem attached to interest groups as agencies of legislative influence.

When we turn to perceptions of the actual decisional choices of legislators, the hierarchy of priorities is noticeably different from that suggested by the expectations respondents had for legislative choice. As the bottom half of Table 7.1 suggests, although conscience was given highest priority in expectational terms, respondents fairly overwhelmingly thought that legislators in fact choose the interest of their district most frequently over the other decisional referents. The second priority in legislative choice insofar as perceptions of what legislators actually do is concerned was party influences. The legislator's judgment or conscience was ranked third in priority; the fourth rank was given to the state as a whole, the fifth to the governor, and the sixth to interest groups. For example, nearly two-thirds of all the respondents indicated a belief that the legislator's conscience ought to take precedence over the interests of his district in legislative choices, but more than half (54 percent) believed that legislators choose district interests over their own conscience. In short, Iowa legislators are generally expected to be trustees: to make their legislative choices mainly in terms of their own best judgment and conscience; however, people tend to think that legislators are delegates: that they represent the interests of their own districts. Although of course a legislator's best judgment may not necessarily be in conflict with the interests of his district as he sees them, these interests represent distinctive analytical foci for legislative representation. [7]

Furthermore, more than half (54 percent) felt that legislators ought to choose the interest of the state as a whole over the concerns of their own district, whereas 70 percent of the respondents believed that legislators actually choose district interests over statewide interests. Again, legislators may not see differences between these two areal foci of representation, but the evidence reflects a gap between expectations about the representational role of the legislator and his performance as perceived by respondents.

It is also interesting to note the role of party influence in perspectives on legislative decision making. Here again, as with the earlier analysis of influence agencies, party influence is generally thought to be greater than it should be. Whereas about three-quarters of the entire group of respondents felt that party influence ought to have priority over interest groups and the influence of the governor, only a small proportion (less than one-fifth) thought that party influences ought to have a higher priority than those of the district, the state, or the legislators' conscience. In contrast, nearly half the respondents (49 percent) felt that party influences were, in fact, given higher priority than those of the district, 61 percent believed that party interests were given higher priority than statewide interests, and 51 percent indicated that party influences had higher priority than the dictates of the legislators' own conscience. Thus it is clear that respondents generally felt that interest groups and the governor have more influence in legislative decision making than they should have.

EXPECTATION AND PERFORMANCE REFERENTS

We showed in Chapter 3 that legislators exhibit higher support levels for the legislature than do lobbyists, attentive constituents, party leaders, or the general public; we might also expect legislators to differ significantly on their rankings of the expectation and performance referents. However, this is *not* the case. Legislators, political influentials (which included lobbyists, attentive constituents, and

Table 7.2   Rankings and Scale Scores for Expectation and Performance Decisional Criteria

	Expectations						Performance					
		Respondents						Respondents				
Referents	Legislators		Political Elite		General Public		Referents	Legislators		Political Elite		General Public	
	R^a	S^b	R	S	R	S		R	S	R	S	R	S
Conscience	1	-1.10	1	-.90	1	-.50	District	1	-.55	2	-.47	1	-.33
State	2	-.78	2	-.74	3	-.45	Conscience	2	-.44	3	-.22	4	-.07
District	3	-.68	3	-.66	2	-.47	Party	3	-.35	1	-.58	2	-.28
Party	4	.22	4	.18	4	.33	State	4	-.20	4	.07	3	-.15
Governor	5	1.11	5	1.01	5	.38	Group	5	.60	5	.51	6	.59
Group	6	1.23	6	1.11	6	.71	Governor	6	.94	6	.70	5	.23
Kendall's Coefficient of Agreement	.602		.538		.331			.323		.279		.214	
Kendall's Coefficient of Concordance	.9746							.8730					

[a] R = Rank

[b] S = Scale Score (Mean of entries from standardized (z) Matrix. See A. Edwards, <u>Techniques of Attitude Scale Construction</u>, pp. 34-37.)

party leaders), and the public all have virtually the same rankings of the referents on the expectation dimension (Table 7.2).[8] Kendall's coefficient of concordance is exceptionally high for both the expectation and performance dimensions, indicating significant *across-group* consensus.[9] Thus all three groups show substantial agreement on the rankings of the referents that should be and on the referents that are in fact used in legislative decision-making. This finding suggests that a person's life experience and position vis-à-vis a legislature play a marginal role in developing his perceptions of which referents *should be* and which referents *are in fact* followed in legislative decision making. This high level of consensus may indicate that the political socialization for elected representatives, political influentials, and the general public is so similar and so effective that once the preferences have been established, they are very resistant to change.

Although the three groups appear to have similar perceptions of the referents on each dimension, one must also evaluate the degree to which the rankings of the individuals within each group agree with one another. The test for *within-group* agreement, Kendall's coefficient of agreement, shows ". . . the extent to which a group of judges agree in their comparative judgments."[10] The coefficient of agreement values indicate for the expectation dimension that if one picked a random pair of respondents from within each group and asked each to judge a random pair of referents, about 80 percent of the time the legislative pair would agree, about 75 percent of the time political influentials would agree, and about 67 percent of the time the public pair would agree, as compared with an anticipated 50 percent probability due to chance—that is, if there were *no* agreement. (On the performance dimension, the comparable agreement values are about 66 percent of the time for legislators, 64 percent for political influentials, and 60 percent for the public.) The higher values among legislators than among influentials, and the higher values among influentials than among the public, indicate that legislators have the highest agreement in their rankings, influentials have the second highest, and the public the lowest. This is the case for each dimension. (Perhaps this finding could have been anticipated for the performance dimension, given a smaller number of legislators than influentials or public and the greater opportunity for legislators to interact and observe one another's behavior, but such explanations seem to be less adequate for the expectation dimension.)

The tendency for all three types of respondent to rank conscience higher than any other expectation referent is a clear indication of support for the trustee model within each group of respondents and parallels the finding when all respondents were combined. The second- and third-ranked expectation referents—wishes of state and district—are both constituent-oriented. Their high position demonstrates the importance attached by respondents of all types to constituent wishes in legislative choice making. Ranked on the lower portion of the scale are three referents whose proper role in legislative decision making is the subject of much debate. Political reformers, among others, frequently argue that steps should be taken to insulate legislators from the pressure exerted on them by the "self-seeking" and "biased" political parties, the governor, and interest groups.[11] The low rankings of these referents is probably predictable, given this widely accepted predisposition.

On the performance demension, a slightly different ordering of the referents is observed. Legislative and public respondents perceive that in their decision making, Iowa legislators actually place wishes of the district first; the influentials rank political party first and district second (Table 7.2). Generally, ranking higher on the performance than on the expectation dimension for all respondents is political party, whereas legislators' conscience and wishes of the state generally rank lower. Although the consensus across types of respondents, as measured by the coefficient of concordance, is lower on the performance than on the expectation dimension, the level continues to be higher than would be expected assuming a random ordering of referents.

One question that might be raised regarding these paired comparison orderings is the degree of consistency displayed by a respondent in his choices among decisional referents. For example, distinguishing a random selection of referents from one that is clearly ordered is an important feature of paired comparison analysis. The strategy we selected required computing a widely used coefficient of consistence for each respondent's ordering of performance and expectation referents.[12] This measure varies between $+1.0$ and 0.0, with a higher score indicating a greater degree of consistency in a respondent's judgments regarding decisional referents. Table 7.3 gives the means of the consistence coefficients and a one-way analysis of variance for both expectation and performance referents when the respondents were separated into the five groups. This analysis demonstrates that on each dimension, legislators as a group showed the greatest degree of

Table 7.3   One-Way Analysis and Mean Scores for Consistence Coefficients of Performance and Expectation Criteria

Type of Referent	Means					Anova		
	Mass Public	Party Leaders	Atten-tives	Lobbyists	Legislators	df	F-ratio	Signi-ficance
Expectations	.729	.901	.917	.830	.946	4,1854	16.73	$p < .0001$
Performance	.658	.847	.815	.626	.877	4,1854	20.23	$p < .0001$

consistency, with the others having lower means. Furthermore, mean scores were lower for each group on the performance than on the expectation dimension. Finally, the F-ratios, indicating differences across the group means, are statistically significant for each type of referent.

To determine that the similar ordering of these referents by legislators, influentials, and public are valid and not the result of some other factor, controls were introduced for personal background and political variables—education, predispositions toward social welfarism, faith in people, representation, and political party identification. The consensus in ranking the criteria by all three types of respondent, demonstrated by the concordance coefficients in Table 7.4, continues to be generally high under these control conditions and approximates the values obtained without controlling. Thus the degree of agreement across types of respondent for each level of the control variable appears to approximate that level observed without any control, and one can conclude that controlling for these variables has little impact on across group agreement.

EXPECTATION–PERFORMANCE DIFFERENTIAL

These findings, together with prior ones, suggest the existence of an expectation-performance differential among Iowa respondents. This possibility can be seen if data from Table 7.2 are rearranged, arraying expectation and performance rankings more closely together. Although some similarity of rankings can be observed across the two dimensions, this agreement is far from complete. Legislators and the public each appear to have a moderate expectation-performance differential and the political influentials a more substantial one. The degree to which the differential exists for each group is seen if one looks at the values for Kendall's rank correlation coefficient tau (τ). The values for tau in Table 7.5 substantiate that the rankings of referents on the performance dimension are *not* identical with the rankings on the expectation dimension for legislators, influentials, or public, although some degree of agreement is evident.

Each *group* of respondents perceives that legislators place a lower priority on their own consciences than the groups believe should be the case, and two groups, legislators and influentials, perceive that statewide interests rank lower than they should. The most dramatic moves upward on the performance rankings are district interests and political parties. Thus each group perceives that political parties and district interests rank too high as referents guiding legislative decision making; and each also sees the legislator's own conscience and, to a lesser extent, statewide interests are ranking too low on the performance dimension. This seems to indicate

Table 7.4   Coefficients of Concordance for Decisional Criteria

Control	Expectations	Performance
Education		
1-11 years	.8730	.7714
12 years	.9238	.7968
13-16 years	.9746	.9111
17 or more years	.8730	.9111
Social Welfare[a]		
High	.8730	.9238
Medium	.9492	.8730
Low	.9746	.8222
Faith-in-People[b]		
High	.9492	.8476
Medium	.9746	.8730
Low	.8730	.8730
Political Party[c]		
Democratic	.8730	.9238
Republican	.9492	.8222
Representation[d]		
High	.9238	.8603
Medium	.9746	.8730
Low	.9111	.9238
No Control	.9746	.8730

All coefficients of concordance are statistically significant at
.05 level.

[a]The "social welfare" variable is based on standardized factor scores
from a rotated factor analysis solution of items relating to ideological
attitudes. The items composing this scale indicate the respondents'
attitudes toward governmental involvement in social welfare issues.
Respondents scoring "High" have a favorable view of government's
role in social welfare areas.

[b]The "faith-in-people" variable is based on standardized factor
scores from a rotated factor analysis solution of items relating
to psychological predispositions. The items composing this
scale indicate the respondents' attitudes toward other individuals.
Respondents scoring "High" have a high level of faith in other
persons.

[c]Since no member of the legislature had an "Independent" party
identification, this level of the control variable was excluded
from analysis.

[d]The "representational" variable is based on standardized factor
scores from a rotated factor analysis solution of items relating
to legislative attitudes. The items composing this scale indicate
the respondents' attitudes toward the legislature as a representational institution. Respondents scoring "High" view the legislature
as an institution that does perform a representational function.

Table 7.5   Rankings for Expectation-Performance Differential

Referents	Legislators		Political Elite		General Public	
	Expectations	Performance	Expectations	Performance	Expectations	Performance
Conscience	1	2	1	3	1	4
State	2	4	2	4	3	3
District	3	1	3	2	2	1
Party	4	3	4	1	4	2
Governor	5	6	5	6	5	5
Group	6	5	6	5	6	6
Kendall's Tau	.47		.20		.47	

that persons, regardless of whether they are citizens, political influentials, or legislators, believe in trustee-oriented decisional criteria but perceive delegate- and party-oriented decisional criteria to be operative.

Previous analysis in this chapter has used groupings of respondents (e.g. mass public, party leaders, attentive constituents, lobbyists, and legislators) as the base for analysis and for making conclusions about decisional referents. Although such aggregate analysis is a widely used and accepted analytical strategy, a complementary analysis of differences in the rankings of expectation versus performance referents *on the individual level* should further illuminate our study of decisional referent.[13] The most plausible strategy for determining whether an expectation-performance differential exists on the individual level, for estimating the magnitude of that differential, and for making comparisons of individual-level differences among respondent types is to calculate a summary measure that assesses the agreement between an individual respondent's expectation and his performance rankings of decisional referents. Kendall's tau was again selected as the most appropriate summary measure, and in this instance, a separate tau coefficient was calculated between the two sets of rankings for each respondent. The distribution of these tau values by type of respondent appears in Table 7.6 and reveals the large number of respondents displaying congruent [$\tau + 0.50$ ($0 + 1.00$)] rather than incongruent [$\tau - 0.50$ ($0 - 1.00$)] patterns. More than two out of every five respondents appear to have exceedingly high levels of congruence ($> +.50$) between the rankings of decisional referents they expect to be used. On the other hand, less than 4 percent have substantial differences from one ranking to the other ($> -.50$). This individual-level evidence further persuades us that a substantial

Table 7.6   Expectation-Perception Differential Scores (Tau) of Influence Agencies

Values of Differential Measure (Tau)[a]	Type of Respondent					
	Mass Public	Party Leaders	Attentive Constituents	Lobbyists	Legis- lators	All Respondents
+0.80 to +1.00	20.6	30.0	19.6	14.2	35.3	21.8
+0.50 to +0.79	25.5	24.5	25.7	15.1	30.3	25.4
+0.20 to +0.49	16.8	12.2	22.0	19.3	16.5	18.0
-0.19 to +0.19	14.3	17.8	15.1	13.1	10.0	14.2
-0.20 to -0.49	7.0	8.8	9.8	13.1	5.1	8.0
-0.50 to -0.79	2.9	3.3	3.6	3.0	1.7	3.0
-0.80 to -1.00	0.8	0.0	0.6	3.0	0.6	1.0
NA	12.2	3.3	3.5	19.2	0.6	8.7
Total %	100.0	99.9	99.9	100.0	100.1	100.1
N	1001	90	484	99	181	1855

	One-way ANOVA (using tau values as scores)		
$x^2 = 81.34$ df = 28 $p < .001$	df	F-ratio	significance
	4,1854	9.18	$p < .0001$

[a]The values of differential measure vary between +1.0 and -1.0. A high positive value denotes <u>high concurrence</u> in the rankings on the expectation and on the perception dimensions. A high negative value denotes <u>high differential</u> between the rankings on the expectation dimension from the rankings on the perception dimension. A value of 0.0 indicates <u>no relationship</u> between the rankings on the expectation and the perception dimensions. For more on Kendall's tau see William L. Hays, <u>Statistics For Psychologists</u>, New York: (Holt, Rinehart and Winston, 1963) pp. 647-655.

performance-expectation differential on decisional referents characterizes only a minuscle number of Iowa respondents, whereas an exceedingly large number perceive that the decisional referents they would prefer to guide legislative decisions do in fact guide those choices. We interpret these findings as an independent indicator of trust among Iowans in their legislature and in the decisions it makes.

When we compare levels of the differential measure across type of respondent, certain interesting and very statistically significant trends develop ($x^2 = 81.34$, $p < .001$). First, substantially higher proportions of legislators—about two out of three—appear to have high congruence ($\tau < +.50$), and somewhat less than half that proportion—29 percent—of the lobbyists have a similarly high level. The other types of respondent—mass public, party leaders, and attentive constituents—hover around 50 percent, with the mass public closely resembling the attentive constituents. Similarly for the two extremely incongruent categories, about 6 percent of the lobbyists have high incongruence, compared with 2 percent of the legislators. Overall, legislators appear to have the greatest propensity for congruence between legislative performance and legislative expectation on decisional referents, whereas lobbyists have the least propensity. The mass public, attentive constituents, and party leaders fall somewhere between legislators and lobbyists, with the public resembling the attentive constituents most closely. The latter finding further reinforces our view that the use of middlemen in legislative-constituent communications may not be greatly imperiled by slippage between views of constituents and middlemen.

A number of interesting but unanswerable propositions are suggested by the preceding analysis.

1.   Are legislators so enamored of the legislature (socialized by their legislative or other experiences) that they fail to perceive substantial decision making that is not consistent with their own expectations for those decisions?

2   Because legislators have a decided advantage in observing the Iowa legislature and its decision-making goals, are their perceptions that a small differential exists between performance and expectations the most accurate ones?

3.   Since lobbyists must become involved with the "give and take" surrounding legislative decision making, and because they are also likely to be unsuccessful in obtaining some or all of their legislative goals, have they as a group generally become pessimistic in their views regarding the degree to which decision making expectations are mirrored in reality?

4.   Because lobbyists have in-depth interaction with legislators and observe firsthand the bargaining that takes place in decision making, might their less optimistic view of expectation-performance congruence reflect this insider's view of legislative politics?

5.   Is the apparently large number of mass public, attentive constituent, and party leader respondents with congruent perspectives on legislative decision making a hopeful sign and an independent indicator of a predisposition toward political system maintenance and a continuation of decision making?

DECISIONAL REFERENTS AND LEGISLATIVE SUPPORT

We undertook two types of analysis to test the hypotheses that perceptions of decisional referents affect support and that the referent differentials, or gaps, between perceptions and expectations in priorities of decisional referents for the legislature affect levels of legislative support. First, we divided our respondents into two groups—general public and elites—and analyzed them separately. Within each of the sample subsets, we constructed four typologies of responses based on combined perceptions and expectations for each pair of decisional referents. For example, in the district-state comparison, we divided the public and the combined elite groups into the following categories: (1) those who said that legislators should choose the district over the state and those who said that they thought legislators actually do make such a choice, (2) those who mentioned that district interests should have the highest priority but believed that legislators in fact would choose the interest of the state as a whole, (3) those who gave highest priority to statewide interests and thought that legislators would actually give statewide interests highest priority, and (4) those who said that legislators should choose state interests over district ones but thought that legislators would choose district interests. The same types of classification were used for all the paired comparisons.

For each set of congruent and incongruent groups, we calculated the average legislative support scores for each typology. If the hypothesis we are examining were to be fully supported, legislative support would be higher in the congruent sets than in the incongruent ones. The results appear in Table 7.7; those which conform to our hypothesis are enclosed in boxes. It is plain from casual inspection of the table that our expectations about the differences in legislative support among congruent and incongruent respondents are borne out in some cases only. For the general public, our expectations are verified in 13 cases; no differences between congruent and incongruent groups materialize in 9 sets of data, and the evidence runs contrary to the hypothesis in 6 cases. In the elite groups, 10 of the comparisons analyzed are in conformity with the hypothesis, but in 11 cases there are no differences between congruent and incongruent groups, and in 7 cases the evidence is contrary to the hypothesis. Therefore, it appears that support for the ''gap hypothesis'' is equivocal at best, paralleling our finding in Chapter 6. It can be said, however, that the hypothesis is supported in more trials that it is refuted. Again, this *may be* sufficient evidence to indicate that differentials between perceptions and expectations can affect support for political institutions in a political system in which support for the legislature is very high and in which there are in great gaps between perceptions about the institution and expectations of it.[14]

Our second strategy for testing the hypothesis that decisional referents and any performance-expectation differential would affect levels of legislative support was to perform a multiple regression analysis. Since the available measures regarding a respondent's ordering of decisional referents consisted of multiple indicators (i.e., the number of times each referent was selected), and since these measures must be viewed as a *set* of related independent variables rather than separate independent variables, problems of potential multicollinearity had to be faced. Inspection of the intercorrelation matrix of these indicators—the number of times

Table 7.7 Perceived and Expected Choices for Legislators Among Decisional Referents and Legislative Support: Public and Combined Elite Groups

Decisional Referents		Mean Legislative Support Scores Public				Combined Elite Groups			
(1)	(2)	Should Choose (1) and Do Choose (1)	Should Choose (1), do Choose (2)	Should Choose (2), do Choose (2)	Should Choose (2), do Choose (1)	Should Choose (1), do Choose (1)	Should Choose (1), do Choose (2)	Should Choose (2), do Choose (2)	Should Choose (2), do Choose (1)
District-State		-.38	-.72	-.28	-.26	.42	.05	.60	.49
District-Conscience		-.42	-.53	-.24	-.40	.36	.41	.51	.48
District-Party		-.40	-.31	-.45	-.61	.55	.41	.20	.28
District-Group		-.39	-.40	-.87	-.57	.48	.40	.30	.83
State-Conscience		-.47	-.49	-.32	-.41	.33	.30	.50	.50
State-Group		-.35	-.42	-.65	-.62	.47	.46	.54	-.46
State-Party		-.39	-.30	-.44	-.53	.60	.43	.29	.54
State-Governor		-.27	-.46	-.78	-.58	.51	.29	-.30	.10
Conscience-Party		-.33	-.36	-.53	-.46	.51	.43	.33	.48
Conscience-Group		-.31	-.40	-.58	-.57	.52	.42	-.14	.18
Conscience-Governor		-.28	-.41	-.59	-.57	.50	.37	-.43	.48
Party-Group		-.33	-.58	-.46	-.53	.47	.44	.46	.45
Party-Governor		-.28	-.52	-.60	-.45	.48	.31	.17	.31
Group-Governor		-.43	-.40	-.48	-.34	.47	.54	.37	.41

each referent was selected—indicated that no pair of independent variables appeared to have excessively high levels of intercorrelation. Thus multiple regression analysis proceeded, mindful of these potential problems. The analysis showed that five of the independent variables had a multiple R of .35, thus explaining about 12 percent of the total variance in level of legislative support (see Table 7.8). This figure is considerably lower than those resulting from analyses in previous chapters, suggesting that one's perceptions of decisional referents have little impact on levels of support.

A legislature is, among other things, a place where influence is exerted and decisions are made. We have attempted to map some of the perspectives citizens and political leaders have of the structure of legislative influence and decision making. In this examination we have show that:

1.   Significant agreement exists within each group and for each dimension (expectation and performance) on judgments of criteria.

Table 7.8   Decisional Referents as Related to Legislative Support: Multiple Effects for the Combined Public and Elite Samples

Variables in the Regression Analysis	Zero-order Correlation with Legislative Support	Standardized Regression Coefficients (betas)
Should choose conscience	.19	.28
Should choose state interests	.14	.23
Should choose political party	.03	.16
Do choose governor	-.25	.13
Should choose district interests	.02	.11

Multiple R = 0.35

Multiple R^2 = 0.12

$X_1 = -1.96 + .18X_2 + .23X_3 + .14X_4 - .09X_5 + .11X_6$

$X_1 =$ legislative support

$X_2 =$ should choose conscience

$X_3 =$ should choose state interests

$X_4 =$ should choose political party

$X_5 =$ do choose governor

$X_6 =$ should choose district interests

2.   Legislators, influentials, and public agree substantially on the rankings of six criteria for each dimension, even when control factors are introduced.

3.   The criteria rankings of the performance dimension are *not* the same as those on the expectation dimension.

4.   A moderate performance-expectation differential exists; it is especially accentuated among lobbyists and least noticeable among legislators.

5.   Respondents' perceptions of decisional criteria are only slightly related to levels of legislative support.

6.   Levels of performance-expectation differentials do not seem to be an especially potent explanatory variable of legislative support, especially when the effects of other variables are taken into account.

We hypothesized that where influence and decision-making behavior are perceived to be grossly different from the conditions expected, support for the legislature would be relatively low. We have been able to show that this is true to some extent, even in the highly supportive political environment of the legislative body we are investigating. And yet it seems very clear that at least in this case, perspectives on legislative influence and decision making play a relatively small part in accounting for differences in support for the legislature.

The failure of legislators, influentials, and public to rank criteria similarly on the performance dimension and on the expectation dimension is an indication of potential system crisis. If individuals believe that an institution is not performing in a manner consistent with their expectations, they are likely to reconsider their levels of support for that institution. To the extent that the perception-expectation differential in Iowa is salient in orienting individuals to politics, a high level differential may foster a lower level of system affect.

NOTES

1. James G. March, "Theory of Organizational Decision-Making," in *Essays on the Behavioral Study of Politics*, Austin Ranney, ed. (Urbana, Ill., 1962), p. 196; Herbert A. Simon, *Administrative Behavior* (New York, 1947), p. 67.

2. Whether called criteria or referents, these are the "low-level" factors guiding the direction of decisions being made.

3. Roger H. Davidson, *The Role of the Congressman* (New York, 1969), p. 22; Cleo H. Cherryholmes and Michael J. Shapiro, *Representatives and Roll Calls: A Computer Simulation of Voting in the Eighty-Eighth Congress* (Indianapolis, Ind., 1969); Leon S. Cohen, "The Application of Role-Theory to the Study of Legislative Behavior," a paper read at the 1969 Annual Meeting of the American Political Science Association; Heinz Eulau, "Logics of Rationality in Unanimous Decision-Making," in *Rational Decisions*, Carl J. Friedrich, ed., Nomos Vol. VII (New York, 1964), pp. 26–54; Harvey C. Mansfield, Jr., "Rationality and Representation in Burke's 'Briston Speech,'" in *Rational Decisions*, pp. 197–216; J. Roland Pennock, "Reason in Legislative Decision," in *Rational Decisions*, pp. 98–106; Richard C. Snyder, "A Decision-Making Approach to the Study of Political Phenomena," in *Approaches to the Study of Politics*, Roland Young, ed. (Evanston, Ill., 1958), p. 36; Sidney Ulmer, *Political Decision-Making* (New York, 1970), especially pp. 3–14; John C. Wahlke, "Policy Determinants and Legislative Decisions," in *Political Decision-Making*, pp. 76–77; Donald R. Matthews and James A. Stimson, "Decision-Making by U.S. Representatives: A Preliminary Model," in *Political Decision-Making*, pp. 16–17; John C. Wahlke, Heinz Eulau, William Buchanan, and LeRoy C. Ferguson, *The Legislative System: Explorations in Legislative Behavior* (New York, 1962).

4. See L. L. Thurstone, "A Law of Comparative Judgment," *Psychological Review*, Vol. 34 (1927), 273–286; L. L. Thurstone, "Psychophysical Analysis," *American Journal of Psychology*, Vol. 38 (1927), 368–389; Warren S. Torgerson, *Theory and Methods of Scaling* (New York, 1958); and Allen L. Edwards, *Techniques of Attitude Scale Construction* (New York, 1957), pp. 19–81.

5. Fred N. Kerlinger, *Foundations of Behavioral Research: Educational and Psychological Inquiry* (New York, 1964), p. 497.

6. See Torgerson, *Theory and Methods of Scaling*, pp. 155–163; Edwards, *Techniques of Attitude Scale Construction*, pp. 19–37; and L. L. Thurstone, "The Method of Paired Comparisons for Social Values," *Journal of Abnormal and Social Psychology*, Vol. 21 (1927), 384–400.

7. The instructions given the respondent provide insight about the task given him with these questions:

We hear a lot these days about disputes that arise over issues facing each session of Iowa's General Assembly. When these conflicts arise, the legislator might have to make a decision that will favor one person or group rather than another.

Which one *should* the legislator choose if the conflict was between district and state?

. . .

For these last few questions I've been asking you what you think about the choices a legislator *SHOULD* make when conflicts arise in the legislative process. I wonder if you could tell me for the following situations which choice members of the Iowa legislature *WOULD IN FACT MAKE* if the conflict arose.

Which one *would in fact* the legislator choose if the conflict was between district and state?

A total of 30 questions had to be asked to present all possible pairs of criteria, once for expectations and once for performance.

8. Herbert McClosky's finding that "Political Influentials"—delegates to the 1956 Republican and Democratic National Conventions—rather than the general electorate" . . . serve as the major repositories of the public conscience and as carriers of the Creed" stimulated numerous studies on elite-mass differences. Herbert McClosky. "Consensus and Ideology in American Politics," *American Political Science Review,* Vol. 58 (June 1964), 374.

9. See William L. Hays, *Statistics for Psychologists* (New York, 1963), pp. 656–658; and Sidney Siegel, *Nonparametric Statistics for the Behavioral Sciences* (New York, 1956), pp. 229–238.

10. Edwards, *Techniques of Attitude Scale Construction,* p. 76.

11. For a recent example of this position, see Mark J. Green, James M. Fallows, and David R. Zwick, *Who Runs Congress?* (New York, 1972).

12. See Edwards, *Techniques of Attitude Scale Construction,* pp. 70–76.

13. Such an individual-level analysis was not feasible regarding differing *patterns* of referent rankings, since a total of 144 differing patterns would be possible from all possible combinations of six referents. This was too unwieldy for meaningful analysis.

14. For a brief recent comment in this connection, see Jack Dennis, "Support for the Institution of Elections by the Mass Public." *American Political Science Review,* Vol. 64 (September 1970), 834–835.

8 SOCIAL AND POLITICAL ORIENTATIONS

Thus far we have analyzed factors in the structural location of our respondents as they affect support for the legislature, and we have examined respondents' more specific perspectives on legislators and the legislature. We turn now to a number of variables that are by and large more distant from respondents' concerns with the legislature as such and with the process of representation. The factors we wish to deal with in this chapter are saliency, potency, pride, trust, traditionalism, and liberalism. As we suggested in Chapter 2, we originally conceived some of these factors to be in the so-called predispositional category and some to be phenomenal factors, but we deal with them together here as a matter of convenience.

We attempted to choose variables that could reasonably be linked hypothetically to legislative support, and these are both theoretically and intuitively interesting. For example, it was our hypothesis that support for the legislature should be influenced by the relative *saliency* of different levels of government to our respondents. We thought that respondents for whom the state level of government was particularly salient—that is, those who were most interested and concerned about what was happening at the state level of government—would be more likely to support the state legislature than those for whom national or local levels were the more salient ones.

Again, we hypothesized that those who exhibited the greatest degree of political *potency* with respect to the potentialities for influencing the legislature would be most likely to exhibit high support for the legislative institution. We thought, also, that we could expect support for the legislature to be influenced by the degree of *pride* our respondents exhibited in the state government. We inquired of our respondents what they were proud of as Iowans and as Americans, expecting those who exhibited pride in the institutions of the state government to be especially supportive of the state legislature.

Furthermore, we posited a relationship between the degree to which our respondents exhibited faith in other people and the extent of their faith in, or support of, the legislature. Accordingly, we scored our respondents on a scale of *interper-*

sonal trust. Finally, we thought that our respondents' degrees of support for the legislature would be affected by their *ideological orientations.* We submitted two ideological scales to our respondents, one dealing with attitudes toward change (traditionalism), the other focusing attention principally on the attitudes toward the role of the welfare state (instrumental liberalism).

In our attempt to develop an explanatory system that would account for the maximum amount of variance in support for the legislature among our respondents, we assumed that each of these factors would bear a significant bivariate correlation to legislative support. We also hoped that each of them would contribute substantially to a multivariate explanation of variation in support.

SALIENCY OF LEVELS OF GOVERNMENT

The concept of political salience has come to have a number of different meanings in political analysis.[1] It is used to refer to general orientations toward political objects and goals or, as it has in the hands of some investigators, to refer to more specific aspects of politics such as issue domains or geopolitical units. Our use of the concept is in the most restricted sense: to perceive interest in, and awareness of, political units of government.

It has been suggested that people develop salience maps with respect to geopolitical units and that their perspectives on politics develop in the light of their varying salience maps.[2] Dahl once argued as follows in an essay on "The City in the Future of Democracy":

> An American state is infinitely less important to citizens of that state than any democratic nation-state is to its citizens. Consequently, the average American is bound to be much less concerned about the affairs of his state than of his city or county . . . [Furthermore,] it cannot even be said that the states, on the whole, can tap any strong sentiment of loyalty or like-mindedness among their citizens.[3]

Some national sample survey data seem to indicate that Dahl's assertions were correct. However, the Iowa evidence does not support this conclusion about the salience of levels of government for our respondents. We asked our respondents—samples of the public, attentive constituents, party leaders, and lobbyists—the following question: "of these three levels of government—national, state, and local—which would you say that you were most interested in and followed the most closely?" Reactions to this question are displayed in Table 8.1: generally, Iowans exhibit a substantially greater degree of state-level salience than has been assumed to hold among American citizens. Only party

Table 8.1   Saliency of Levels of Government for Public and Elite Groups

Most Salient Level	Public	Attentive Constituents	Party Leaders	Lobbyists
National	22.0	31.2	40.0	16.2
State	45.3	36.2	33.3	54.5
Local	21.7	22.9	12.2	17.2
Don't Know	11.1	9.7	14.4	12.1
Total	100.1	100.1	99.9	100.0

leaders showed somewhat more national-level salience than salience for the state level of government. In the general public, 45 percent indicated that they paid closest attention to the state level of government, compared with 36 percent among attentive constituents, 33 percent among lobbyists. In the general public and among lobbyists, national and local salience occurred to approximately an equal extent, whereas attentive constituents and party leaders exhibited a greater degree of national than local salience. Although we have not eliminated the apolitical respondents from these calculations—those who pay no attention to public affairs and politics—adjusting our evidence in this respect does not fundamentally alter the conclusions that can be drawn from it.

Again, with national sample survey evidence, it has been shown that "as the salience of a state's politics rises, so does the evaluation of that government's performance."[4] Our evidence from the Iowa data certainly confirms this finding. For our respondents, national salients tend to feel that the national government is doing the best job of accomplishing what it is supposed to do, state salients tend to rate the state level highest, and local salients the local level highest (Gamma = .28). But is there a significant linkage between the salience of levels of government and support for the legislature? In Table 8.2 we make comparisons for the general public and the combined elite groups among those who are mainly national, state, or local salients in terms of their relative levels of support for the legislature. The evidence demonstrates that for the general public, there is a relationship, however slight, between salience of levels of government and support for the legislature. This relationship does not, however, hold for the combined elite groups. In the general public, support for the legislature is highest for state salients and lowest for local salients.

Table 8.2   Saliency of Levels of Government and Legislative Support

Legislative Support	Public National	Public State	Public Local	Elite Groups National	Elite Groups State	Elite Groups Local
High	18.9	20.5	7.6	50.8	44.5	43.6
Medium	30.7	27.5	30.6	29.3	33.5	31.6
Low	50.4	52.0	61.9	19.9	22.0	24.8
Total	100.0	100.0	100.1	100.0	100.0	100.0

If we focus on the relative degrees of state-level salience, the relationship between state salience and support for the legislature is weak indeed. Table 8.3 indicates the varying levels of legislative support, both in the general public and in the combined elite groups, among those for whom the state is the most salient level of government, those for whom the state is the second most salient government level, and those for whom the state level is not mentioned as a salient level of government. In the general public, there is no important relationship between state salience and support for the state legislature (Gamma = .05). In the combined elite groups, the relationship between the two attitudes is, somewhat negative (Gamma = −.14).

Although the salience of levels of government does appear to bear a certain relationship to general, affective orientations to the same levels of government, in

Table 8.3 Saliency of State Level and Legislative Support

Legislative Support	Public State Most Salient	Public State Second	Public State Not Salient	Elite Groups State Most Salient	Elite Groups State Second	Elite Groups State Not Salient
High	20.8	15.5	10.9	44.5	50.0	56.6
Medium	27.9	30.5	37.0	33.5	29.5	27.1
Low	51.3	54.1	52.2	22.0	20.5	16.3
Total	100.0	100.1	100.1	100.0	100.0	100.0

the Iowa evidence state salience is not significantly related to support for the state legislature. In addition, support for the legislature is not influenced by respondents' beliefs about what level of government is doing the best job. No differences in legislative support among Iowans occur between those who think the national government is doing the best job, those who give the highest evaluation to the state level, and those whose affective orientations seem to be greatest for the local level of government (Gamma = .03). Furthermore, if we examine only the respondents in the general public who gave the highest performance evaluations to the state level of government, and for these respondents compare the salience of levels of government in terms of support for the legislature, we again find no important relationship between the two attitudes (Gamma = .16).

POLITICAL POTENCY

We hypothesized that our respondents would exhibit some measure of support for the legislature to the degree that they could display feelings of political potency with respect to their actual or projected dealings with the legislature. We asked all our respondents except legislators how likely they thought it would be that they could influence the legislature if they tried to do so, how likely it would be that they would try to influence the legislature if the occasion arose, and to what extent they had actually tried to influence the state legislature. We expected those who exhibited a high degree of political potency—that is, those who said it would be very likely that they could influence the legislature and that they would try if the occasion arose—and those who indicated that they had often tried to influence the legislature, to be much more supportive of the legislature than those who were relatively impotent politically.

Comparisons of four sample groups appear in Table 8.4. Again, differentiation between the general public and the elite groups is very marked. The elite groups constitute a much more politically potent set of individuals than people in the general population. Furthermore, most people in the general population (73 percent) report never having tried to influence a legislator, whereas a very large majority of the people in the leadership groups report having done so.

In our entire set of samples, there is a fairly strong connection between degrees of political potency and support for the legislature when these two factors are compared by themselves. Figure 8.1 graphically reveals the extent of this relationship, indicating relatively high support for the legislature among the politically potent respondents, and relatively low support among the respondents who were relatively impotent politically. However, significant correlations between each of

Table 8.4   Political Potency of the Public and of Attentive Constituents, Party Leaders, and Lobbyists

Potency Items	Public	Sample Attentive Constituents	Party Leaders	Lobbyists
COULD INFLUENCE LEGISLATURE				
Very likely	4.2	10.4	13.5	23.7
Moderately likely	8.2	28.4	33.7	30.9
Somewhat likely	22.2	44.6	33.7	33.0
Not likely	65.4	16.6	19.1	12.4
Total	100.0	100.0	100.0	100.0
WOULD TRY IF OCCASION AROSE				
Very likely	13.7	72.6	75.3	81.8
Moderately likely	14.1	18.2	16.8	11.1
Somewhat likely	30.0	7.1	6.7	6.1
Not likely	42.2	2.1	1.1	1.0
Total	100.0	100.0	99.9	100.0
HAVE TRIED TO INFLUENCE LEGISLATURE				
Often	1.2	36.0	25.8	79.6
Several Times	8.5	50.4	48.3	17.3
Once or Twice	17.2	9.6	19.1	3.1
Never	73.0	4.0	6.7	0.0
Total	99.9	100.0	99.9	100.0

the three potency indicators and support for the legislature occur only among attentive constituents. For them the product-moment correlation between likelihood that they would try to influence the legislature and support level is .12 ($p <$ .01); it is somewhat higher for those who have actually tried to influence the legislature ($r = .17$, $p < .001$). For the general public and the party leaders significant correlations with legislative support occur only in terms of having tried to influence the legislature (for the public $r = .11$, $p < .01$; for the party leaders $r = .23$, $p < .05$).

Lobbyists of course are a group of political actors who have reality-tested the efficacy of their legislative influence on many occasions. For them, neither prior attempts to influence the legislature nor the likelihood that they would engage in such activities if the occasion arose were significantly correlated with the respondents' legislative support. Among lobbyists, however, the likelihood that the respondents could influence the legislature if they tried to do so was significantly

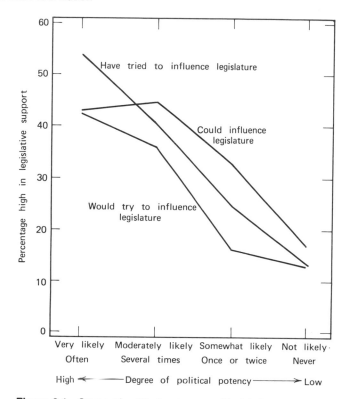

Figure 8.1 Sense of political potency and legislative support.

related to their support for the legislature ($r = .37, \rho < .001$). We conclude that political potency bears a simple relationship to legislative support, but this relationship is not very large, and it is not consistent across all our sample groups.

PRIDE IN STATE AND NATION

We expected to find a linkage between state pride and support for the state legislative body—specifically we believed that those who referred to the state's governmental institutions as aspects of their state about which they had the most pride would exhibit relatively the greatest support for the state legislature. Furthermore, with respect to national pride, we assumed that respondents who were proud of government institutions in general would report greater support for some aspect of it, namely, the state legislature.

Table 8.5 distributes respondents in four of our sample groups across a set of code categories derived from responses to the question, "what kinds of things are you proud of as an Iowan?" Here again we encounter substantial differences between responses from the general population and from the elite groups. In general, elite group respondents were in a position to name more features of Iowa about which they were proud than those in the general population. Whereas more than 10 percent of the mass public respondents could mention nothing that was a source of state pride, only a miniscule percentage of those in the elite groups were in that category. Elite respondents indicated substantially more pride in the state's economy and in the characteristics of its people than did those in the general public. More important, attentive constituents, party leaders, and lobbyists displayed a considerably greater degree of pride in the state's governmental institutions than did the respondents in the mass public. Finally, we note that among all

Table 8.5   Objects of State Pride for Public, Attentive Constituents, Party Leaders, and Lobbyists (in percentages)

Object	Public	Attentive Constituents	Party Leaders	Lobbyists
Nothing	10.2	.2	1.1	1.0
Governmental Institutions	7.1	17.8	15.6	17.2
Social Legislation	3.0	5.8	1.1	6.1
Economy	19.4	42.1	45.6	34.3
Characteristics of the People	26.2	81.0	76.7	76.8
Spiritual Values	1.4	9.7	6.7	6.1
Arts and Sciences	.6	.6	1.1	--
Physical Attributes	75.4	68.4	63.3	62.6
Other	27.2	22.1	25.6	21.2
Number of Responses	1,705	1,199	213	223
Number of Cases	1,001	484	90	99
Average Responses	1.7	2.5	2.4	2.3

sample groups, the highest proportion of responses fell in the category covering the physical attributes of the state.

Table 8.6 treats the same type of evidence with respect to national pride (respondents were asked "what kinds of things are you proud of as an American?"). The proportions in this table make it abundantly clear that unlike state pride, national pride is for Iowans very much a matter of being proud of the institutions of the national government. In this respect, national pride among Iowans takes a shape very similar to that of national population samples, except that Iowans seem, if anything, to exhibit a considerably greater degree of national pride than the population of the country as a whole.[5] Attentive constituents, party leaders, and lobbyists reflect a much greater degree of national pride than do Iowans in the general population, especially with respect to governmental institutions, social legislation, the economy, the characteristics of the people, and the world leadership role of the United States.

Table 8.6   Objects of National Pride for Public, Attentive Constituents, Party Leaders, and Lobbyists (in percentages)

Object	Public	Attentive Constituents	Party Leaders	Lobbyists
Nothing	4.8	.6	--	3.0
Governmental Institutions	108.4	117.1	110.0	84.8
Social Legislation	4.1	9.3	18.9	12.1
Economy	15.6	44.6	43.3	45.5
Characteristics of the People	1.9	10.7	16.7	8.1
Spiritual Values	1.1	4.5	5.6	2.0
Arts and Sciences	.5	1.7	1.1	2.0
Physical Attributes	4.7	4.5	6.7	14.1
World Leadership	5.8	22.7	18.9	20.2
Number of Responses	1,634	1,108	206	198
Number of Cases	1,001	484	90	99
Average Responses	1.6	2.3	2.3	2.0

What, if any, connections do these differences in objects of state and national pride have with relative support for the state legislature? In Table 8.7 we present mean legislative support scores for each object of national and state pride for our entire body of respondents. There it can be seen that in general, mean support scores are higher for objects of national pride than for state pride, but there are some interesting differences between the two with respect to pride in both state and nation. For the respondents who can say nothing about their pride in state and national political systems, support for the state legislature is relatively very low. Those who exhibit pride in the Iowa governmental institutions and the characteristics of its people show positive mean legislative support, and respondents indicating state pride in other respects have mean support scores that are negative.

Although national pride seems to overcome state pride with respect at least to its impact on support for the state legislature, Table 8.7 indicates that pride in governmental institutions in the state and pride in the characteristics of its people cited by respondents who have relatively greater support for the state legislative institution. We have selected two objects of state pride for further consideration, detailed in Table 8.8. These data make it clear that those who mention pride in

Table 8.7   Pride and Legislative Support for All Respondents

Objects	Mean Legislative Support Scores	
	Iowa Pride	National Pride
Nothing	-.44	-.45
Governmental Institutions	.09	.24
Social Legislation	-.33	.20
Economy	-.07	.16
Characteristics of People	.23	.42
Spiritual Values	*	*
Arts and Sciences	*	*
Physical Attributes	-.20	-.16
World Leadership	--	.24
Other	-.21	-.21
Sample Mean	-.08	-.08

*Too few cases for a meaningful Mean.

Table 8.8   State Pride in Governmental Institutions and Characteristics of People and Support for the Legislature

Legislative Support	Governmental Institutions		Characteristics of the People	
	Mentioned	Not Mentioned	Mentioned	Not Mentioned
High	37.0	26.6	39.7	19.9
Medium	28.9	32.1	31.4	32.0
Low	34.1	41.3	28.9	48.1
Total	100.0	100.0	100.0	100.0

Iowa governmental institutions and the characteristics of its people, have a greater tendency to support state legislature than those who do not mention these objects of state pride. For those for whom Iowa's governmental institutions were the biggest source of state pride, 37 percent could be characterized as high in legislative support, whereas among those who did not mention governmental institutions, 41 percent could be characterized as low in support (Gamma = .17). Iowans who had pride in the characteristics of the people of the state were even more supportive of the legislature than were those who did not mention this object of their pride. Nearly 40 percent of those who mentioned this attribute were high in support, whereas very nearly half of those who did not mention characteristics of the people were low in support (Gamma = .38). Our general conclusion is that certain objects of state pride are positively related to support for the legislature, although this relationship is not extremely strong.

TRUST, TRADITIONALISM, AND INSTRUMENTAL LIBERALISM

Variations in our respondents' degrees of interpersonal trust, their attitudes toward social and political change, and their attitudes toward the welfare state were expected to be related to the respondents' support for the state legislature. We anticipated a relationship between faith in people and support for the legislature, thinking that faith in others and faith in the system would go hand in hand. We anticipated also that respondents who were highly traditional would exhibit relatively lower degrees of support for the legislature; likewise, those most willing to

Table 8.9 Trust, Traditionalism, and Instrumental Liberalism for Public and Elite Groups

Items	Percentage Who Agree*				
	Public	Attentive Constituents	Party Leaders	Lobbyists	Legislators
TRUST					
You can't be too careful in your dealings with other people.	82.7	72.5	78.9	73.7	56.4
Most people are more inclined to look out for themselves rather than other people.	81.7	77.2	81.1	71.7	58.6
If you don't watch yourself, other people will take advantage of you.	69.8	54.8	60.0	49.5	50.3
No one is going to care much about what happens to you when you get right down to it.	40.2	26.7	30.0	26.3	31.4
Human nature is fundamentally cooperative.	82.5	88.6	85.6	88.9	87.3
TRADITIONALISM					
If something grows up over a long time there is bound to be much wisdom in it.	62.6	49.2	45.6	39.4	39.2
If you start trying to change things very much you usually make them worse.	37.1	14.2	12.2	12.1	25.4
Our society is so complicated that if you try to reform parts of it you're likely to upset the whole system.	34.0	11.8	10.0	11.1	24.9
I prefer the practical man anytime to the man of ideas.	53.8	37.8	38.9	30.3	49.7

INSTRUMENTAL LIBERALISM

On the whole labor unions have helped the working man and should be encouraged.	64.8	72.3	81.1	69.7	75.7
Most internal problems our society faces, like unemployment, can be solved better by the government than by private enterprise.	38.4	25.4	36.7	28.3	27.1
The only way to provide adequate medical care for the entire population is through some form of socialized medicine.	30.8	24.6	34.4	31.3	19.3
Our federal government should be willing to step boldly into areas like old-age insurance and electric power where private enterprise seems to be faltering and give people the services they need.	48.0	33.5	47.8	44.4	27.6

*Combined "strongly agree" and "agree" responses.

change should be most supportive of the legislature. Finally, we expected those who were high on a scale of welfare liberalism to be more likely to support the legislature than those who could be characterized as relatively nonliberal.

We administered three standard batteries of attitude items to our respondents, and these items are delineated in Table 8.9.[6] The table not only shows the items that define our measures of trust, traditionalism, and instrumental liberalism, but also the total proportions of respondents who agreed with each item for each of our sample groups. For the interpersonal trust items, differences between the general public and the leadership groups were fairly sharp on all but the last of these items, which produced virtually no differences among all samples. Legislators were generally the most trusting.

On the traditional items, again the general public responded in comparatively the most traditionalist manner; the elite respondents indicated lower degrees of traditionalism, although in some respects the legislators were more like the general public than were the other leadership groups. In terms of the total percentage of agreement to the instrumental liberalism items, systematic differences between the general public and the leadership groups are not very great.

In the interest of scaling our respondents on these variables, we factor analyzed their responses to the attitude items. The results appear in Table 8.10. Trust, traditionalism, and instrumental liberalism, as we measured them, produce a very elegant factorial structure, and factor scores were developed for each respondent from the factor loadings in a very straightforward way.

The mean factor scores for each of these dimensions for each of the sample groups are given in Table 8.11; these mean scores make it possible to compare sample groups in a way that is somewhat simpler than making comparisons for each individual item in the data set. We are now in a position to make more precise comparisons between the public and the elite respondents, and among elite groups. We see, as the percentage distributions suggested, that people in the general population are substantially less trusting—have a lower degree of faith in people—than the respondents in the elite groups, and that legislators indicate a relatively high degree of interpersonal trust, with the other elite groups falling between.

Apparently misanthropy is relatively widespread in the mass public, but political leaders, and preeminently legislators, tend to be very trusting of others. With respect to traditionalism, respondents in the mass public are, on the average, very high, whereas those in the leadership groups are relatively low, except that legislators fall somewhere between the general public and the other political leaders in their willingness to accept changes. In this respect, legislators are more like the mass public than are the other leadership groups. With regard to instrumen-

Table 8.10 Factor Analysis of Trust, Traditionalism, and Instrumental Liberalism

Items		Factor Loadings*	
	I	II	III
TRUST			
Can't be too careful	-.705		
Look out for selves	-.777		
Others take advantage	-.795		
No one is going to care	-.624		
TRADITIONALISM			
Long time things wise		.650	
Change makes things worse		.811	
Reform upsets the system		.760	
Prefer practical man		.577	
INSTRUMENTAL LIBERALISM			
Encourage labor unions			.555
Government should solve problems			.744
Socialized medicine			.813
Provide government services			.806

*All loadings greater than .300 are shown.

Table 8.11 Mean Factor Scores for Trust, Traditionalism, and Instrumental Liberalism for Public and Elite Groups

Sample Group	Trust	Traditionalism	Instrumental Liberalism
Public	-.17	.23	-.11
Attentive Constituents	.13	-.34	.18
Party Leaders	-.04	-.49	-.17
Lobbyists	.16	-.43	.01
Legislators	.48	.00	.25

tal liberalism, the general public is relatively low and legislators are relatively high on the scale, with attentive constituents and lobbyists falling between the two extremes. The low mean instrumental liberalism score for party leaders is due largely to the very powerful correlation between the scale and party identification in this elite group.

We adopted multiple regression analysis to assess the influence of these three attitude variables on support for the legislature. The correlation coefficients, variance explained, and the weights attached to each component in the analysis are presented in Table 8.12. For the general public, the multiple relationship between trust, traditionalism, and instrumental liberalism, and support for the legislature, is not extraordinarily great. The simple correlation in the public sample between traditionalism and legislative support is .25, and the addition of interpersonal trust and instrumental liberalism does not dramatically increase the coefficient. Additionally, the regression weight attached to traditionalism for the general public is larger than for the other two scales.

In the general public, then, there is a relationship of some importance between unwillingness to change and support for the legislature. For the elite groups, however, substantial improvement in the relationship to support for the legislature is gained by combining the three items, since the multiple correlation substantially exceeds any of the simple correlations among these variables. From 10 to nearly 20 percent of the variance in legislative support in the elite groups can be accounted for by these three scales, although the regression weights indicate some variation in the relative importance of each component.

It may be of interest to consider the effect of variations in party identification on traditionalism, instrumental liberalism, and interpersonal trust, since differences in party attachment may be thought to be affecting the relationship between these scales and legislative support. In none of our samples is there any relationship between party identification and interpersonal trust. Democrats are no more

Table 8.12   Regression of Trust, Traditionalism, and Instrumental Liberalism on Legislative Support

Sample Groups	Multiple R	R²	Trust	Traditionalism	Instrumental Liberalism
Public	.28	.08	.07	.21	.15
Attentive Constituents	.35	.12	.21	.23	.23
Party Leaders	.43	.19	.22	.28	.38
Lobbyists	.32	.10	.15	.24	.18
Legislators	.37	.11	.17	.23	.34
Total Sample	.40	.16	.18	.27	.24

trusting than Republicans, and strength of party identification does not influence the degree of faith in people exhibited by our respondents. Furthermore, except for legislators, there is no significant correlation in our sample groups between traditionalism and party identification. Generally, Democrats and Republicans do not differ in their willingness to change. Legislators constitute a somewhat unusual group of elite respondents here because for them there is, in fact, a rather substantial relationship between party identification and traditinalism. The mean traditionalism scores are much higher for Republican legislators than for Democratic legislators; interestingly enough, the standard deviation for Democrats is small (averaging about .8), whereas the standard deviation for Republicans on our measure of traditionalism is relatively large (averaging about 1.3).

For instrumental liberalism, however, there is a substantial correlation for each sample group with variations in partisan identification. This relationship is especially strong for party leaders, which probably accounts for the very high regression weight for this scale in the analysis of Table 8.12. Party differences on instrumental liberalism such that Democrats are significantly more liberal than Republicans are to be expected. However, as we demonstrated in Chapter 2, differences in party identification are not significantly correlated with diffuse legislative support. Thus since party identification is significantly related to instrumental liberalism but not to support for the legislature, our evidence does not show any contaminating effects of party identification in the simple correlations between instrumental liberalism and support.

SOCIOPOLITICAL ORIENTATIONS AND LEGISLATIVE SUPPORT

When all the variables considered in this chapter—salience, potency, pride, trust, traditionalism, and instrumental liberalism—are taken together in terms of their multiple effects on support for the legislature, they yield a multiple correlation coefficient of .46, which means that these variables alone can account for about one-fifth ($R^2 = .21$) of the variance in legislative support, when all our respondents are lumped. Table 8.13 shows the weights for each variable in the regression analysis and the simple correlations they bear to legislative support. These results clarify the pattern of relationships between these sets of variables and legislative support. In general, summarizing across both public and elite respondents, the salience of the state governmental level has little to do with support for the legislature. Moreover, although feelings of potency about involvement in state politics, pride in state governmental institutions, and faith in people are modestly correlated with legislative support in bivariate terms (compared with the effects of

Table 8.13   Salience, Potency, Pride, Trust, and Ideology Related to Legislative Support: Multiple Effects for the Combined Public and Elite Samples

Variables in the Regression Analysis	Zero-order Correlations with Support	Standardized Regression Coefficients (beta's)
Salience	.02	.02
Potency	.26	.15
Pride	.20	.15
Trust	.18	.14
Traditionalism	.28	.24
Instrumental Liberalism	.23	.21

traditionalism and instrumental liberalism), the first-mentioned attitudes carry less weight in the combined analysis. The regression weights indicate that among these six independent variables, traditionalism and instrumental liberalism are the most substantial correlates of legislative support.

What do these relative findings mean? They appear to show that certain kinds of social and political orientations that have been thought to influence the stability of political regimes may not be as important some have assumed. We believe it is fair to summarize the implication of much political research by saying that the citizen in a "civic culture" is oriented to major political objects in an allegiant way by virtue of some mix of high salience for the relevant system level, strong feelings of potency about political participation, pride in the political institutions at that level, and substantial propensity to have faith in others in the system.[7] The particular evidence adduced here, however, raises real doubt about these assumptions. Furthermore, the relative impact of these factors is even more drastically diminished when levels of political stratification are introduced into the multiple regression analysis. Now we are assessing the direct effects of these independent variables on legislative support. In most other research, the treatment of these kinds of variables has been much more simplified than ours. Earlier in this chapter, we gave evidence of the existence of some bivariate effects for these variables. When a full set of predictors are assessed together, however, it can be seen that salience, potency, pride, and trust are relatively weak in the face of ideological factors. It is possible, of course, that support for the legislature is indirectly affected by these factors even though their relative direct effects are not so great. It may be that salience, potency, pride, and trust have an important bearing on the quality and quantity of political participation, and through political participation, they influence allegiance to the legislative institution as one significant political object. We have not attempted to ferret out such causal paths.

In the framework of the set of variables considered in this chapter, ideological orientations take on an important and relatively unexpected meaning. It turns out that both conservative-traditional and liberal-welfare service orientations provide an important basis for the reservoir of support accruing to the legislature. The linkage between traditionalism and legislative support means that the urge to defend established political values and acceptance of the status quo constitute primitive beliefs that fairly powerfully contribute to support for one element of the regime, the legislature. The connection between instrumental liberalism and legislative support means that in the measure that citizens are satisfied with the service state and accept the values of positive welfare policies, their relation to the legislative element of the political regime is strongly allegiant.

In a speculative vein, we suggest that the evidence presented here corroborates the partial theory that support for the political regime—thus, perhaps, political stability—flows more strongly from traditional values related to the effectiveness of the system and the perceived benefits stemming from it than from a sense of pride in the structures of government, personal feelings of political efficacy, or a sense of social trust. The primitive political ideology of the common man, explicated in detail in the case studies examined by Robert E. Lane, appears to us to play a profound role in undergirding the legitimacy accorded to the regime. As Lane has said of the men of Eastport:

> . . . Elected officials are seen as responsive to the will of the people, that is, the common men of Eastport. Congress is a warm and friendly place for common people to visit; it is not just a rich men's club. The Executive, while occasionally delinquent, is rarely indifferent to the public needs—the needs of the great financial interests are not his principal concern. . . .

> . . . If they think of government as affecting their lives at all, these Eastport men think of it is giving benefits and protections . . . by the change in policy so dramatically effected in the thirties, the government became, with certain residual doubts, an ally, a friend. . . .[8]

Our discovery of the relative importance of factors of traditionalism and instrumental liberalism in accounting for degrees of support for the legislature buttresses this interpretation.

NOTES

1. On the general concept of political salience, see Angus Campbell, Philip E. Converse, Warren E. Miller, and Donald E. Stokes, *The American Voter* (New York, 1960), pp. 317–321, and Moshe M. Czudnowski, "A Salience Dimension of Politics for the Study of Political Culture," *American Political Science Review,* Vol. 62 (September 1968), 878–888.

2. See M. Kent Jennings and Harmon Zeigler, "The Salience of American State Politics," *American Political Science Review,* Vol. 64 (June 1970), 523–535.

3. Robert A. Dahl, "The City in the Future of Democracy," *American Political Science Review,* Vol. 61 (December 1967), 968.

4. Jennings and Zeigler, "The Salience of American State Politics," 528.

5. Compare the findings of the Five Nations Study reported in Gabriel A. Almond and Sidney Verba, *The Civic Culture* (Princeton, N.J., 1963), pp. 101–105.

6. The items for these measures are derived from Morris Rosenberg, *Society and the Adolescent Self-Image* (Princeton, N.J., 1965), pp. 309–311; Herbert McClosky, "Conservatism and Personality," *American Political Science Review,* Vol. 52 (March 1958), 27–45; Herbert McClosky, "Consensus and Ideology in American Politics," *American Political Science Review,* Vol. 58 (June 1964), 361–382; and John P. Robinson, Jerrold G. Rusk, and Kendra B. Head, *Measures of Political Attitudes* (Ann Arbor, Mich., 1968), pp. 79–160.

7. Almond and Verba, *The Civic Culture,* especially pp. 489–493.

8. Robert E. Lane, *Political Ideology: Why the American Common Man Believes What He Does* (New York, 1962), p. 474. See also Marian Roth and G. R. Boynton, "Communal Ideology and Political Support," *Journal of Politics,* Vol. 31 (February 1969), 167–185.

9 DETERMINANTS OF LEGISLATIVE SUPPORT IN IOWA

Having considered the effects of variables representing predispositional, structural, and phenomenal factors on levels of legislative support using bivariate and limited multivariate analysis, we must now begin to integrate this previous analysis into a more encompassing view. In addition, we are ready to test the explanatory model outlined in Chapter 2, where we postulated that combinations of variables representing the three clusters of factors just named would be significantly related to levels of legislative support. Now our task is to synthesize previous analyses and to reevaluate the relationships already identified, to develop a specific and parsimonious explanation. We highlight the variables having sizable and independent relationships with support and exclude from the model variables having negligible or spurious relationships. In doing this, we employ a basic multiple regression approach and path analysis. This combination of techniques permits us to take a moderate step toward confirming the plausibility of our model in causal terms and provides a means for assessing the impact of direct and indirect paths from our independent variables to legislative support.

Several problems pervade such an analysis. Initially we discussed an extraordinary number of independent variables. In preceding chapters, more than 60 independent variables have been used. Although some of these are discarded from future analysis because they appear to have no significant independent relationship to support, a large number of variables are still included. Such a large number of variables makes multivariate analysis unwieldy. Furthermore, the situation poses related theoretical and methodological problems. For example, using many different variables raises questions about the degree to which each is an independent indicator and can contribute some unique explanatory power to the analysis. The variables included in each cluster undoubtedly have some measurement overlap, thus raising the methodological problem of multicollinearity. All multivariate analyses, but especially those using correlation and regression, must be sensitive to those situations when ". . . the correlation between two or more independent variables is high, [because] the sampling error of the partial slopes and partial correlations will be quite large.''[1] The difficulty with multicollinearity is that a number of differing combinations of coefficients for the variables will equally satisfy the prerequisites for the regression analysis. Thus the investigator has considerably *less* assurance that the solution and coefficients he proposes accurately represent the multivariate relationship among the factors studied. A third problem, idiosyncratic to the Iowa study, relates to the systematic absence of some data. Certain information was not gathered from some respondents (e.g., income, subjective class identification, political knowledge, and political participation questions were not asked of legislators). None of these difficulties individually or taken together poses insurmountable analytical problems, but certain research strategies were not plausible, and extreme caution had to be exercised throughout the regression and path analyses.

The first step before testing the model or conducting multiple regression was to determine the appropriate indicators. If, as might be anticipated, the individual variables identified with each of the factors arranged in Figure 2.2 form a "coherent, well-integrated" unit, a summary measure of that factor may be appropriate. This suggestion assumes that all variables included within a factor measure one single factor. On the other hand, these variables may measure a variety of features, each one being a unique aspect of the factor, therefore having little if any measurement overlap. To test this possibility, a separate factor analysis was conducted for each respondent type and for the variables included in each factor of the model—structural-social, structural-political, political-predispositional, and phenomenal. If significant variable overlap exists within each factor, as indicated by the factor structuring and the explained variance, a single summary indicator for each factor might be appropriate. The results of the factor analysis in terms of the factor structure, the number of factors, and the explained variance clearly indicated that considerable measurement *diversity* exists across the variables within each factor, except possibly for the structural-social factor. This is the case for respondents of all types. Therefore, we decided *against* any effort to generate a single indicator for each factor and used instead the variables as originally conceived and measured. Indirectly, these findings indicate that multicollinearity among variables within factors should *not* be a problem. The inspection of subsequent intercorrelation matrices for each group of respondents suggests that across-factor independent variables are not related to any significant degree.

In the following sections, we present results from a multiple regression analysis using independent variables that had statistically significant relationships with legislative support controlling for all other independent variables. Path analysis is undertaken to identify the magnitudes of direct and indirect effects. The net result is the identification of a parsimonious set of independent variables and their relationships with support, permitting us to draw conclusions regarding our model postulated in Figure 2.2

MULTIPLE EFFECTS ON LEGISLATIVE SUPPORT

Partial correlational analysis for all respondents identified 21 separate independent variables that had significant independent impact on level of support. Table 9.1 lists these variables with their zero-order correlations and betas. The multiple R for these variables was .65, indicating that the items explain about 43 percent of the variance in level of support for the legislature. We note the possible existence of spurious relations because the multiple R and percentage of explained variance are only moderately higher than similar values from preceding chapters and because many formerly significant relationships disappear. Also, the sizable standardized regression coefficients for the "leadership status" variables indicate the advisability of further analysis by respondent type.

As seen in Table 9.1, variables from all three explanatory factors—structural, political-predispositional, and phenomenal—continue to have significant independent effects on legislative support when controlled for other variables. Furthermore, both social and political-structural variables have this independent effect. This suggests to us that in the development of legislative support, a wide variety of variables have independent impact. These variables include a diverse set of social and political experiences as well as attitudinal and perceptual mechanisms operating within the respondents. The greatest erosion in the number of variables having significant independent relationships from the potential number discussed in previous chapters appears to be among the phenomenal variables studied. Of the more than 30 individual variables included as phenomenal, fewer than one in four remain, and many of these appear to have minor effects at best. The most significant variables seem to grow from our respondents' relationships with the legislature, but it has a very significant impact on overall support and, as shown in tion equation using these 21 variables underscores this observation (see Table 9.1 for the variable designation by number):

$$X_1 = -2.19 - .04X_2 + .06X_4 + 1.76X_5 + 1.24X_6 + .71X_7 \ a \ 1.14X_8 + 2.24X_9 + .06X_{10} - .05X_{11} - .19X_{12} + .08X_{13} + .04X_{14} - .06X_{15} + .03X_{16} - .21X_{17} + .12X_{18} - .07X_{19} + .22X_{20} + .19X_{21} - .01X_{22}$$

In addition to analyzing support for all respondents, we considered the effects of

Table 9.1 All Factors and Legislative Support for All Respondents: Multiple Effects

Variables in the Regression Analysis	Variable Number for Regression Equation	Zero-order Correlation With Support	Standardized Regression Coefficients (betas)
STRUCTURAL FACTOR (SOCIAL)			
Subjective Class Identification[a]	2	-.26	-.06
Income	3	.35	.11
STRUCTURAL FACTOR (POLITICAL)			
Political Knowledge	4	.43[f]	.28
Leadership Status[b]/			
Public	5	-.45	.91
Attentive Constituents	6	.27	.57
Party Leaders	7	.06	.16
Lobbyists	8	.12	.27
Legislators	9	.25	.70
POLITICAL-PREDISPOSITIONAL FACTOR			
Ideological Orientation/ Traditionalism	10	.28	.06
Political Potency-Likelihood of Taking Political Action	11	-.32	-.07
Political Potency-Prior Attempts to Influence Decisions	12	-.40	-.23
Political Involvement (Participation)	13	.35[f]	.10
PHENOMENAL FACTOR			
Influence Agents/Should be Influenced by Pressure Groups	14	-.11	.04
Are Influenced by Republican Agents	15	.00	-.07
Decisional Referents/Decisions Should be Influenced by State Level Considerations	16	.14	.03
Consistency of Should Dimension Decisional Referents	17	-.27	-.04
Perception-Expectation Differential Differential Between Should and Are Influenced Agents[c]	18	-.07	.14
Net Differentials Between Should and Are Influence Agents[d]	19	-.11	-.09
Representativeness Factor	20	.33	.22
Compromise Factor	21	.27	.19
Political Mobilization	22[e]	.03[f]	-.06

[a]Respondents, except legislators, were asked whether they considered themselves to be middle or working class.

[b]For this analysis, leadership status was constructed as a series of "dummy variables."

[c]The formula for calculating this differential was $\dfrac{\sum \left| S_i - D_i \right|}{N}$

S_i = Should rating influence agent i
D_i = Do rating influence agent i
N = Total number of agents rated

[d]The formula for calculating this net differential was

$$\frac{\sum \left| S_i - D_i \right|}{M}$$

The numerator is the same as c above. M = Total number of agents where a difference in the should and do ratings was detected.

[e]Diffuse Legislative Support will be designated Variable 1.

[f]These zero-order correlations differ somewhat from ones presented in earlier chapters because the values used for these independent variables differed from the ones used previously. For example, political knowledge included seven rather than two questions, political knowledge included five rather than two variables, and for political mobilization we used a Likert-type, summed rating scale rather than factor scores.

these independent variables on the two previously identified dimensions—
—compliance and commitment. In each case, variables from all three factors had
significant independent effects, but in each instance the number of variables
having such a relationship was smaller than for the general measure of support. As
the analysis presented in Table 9.2 reveals, the most striking differences for the
compliance dimension are the absence of an independent relationship for the

Table 9.2   All Factors and Compliance Dimension for All Respondents: Multiple Effects

Variables in the Regression Analysis	Variable Number for Regression Equation	Zero-order Correlation with Compliance Factor	Standardized Regression Coefficients (betas)
STRUCTURAL FACTOR (SOCIAL)			
Education	2	.30	.14
POLITICAL-PREDISPOSITIONAL FACTOR			
Ideological Orientation/ Traditionalism	3	.22	.06
Political Potency-Likelihood of Taking Action	4	-.24	-.11
Salience of State Politics	5	-.19	-.07
PHENOMENAL FACTOR			
Influence Agents/ Should be Influenced by Pressure Groups	6	-.14	-.10
Should be Influenced by Experts	7	.11	.07
Decisional Referents/ Decisions Should be Influenced by State Level Considerations	8	.14	.06
Decisions Should be Influenced by District Level Considerations	9	.03	-.04
Perception-Expectation Differentials/ Differential Between Should and Are Influence Agents	10	.00	.10
Net Differential Between Should and Are Influences Agents	11	-.04	-.07
Representativeness Factor	12	.23	.21
Compromise Factor	13[a]	.19	.14

[a]Compliance will be designated variable 1.

structural-political variables—especially for the leadership status variables—and the smaller percentage of explained variance (multiple $R = .45$, explaining about 21 percent of the variance). Thus sample designation appears to have no independent impact on the compliance predisposition respondents have toward the Iowa legislature, but it has a very significant impact on overall support and, as shown in Table 9.3, on the commitment dimension. The mass public indicates a predisposition to comply with legislative decisions as great as that reported by legislators, attentive constituents, party leaders, or lobbyists. On the other hand, when we consider the commitment dimension, the leadership variables have an important impact, suggesting that status differentiation does influence the respondent's

Table 9.3 All Factors and Commitment Dimension for All Respondents: Multiple Effects

Variables in the Regression Analysis	Variable Number for Regression Equation	Zero-order Correlation with Commitment Factor	Standardized Regression Coefficients (betas)
STRUCTURAL FACTOR (SOCIAL)			
Subjective Class Identification	2	-.18	-.04
Income	3	.22	.05
STRUCTURAL FACTOR (POLITICAL)			
Political Knowledge	4	.30	.24
Leadership Status/			
Public	5	-.32	.72
Nominees	6	.17	.46
Party Leaders	7	.03	.12
Lobbyists	8	.08	.22
Legislators	9	.24	.58
POLITICAL-PREDISPOSITIONAL FACTOR			
Political Potency-Prior Attempts to Influence Decisions	10	-.27	-.18
Political Involvement	11	.23	.06
PHENOMENAL FACTOR			
Decisional Referents/ Decisions Are Influenced by Interest Groups	12	.03	.06
Representativeness Factor	13	.24	.17
Compromise Factor	14[a]	.18	.14

[a]Commitment will be designated variable 1.

commitment to the legislature. (The multiple R for the commitment dimension is .48, explaining about 23 percent of the variance.)

The appearance of "education" in place of other social status variables for compliance indicates a variation in the nature of the relationship; that is, level of education rather than social or economic differentiation affects feelings of compliance. When we examine commitment, we find that the impact of structural-social variables is through social and economic differences. Thus feelings of compliance with the legislature seem to be affected by differences in educational level, whereas a commitment to the legislature is affected more by perceived social position and income. Thus perhaps the findings of Easton and others regarding the political socialization of obedience through early school experiences may be reinforced by later educational experiences, with the result that feelings of compliance with the legislature become even more ingrained throughout the educational experience.[2] On the other hand, an increase in one's perceived social status or income has a positive effect on feelings of legislative commitment.

Considering the political-predispositional and phenomenal factors, almost entirely different sets of variables are related independently to compliance and to commitment. The only common variables are the representativeness and compromise factors. This indicates to us that the structural, political-predispositional, and phenomenal variables that affect compliance differ from those affecting commitment.

LEGISLATIVE SUPPORT AND THE MASS PUBLIC

Because of the pronounced effect of the leadership status variables on levels of legislative support and the systematic interaction between these statuses and other structural, political-predispositional, and phenomenal variables, we decided to examine the relationships between all other independent variables and support within each leadership status category. To reduce potential measurement error, all factor scores from prior factor analyses that did not differentiate by type of respondent were generated again, but this time a separate factor analysis was conducted within each category. Subsequent inspection of a product-moment correlational analysis of variables demonstrated that this may have been unnecessary from the standpoint of numerical values; however, to assure a normal distribution of scores on these variables, especially on legislative support, and to maximize variance within each category of respondents, generating these new scores seemed to be an important strategy.[3] Thus all subsequent analysis in this chapter uses indicators of the variables that were generated separately for each category of respondents.

Multiple regression analysis for the mass public identified six variables with significant independent effects on legislative support. Together these variables had a multiple $R = .50$, explaining about one-quarter of the total variance. This is only slightly more than one-half the total variance explained when all respondents are analyzed together, but the number of variables used is considerably smaller. Even when the number of independent variables in the mass public analysis is increased substantially to 49, the multiple $R = .54$, a very minor increase of .04. Note that the six variables in the final regression include one each from the social-structural, political-structural, and political-predispositional factors and three from the phenomenal factor (Table 9.4). According to the standardized regression coefficients, two of the phenomenal variables—representativeness and compromise factors—seem to have the greatest effect, whereas each variable from the structural and the political-predispositional factors has a somewhat smaller effect.

Table 9.4   All Factors and Legislative Support for Mass Public: Multiple Effects

Variables in the Regression Analysis	Variable Number for Regression Equation and Path Analysis	Zero-order Correlation with Support	Standardized Regression Coefficients (betas)
STRUCTURAL FACTOR (SOCIAL)			
Subjective Class Identification	2	-.14	-.06
STRUCTURAL FACTOR (POLITICAL)			
Political Knowledge	3	.28	.19
POLITICAL-PREDISPOSITIONAL FACTOR			
Ideological Orientation/ Traditionalism	4	.25	.14
PHENOMENAL FACTOR			
Influence Agents/ Should be Influenced by Populist Agents	5	.11	.09
Representativeness Factor	6	.28	.25
Compromise Factor	7[a]	.28	.25

[a]Support will be designated variable 1.

This analysis indicates that variation in levels of support is most closely related to other perceptions a person has of the legislature. An important analytical question must be asked: how much of this effect is a direct result of these phenomenal variables, and how much is due to the indirect effects of other variables acting through them? Using path analysis, it is possible to assess the comparative direct and indirect effects for the mass public using six identified variables. At the outset, all paths from variables within each factor to the variables in each succeeding factor were examined to determine their significance. If the analysis indicated an insignificant value, that path was removed from the model. The final, refined model (Figure 9.1) indicates that our postulated links among independent variables to legislative support are not as pervasive as our earlier general model hypothesized. More specifically, one path between a social-structural and political-predispositional variable($P_{4,2}$), together with some of the paths from the social-structural variables and the political-predispositional variables to the phenomenal variables ($p_{6,2}$; $p_{7,2}$; $p_{5,4}$) were insignificant and were therefore removed from the model. Furthermore, the remaining paths to the phenomenal variables do not appear to be very substantial. All this suggests that for the most part, the relationship between each of these independent variables and legislative support is independent and direct. (The model in Figure 9.1 explains about 19 percent of the variance through direct paths and about 5 percent through indirect paths, leaving 75.5 percent for residual variables not included in the model.) Among the mass public in Iowa, the effects of these independent variables are mainly direct.

LEGISLATIVE SUPPORT AND THE ATTENTIVE ELITE

Among respondents nominated by legislators as attentive constituents, a great number and variety of variables were found to affect level of legislative support. Eleven independent variables representing each type of factor had a multiple $R = .52$, indicating an ability to explain about 27 percent of the variance (see Table 9.5; using 50 variables, $R = .60$, $R^2 = .36$). As with the mass public, the variables showing the greatest impact appear to be the phenomenal ones, followed closely by the political-predispositional ones. Three structural variables that had insignificant relationships with support for the mass public were found to have sizable independent relationships to support among attentives; these variables were size of place of residence, age, and party identification. Thus among nominated respondents, those residing in cities and towns, being younger, and

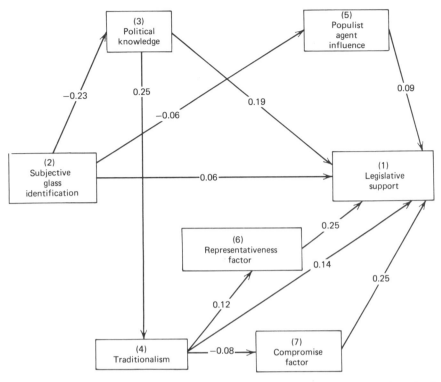

Figure 9.1 Explanatory model of legislative support among mass public respondents (path coefficients).

having a strong Republican Party affiliation are more likely to have higher levels of support.

Given this large number of independent variables and all the potential paths, an exceedingly complex explanatory model results; however, path analysis simplified the final version somewhat because certain possible paths proved to be insignificant (see Figure 9.2). The direct paths between these independent variables and support now explain about 25 percent of the variance, and the indirect paths explain the remaining 2 percent. Again, the greatest effect is through the direct paths of independent to the dependent variables. This finding reinforces further our conclusion that the hypothesized interrelationships of independent variables from Figure 2.1 do not seem to be as extensive in their impact on support as postulated. Phenomenal and political-predispositional variables have a considerable independent effect on levels on legislative support.

Table 9.5   All Factors and Legislative Support for Attentives: Multiple Effects

Variables in the Regression Analysis	Variable Number for Regression Equation and Path Analysis	Zero-order Correlation with Support	Standardized Regression Coefficients (betas)
STRUCTURAL FACTOR (SOCIAL)			
Size-of-Place of Residence	2	-.10	-.13
Age	3	-.19	-.15
STRUCTURAL FACTOR (POLITICAL)			
Party Identification	4	.14	.12
POLITICAL-PREDISPOSITIONAL FACTOR			
Ideological Orientation/			
Traditionalism	5	-.19	.12
Institutional Liberalism	6	.17	.12
Interpersonal Trust	7	-.17	-.11
Political Potency - Prior Attempts to Influence Decisions	8	-.18	-.13
PHENOMENAL FACTOR			
Influence Agents/ Should be Influenced by Partisan Agents	9	-.07	.07
Perception-Expectation Differential/ Differential Between Should be and Are Influenced	·10	-.02	.13
Representativeness Factor	11	.28	.28
Compromise Factor	12[a]	.20	.18

[a]Support will be designated variable 1.

LEGISLATIVE SUPPORT AND PARTY LEADERS

In sharp contrast with the findings and explanatory models suggested for the mass public and attentive constituents are those appropriate for party leaders. Not only is the number of variables smaller, but also the scope of the independent variables, only three politically based independent variables have an impact on levels of support. (This finding may have resulted partly because Iowa party leaders resemble one another in their background experiences, as can be seen in Table 3.1.) Note further in Table 9.6 that no phenomenal or social-structural variables have independent relationships with legislative support among party leaders.

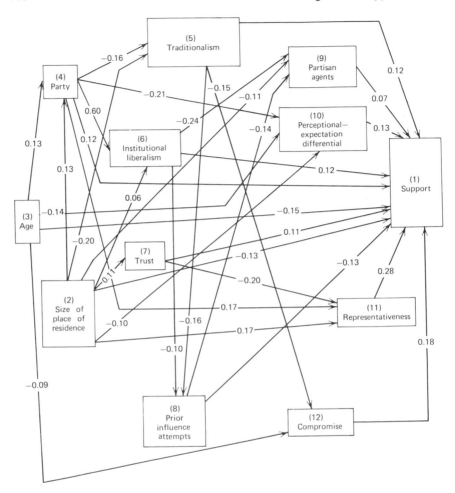

Figure 9.2 Explanatory model of legislative support among nominated respondents (path coefficients).

Using the three politically based variables, the multiple R is .43, explaining about 18 percent of the variance. According to the standardized regression coefficients, party identification has a somewhat greater effect than the other two predispositional variables.

The explanatory model developed from these data show significant paths existing *only* directly from the independent variables to support (Figure 9.3). Thus all 18 percent of the explained variance seems to be the direct result of these political variables. The direct nature of this effect, the highly political nature of

Table 9.6   All Factors and Support for Party Leaders: Multiple Effects

Variables in the Regression Analysis	Variable Number for Regression Equation and Path Analysis	Zero-order Correlation with Support	Standardized Regression Coefficients (betas)
STRUCTURAL FACTOR (POLITICAL)			
Party Identification	2	.31	.37
POLITICAL-PREDISPOSITIONAL FACTOR			
Ideological Orientations/ Traditionalism	3	.18	-.18
Political Potency - Likelihood of Taking Political Action	4[a]	-.14	.23

[a]Support will be designated variable 1.

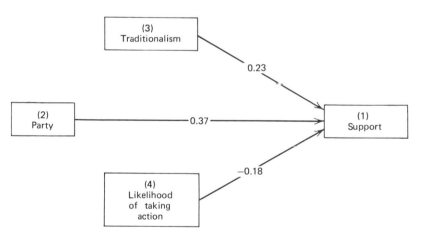

Figure 9.3   Explanatory model of legislative support among party leader respondents (path coefficients).

these independent variables, and the type of respondent under study indicate to us that the partisan-political orientation of party leaders makes these individuals more sensitive to influence on level of support from politically based factors. Another interesting feature of our findings is the absence of effect from phenomenal variables. Levels of support among all other types of respondent are very significantly related to perceptions of the legislature, especially their views regarding representativeness and compromise in the Iowa legislature, but this relationship is absent among party leaders—suggesting a differing orientation for these respondents. More specifically, their general views of the legislature do not appear to affect levels of support.

LEGISLATIVE SUPPORT AND THE LOBBYISTS

Lobbyists, who, next to legislators, have the greatest daily contact with the legislature among our Iowa respondents, were overwhelmingly influenced in their level of legislative support by the independent variables hypothesized to be "closest in time" to support—that is, phenomenal variables. These variables have the largest betas for lobbyists, which suggests that the lobbyists' levels of support are closely related to their other perceptions of the legislature (see Table 9.7). The effects of both types of structural variables—social and political—are absent for lobbyists. Furthermore, only the salience of state politics has an independent impact in addition to the four phenomenal variables. (The greater was the perceived salience of state politics, the higher the level of support.) Lobbyists, like party leaders, seem to be affected in their levels of support primarily by variables that are associated with adult political life. (Again, the absence of variance for many

Table 9.7   All Factors and Legislative Support for Lobbyists: Multiple Effects

Variables in the Regression Analysis	Variable Number for Regression Equation and Path Analysis	Zero-order Correlation with Support	Standardized Regression Coefficients (betas)
POLITICAL-PREDISPOSITIONAL FACTOR			
Salience of State Politics	2	-.25	-.25
PHENOMENAL FACTOR			
Influence Agents/ Should be Influenced by Citizen Opinions	3	.23	.30
Decisional Referents/ Decisions Should be Influenced by District Concerns	4	-.25	-.23
Representativeness Factor	5	.41	.36
Compromise Factor	6[a]	.34	.23

[a]Support will be designated variable 1.

background variables may be an important contributing factor to this outcome.) Together, these five variables have a multiple $R = .60$ with support and an explained variance of 36 percent. To these insiders, then, support is most affected by the lobbyists' other images of politics and the legislature and apparently is immune to effects from social background factors. Only to the extent that lobbyists and party leaders are recruited in terms of their social backgrounds do these variables appear to affect their levels of legislative support.[4]

The path analysis for these data shows that the only significant paths are the direct ones between the independent variables and support (see Figure 9.4). Thus in their relationship with support, phenomenal variables do not appear to be affected by the relative salience of state politics.

LEGISLATIVE SUPPORT AND THE LEGISLATORS

Among legislators whose levels of support are, on the average, higher than among other groups, a number of diverse independent variables appear to have some

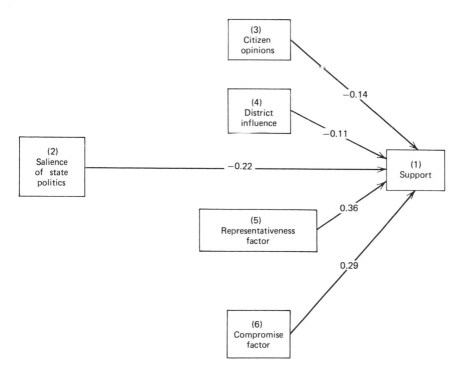

Figure 9.4 Explanatory model of legislative support among lobbyist respondents (path coefficients).

impact. Noticeably absent are the purely political variables that were found to have a significant effect among the other types of elite respondents (see Table 9.8). Political party, salience of politics, and related variables have no significant independent relationships to legislators' levels of support. The lone politically based variable showing any independent effect is a liberal ideology. Taken together, these seven social-structural, political-predispositional, and phenomenal variables have a multiple $R = .55$, explaining about 30 percent of the variance in levels of legislative support. Although the most significant betas are observed relationships for the phenomenal factors, the variables of age, education, and institutional liberalism all have sizable independent relationships. Thus among legislators, higher levels of education, being younger, and having a low level of instrumental liberalism are associated with higher levels of legislative support. Regarding the phenomenal variables, higher levels of support among legislators are associated with (1) the high salience of state-level politics, (2) consideration of

Table 9.8   All Factors and Legislative Support for Legislators: Multiple Effects

Variables in the Regression Analysis	Variable Number for Regression Equation and Path Analysis	Zero-order Correlation with Support	Standardized Regression Coefficients (betas)
STRUCTURAL FACTOR (SOCIAL)			
Education	2	.21	.12
Age	3	-.22	-.18
POLITICAL-PREDISPOSITIONAL FACTOR			
Ideological Orientations/ Institutional Liberalism	4	.24	.15
PHENOMENAL FACTOR			
Decisional Referents/ Decisions Should be Influenced by State Considerations	5	.01	.14
Decisions Should be Influenced by Legislator's Conscience	6	.19	.22
Representativeness Factor	7	.30	.28
Compromise Factor	8[a]	.29	.27

[a]Support will be designated variable 1.

the conscience of the legislator in decision making, (3) belief that the Iowa legislature represents its citizens well, and (4) belief that the legislature is a place for compromise in decision making,

The explanatory model for these data indicate again the predominance of direct paths in explaining the variance in legislative support—direct effects equal 29 percent and indirect effects equal 2 percent (see Figure 9.5). Only the obvious interrelationship of age to education was found to have a significant indirect effect on the dependent variable. This levels of legislative support for legislators appear to entail independent effects from all these seven independent variables.

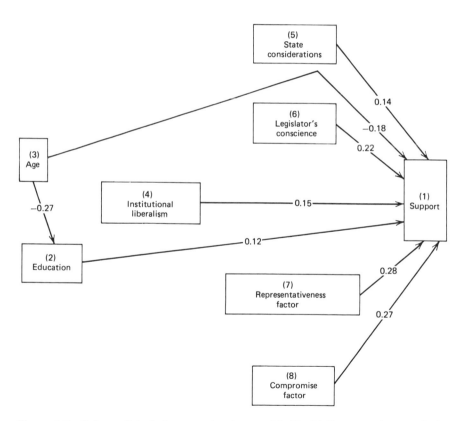

Figure 9.5 Path coefficients for an explanatory model of legislative support among legislators.

CONCLUSIONS AND IMPLICATIONS

The multivariate data analysis and model testing conducted for these Iowa data suggest several important conclusions and implications regarding the development of legislative support.

1.   Differing clusters of independent variables are associated with support accorded to the legislature by different types of respondents. Among mass public, attentive constituent, and legislator respondents, a wide variety of variables independently affect levels of legislative support, including structural, political-predispositional, and phenomenal variables. On the other hand, legislative support by party leaders and lobbyists tends to be affected by clusters of variables that are more limited in scope—predominantly political and legislative perceptual.

2.   Within each group of respondents, the strongest independent relationships with legislative support, as indicated by the betas, are usually from the phenomenal variables. Most impressive is the relationship between levels of legislative support and respondents' perceptions of both rerpesentativeness and compromise. This suggests that legislative support may be one aspect of a more general image developed of the legislature. That is, support for the legislature for most people cannot be developed if their other views of that institution and its processes, especially their views regarding representativeness and compromise, are not included.

3.   The interrelationship of the independent variables, providing indirect as well as direct effects on legislative support, first postulated in Chapter 2, does not seem to be fully supported by path analysis; rather, it would be more realistic to expect an independent, direct effect of these variables on legislative support. Structural, political-predispositional, and phenomenal variables exhibit some interrelationships, especially among attentive constituents and to a lesser extent in the mass public, but not to the extent that direct effects are overwhelmed by indirect onces. A more reasonable explanatory model is perhaps like that in Figure 9.6

4.   Political and partisan variables have pronounced effects on the levels of legislative support displayed by party leaders and lobbyists. This suggests that among party leaders and lobbyists, legislative support is an extension of political and partisan considerations.

5.   A number of the variables included in the original model demonstrated no significant independent relationships with legislative support. Most noticeable were levels of political knowledge and involvement, legislative pride, political opportunism, and political mobilization. Among Iowa respondents, these vari-

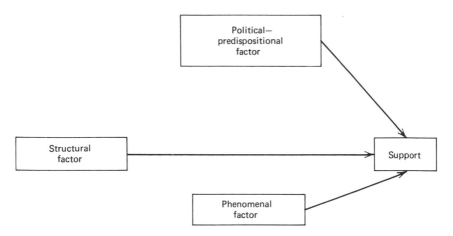

Figure 9.6 Alternate explanatory model for legislative support.

ables do not appear to be important as independent contributors to an explanation of variations in legislative support.

6. Finally, in spite of our best efforts to collect a wide range of data and carefully analyze it, a substantial amount of variance in legislative support remains unexplained. For two types of respondent—legislators and lobbyists—a very reasonable amount of variance has been explained (30 and 42 percent, respectively); for the others it is a more modest amount (18 percent for chairmen, 25 percent for the mass public, and 27 percent for the attentive constituents). Perhaps in other settings, using different operational measures, a greater percentage of explained variance could have been constructed.

NOTES

1. H. M. Blalock, "Correlated Independent Variables: The Problem of Multicollinearity," *Social Forces,* Vol. 42 (December 1963), 233–237.

2. The socialization of obedience to political authority is a well-documented feature of political learning in the United States. See, for example, David Easton and Jack Dennis, *Children in the Political System* (New York, 1969), especially Chapters 5, 7, and 8.

3. Exceedingly high intercorrelations exist between the legislative support scores generated when all respondents were combined together and when separate scores were calculated for each type of respondent. The Pearsonian product-moment correlations were:

Mass public	$r = .996$
Nominees	$r = .998$

Party leader	$r = .981$
Lobbyists	$r = .996$
Legislators	$r = .997$

4. For a further elaboration of this, see Donald R. Matthews, *Social Background of Political Decision-Makers* (New York, 1954); and Ronald D. Hedlund, ''Psychological Predispositions: Political Representatives and the Public,'' *American Journal of Political Science*, Vol. 17 (August 1973), 489–505.

10 CROSS–STATE COMPARISONS FOR LEVELS OF LEGISLATIVE SUPPORT

Whenever political scientists undertake model building from existing data, one of the critical concerns must be the adequacy of those data for generalizing. If the data are faulty or inappropriate, the model will suffer accordingly. In the present case, independent checks on our Iowa data suggest that the information collected probably reflects quite accurately the sentiments of the individuals studied within the tolerances of survey research data. Thus we believe we have accurate information on levels of legislative support for the Iowa legislature; however, related questions must be asked. How adequate are these data and conclusions for other territorial units in the United States, and for the political system in general? Can we use these data to build an adequate model of legislative support, applicable to other states? Throughout this book we have tried whenever appropriate to relate our findings to the political experiences and culture of Iowa, while preserving the general nature of our data. The findings presented to this point are drawn entirely from Iowa and this book remains essentially an in-depth case study of one state. But in addition to the data already reported, we had access to a comparable but more limited set of data on levels of support for state legislatures in 13 other states and for the nation as a whole. These data provide a basis for testing whether it is possible to generalize from our explanatory model.

CROSS–STATE DATA

During 1968 the Institute for Research in Social Science at the University of North Carolina conducted a study of comparative state elections.[1] Included in their survey instrument were some of the questions asked in Iowa. Using a multistage research design, samples were drawn for 13 states. In addition, the samples were appropriately supplemented with additional interviews, making it possible to generate a national sample, also. Using these data, we generated a series of analytical variables to measure legislative support, socioeconomic status, political involvement, and general participation. We examined these analytical variables

195

together with other raw data to assess their individual and combined effects on levels of support. A separate analysis was conducted for each state and for the national sample. Intended to identify and assess the factors that contribute to developing legislative support, the analysis included multiple regression and path analyses.

Since the data collected for the 13 states differed somewhat from the Iowa data, certain theoretic, analytic, and measurement modifications were introduced. The first involved a reassessment of the model to be tested. The model suggested by the Iowa data (Figure 9.6) was taken as the initial one. No evidence existed for automatically rejecting this model, although the possibility of greater interaction among the social-structural, political-structural, political-predispositional, and situational factors was expected for these other data.

The second difference was one of measurement. Although similar data were collected from the 13 states and for Iowa, different questions were sometimes used. For example, political participation information was collected using different question wording and differing response categories. Furthermore, a greater number and variety of political forms were tapped for the 13 states than for Iowa; however, the same seven questions composing our legislative support scale were asked with virtually no differences in wording or response categories. Thus, although the same questions were not always used, comparable information was collected.

A third difference relates to the adequacy of measurement of the assorted dimensions within each set of factors. Because of a drastic reduction in the number of independent variables—less than 15 compared with the more than 60 used in Iowa—the cross-state analysis is limited in its capacity to measure the wide variety of contributing factors. The largest reduction in the number of variables was for the phenomenal and the political-structural factors. Figure 10.1 contains the model we propose to test and lists the variables being used to indicate each factor. When the operational indicators of each factor in this figure are compared with those for Iowa (Figure 2.2), the differences in measurement become obvious.

Finally, the abundant detail found in our exploration of legislative support in Iowa is not supplied to the same degree for the 13 states nor for the national sample. Because the data for the analysis in this chapter are considerably more limited in scope than the data in the Iowa analysis, they do not provide as much explanation as is made available in the preceding work.

OPERATIONAL MEASURES

Since somewhat different questions were asked in the 13-state study, and since

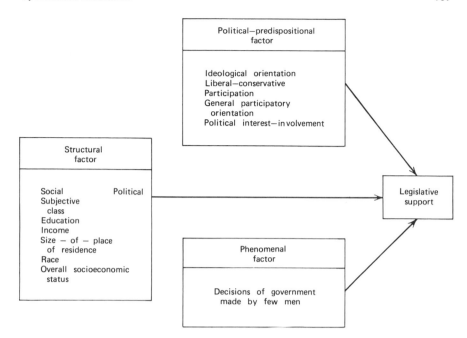

Figure 10.1 Explanatory model for legislative support in 13 States.

differing outcomes sometimes were observed when individual questions were combined, we must describe briefly the operational measures chosen and compare them with those used in Iowa. Regarding the social-structural variables, no basic measurement difference occurred except that race and an analytic variable for socioeconomic status were included for the other states but not for Iowa. Race was excluded in Iowa because the vast majority of the population is white; less than 1 percent of our mass public sample was nonwhite. (Race is a "dummy variable," where white is the low score.) The analytic variable socioeconomic status was derived from a factor analysis of the variables education, income, and occupation. (Low score on this variable is "middle class.") No data from any political-structural variables are included in this analysis.

The political-predispositional factor was operationalized using four variables. The first—liberalism-conservatism—was measured by a set of self-rating questions allowing respondents to indicate their perceived proclivity for a liberal or conservative orientation. Participation, the second variable, is a summated score for six forms of electoral participation—paying attention to government, discussing politics and campaigns, wearing campaign buttons, contributing to a campaign, working for a candidate, and attending meetings. The remaining two variables resulted from a factor analysis of eight items identifying both election and interelection political activities. The variable, general participatory orientation, is found from the factor scores calculated from the first principal component in the factor analysis. The second—political interest–involvement—consists of the rotated factor scores of interelection political activity.

Only one phenomenal variable was included here. The question asked respondents about the degree to which decisions in the name of government were made by a few men.

Finally, the dependent variable was a factor analysis of five items similar to those used in Iowa. Table 10.1 summarizes this factor analysis. (The lower the score on this factor, the higher the level of support.)

DETERMINANTS OF LEGISLATIVE SUPPORT IN OTHER AMERICAN STATES

The initial step in identifying which variables affect the level of legislative support involved submitting the data for each of the 13 states to a multiple correlation-

Table 10.1   Factor Analysis of Legislative Support for Respondents in All States

Diffuse Legislative Support Items	Principal Component Loading
Times when citizens take law into own hands	.739
Times when governor should take law into his own hands	.692
All right to break law if you disagree with it	.650
If passed laws people disagreed with, do away with legislature	.624
Wouldn't make much difference if legislative powers were reduced	.580
% of Total Variance	43.5%

regression analysis.[2] Examination of partial relationships with legislative support indicates that some variables have significant independent effects and others do not. Further refinement was then undertaken by removing variables one at a time from the analysis and determining the effects of this alteration. After a parsimonious set of independent variables had been identified for one state, a similar process was applied for all other states.

This state-by-state analysis presented in Table 10.2 shows the degree of consistency across states. For example, in all states except Florida, Louisiana, and

Table 10.2   Independent Variables and Legislative Support in 13 States: Multiple Effects

Variables in the Regression Analysis	Zero Order Correlation with Support	Standardized Regression Coefficients (betas)
STATES IN NORTHEASTERN UNITED STATES		
MASSACHUSETTS		
Subjective Class	.25	.06
Race	.11	.07
Education	-.33	-.07
Participation	-.85	-.82
Multiple R = .86	R^2 = .75	
NEW YORK		
Race	.32	.12
Education	-.15	.15
Income	-.13	.10
Participation	-.80	-.76
Political Interest/Involvement	-.38	-.24
Multiple R = .84	R^2 = .70	
PENNSYLVANIA		
Race	.20	.25
Education	-.05	.16
Income	-.08	.16
Participation	-.75	-.82
Political Interest/Involvement	-.23	-.30
Multiple R = .84	R^2 = .71	

Table 10.2   (Continued)

ALABAMA

Race	-.19	.38
Education	-.25	-.83
Socio-economic Status	.05	.75
Subjective Class	-.06	.65
Ideology	-.23	-.38
Governmental Decisions	-.09	.29

Multiple R = .44 R^2 = .20

FLORIDA

Ideology	-.33	-.43
General Participation	-.01	.21
Political Interest/Involvement	-.22	-.37
Governmental Decisions	-.10	.23

Multiple R = .45 R^2 = .20

LOUISIANA

Ideology	-.20	-.19
Participation	-.14	-.21
Political Interest/Involvement	-.20	-.26
Governmental Decisions	.05	.19

Multiple R = .36 R^2 = .13

NORTH CAROLINA

Income	-.28	.26
Socio-Economic Status	.13	.05
Participation	-.75	-.77
Political Interest/Involvement	-.38	-.32

Multiple R = .79 R^2 = .63

TEXAS

Education	.30	.39
Income	.17	.17
Subjective Class	.54	-.34
Participation	-.55	-.63
Political Interest/Involvement	-.50	-.60
Governmental Decisions	.43	.29

Multiple R = .86 R^2 = .73

Table 10.2   (Continued)

ILLINOIS

Income	.22	.18
Ideology	-.13	-.12
Participation	.15	.10
Governmental Decisions	.22	.22

Multiple R = .34 R^2 = .12

MINNESOTA

Education	-.37	-.13
Participation	-.86	-.82

Multiple R = .86 R^2 = .75

OHIO

Education	-.26	.13
Income	-.22	.10
Participation	-.80	-.79
Political Interest/Involvement	-.36	-.24

Multiple R = .81 R^2 = 66

SOUTH DAKOTA

Race	.04	.15
Education	-.16	.12
Income	-.18	.15
Participation	-.77	-.88
Political Interest/Involvement	-.38	-.26

Multiple R = .85 R^2 = .73

STATES IN WESTERN UNITED STATES

CALIFORNIA

Ideology	.13	.10
Participation	.25	.21
Governmental Decisions	.21	.15

Multiple R = .31 R^2 = .10

California, social-structural as well as political-predispositional variables have an independent impact on support. Even though the social-structural variables showing the relationship sometimes differ from state to state, the overall finding suggests that social background experiences have an independent effect on support in addition to any indirect effects through other factors. Furthermore, the interrelated nature of the social-structural variables in most states indicates that underlying social stratification experiences have an independent impact on support levels. This independent effect of social background on support parallels our findings for the mass public sample in Iowa.

A second fairly consistent finding for the 13 states is the absence of a significant independent effect for the lone phenomenal variable studied—governmental decisions. Only in Alabama, Florida, Louisiana, Texas, Illinois, and California did a respondent's belief that decisions made in the name of state government were made by a handful of men affect his level of support, and only in Texas is the independent effect a sizable one. (The finding that four of the deviant states are in the South suggests a possible systematic effect for region.) This widespread absence of affect for phenomenal factors is in sharp contrast with our findings in Iowa. One major reason for this difference may be that far fewer phenomenal dimensions were studied for the 13 states than for Iowa. A single-question indicator of governmental perceptions is much less adequate than the scales developed for Iowa. Systematic information regarding such dimensions as representativeness and compromise is lacking for the 13 states. This absence of more complete data on other dimensions in the phenomenal factor precludes our stating that other phenomenal variables have no effect on level of legislative support.

A third similarity across the 13 states is the persistent effect of variables related to participation and political involvement. In every state except Alabama, those variables have significant independent effects, and in 10 of the 13 states the largest betas are found for participation and political involvement variables. As one considers which of these participatory variables seems to be most important, the dominance in 10 states of the "participation" variable in terms of betas indicates that this variable deserves special attention. More than any other variable, this measure of participation has a pervasive and potent effect on legislative support. This strong relationship suggests that for certain states, support is largely a function of participation; however, this finding contradicts some of our Iowa results. For example, among mass public respondents in Iowa (see Table 9.4), no variable purporting to measure any aspect of participation was found to have an independent effect on support; yet if we look at all Iowa respondents together, or even at some of the elite respondents, we find hints that participation has an independent effect nevertheless. If it can be said that leadership status is one measure of participation and the political potency variables indicate a kind of involvement, the analysis presented in Table 9.1 suggests that participatory variables also have significant effects on legislative support in Iowa, but not to the same extent as in the 13 states.

Finally, in Table 10.2 we notice some obvious differences when states are grouped by region. The three Northeastern states—Massachusetts, New York, and Pennsylvania—all exhibit multiple R's in excess of .80, thus explaining more than 70 percent of the variance in legislative support. For three of the four Midwestern states—Minnesota, Ohio, and South Dakota—similarly high multiple R's are found. On the other hand, for Southern and Western states—except North Carolina and Texas—much lower R's (between .30 and .45) appear, indicating a more modest level of success in explaining variance. This level of explained variance is slightly below the 25 percent of explained variance found for the Iowa mass public.

In summary, our findings from the 13 states are as follows:

1. A wide variation in the amount of explained variance exists across these states, from a high of 75 percent in Massachusetts and Minnesota to a low of 10 percent in California.

2. A sectional difference may contribute to these state differences, but anomalies (e.g., Texas, North Carolina, and Illinois) suggest the effects of other statewide variables as well.

3. Participatory variables, in general, have a great effect on legislative support, with the variable "participation" having a most significant positive impact in developing such support.

4. Although less important than the participatory variables, the social background variables generally have a significant independent effect on support.

5. Although the State of Iowa shows some differing trends in the variables found to explain legislative support, the findings for Iowa are not incompatible with the findings from the other states.

Of major significance, however, is the smaller amount of variance we were able to explain using many more variables for the mass public in Iowa than we selected for two states adjoining and resembling Iowa—Minnesota and South Dakota.

DETERMINANTS OF LEGISLATIVE SUPPORT WITH A NATIONAL SAMPLE

These 13-state data sets were supplemented by interviews in other states; thus when all the interviews were taken together and multiplied by an appropriate weighting factor a sizable, valid national sample resulted.[3] These data can be used to ascertain which individual-level variables for a national sample contribute toward the development of diffuse support for state legislatures. Given our state-level findings, we expect variables related to participation and social background experiences to be significantly related to legislative support. The appropriate multiple regression analysis, summarized in Table 10.3, indicates that the social-structural variables of race, education, and income, and the political predispositional variables of ideology, participation, and political interest–involvement all have significant independent relationships with the dependent variable. The largest betas appear for participation, ideology, race, and income. These findings indicate that on a national level, participatory predispositions have the greatest effect on legislative support, whereas ideology and socioeconomic variables also have substantial independent effects.

Prior studies of political and general social involvement have almost uniformly indicated a strong positive association of participatory, ideological, and political variables with prior social background experiences. Thus one question that must be asked relates to the amount of variance in the dependent variable explained by the direct paths from each independent variable to legislative support, and the amount of variance explained by the indirect paths. Recall that in the Iowa analysis, indirect paths generally were much less important than direct paths, and most paths among independent variables were weak or nonexistent. Path analysis on the national sample (Figure 10.2) suggests a different set of conclusions. Several indirect paths exist for the national sample and appear to have an impact on legislative support. The existence of indirect paths between social-structural and political-predispositional variables suggests that our original model—Figure 2.2,

Table 10.3 Independent Variables and Legislative Support for National Sample: Multiple Effects

Variables in the Regression Analysis	Zero-Order Correlation with Support	Standardized Regression Coefficients (betas)
Race	.10	.48
Education	.04	.24
Income	.03	.42
Ideology	-.10	-.54
Participation	-.34	-.78
General Participation	-.09	-.17
Political Interest/Involvement	-.37	-.30
Multiple R = .72	R^2 = .52	

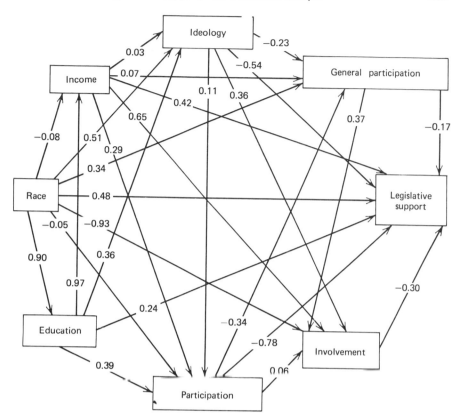

Figure 10.2 Explanatory model of legislative support for national sample (path coefficients).

with its postulated associations among independent variables—is more adequate for describing our national sample than the model suggested for Iowa—Figure 9.6.

A number of possible explanations might be offered for this divergence of findings. The most plausible relates to the nature of the Iowa setting. As we noted in Chapter 1, Iowa has a very homogeneous population, and the effects of many variables are all in the same direction. Iowans so greatly resemble one another in social and political experiences that variation, sufficient to indicate significantly different patterns, does not exist. Thus in Iowa, the high degree of consistency across experiences removes much potential for interaction among these factors, with the resulting depression of divergence among background experiences.

As a kind of check on this notion, we selected South Dakota, a state we believed to be as socially homogeneous as Iowa, and submitted our data to path analysis.

The resulting model indicates that our expectations were not met entirely (see Figure 10.3). Certain paths among the independent variables are significant, which means that a sizable amount of the total variance in legislative support in South Dakota appears to result from the indirect paths.

LEGISLATIVE SUPPORT AND THE LEGISLATURE

Throughout this study of support for state legislatures, the primary concern has been to explain why differing levels of support exist. Our case study of Iowa, our modest comparisons with 13 other states, and our analysis of national sample data have each suggested an explanatory model of legislative support. Although considerable overlap exists for many aspects of these models, the persistence of some variation indicates that systematic differences are probably associated with the cultural, political, and legislative systems being studied. State and regional differences appear to be reflected in differing levels of legislative support and in the relationships of the independent variables to support. Although we have not systematically examined these relationships, their existence seems to be confirmed when we compare Tables 9.4, 10.2, and 10.3

Remarkably stable throughout our analysis has been the continued appearance

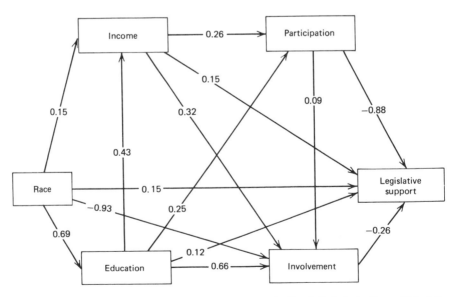

Figure 10.3   Explanatory model of legislative support for South Dakota (path coefficients).

Table 10.4 Summary of Multiple Relationships with Support for Legislatures

Sample	Number of Variables with a Significant Independent Relationship	Type of Factors Represented In Explanatory Model				Multiple R	Percent Total Variance Explained
		Social Structural	Political Structural	Political Predispositional	Phenomenal		
Iowa-Mass Public	6	Yes	Yes	Yes	Yes	.50	25%
Iowa-Nominated Elite	11	Yes	Yes	Yes	Yes	.52	27%
Iowa-Party Leaders	3	No	Yes	Yes	No	.43	18%
Iowa-Lobbyists	5	Yes	No	Yes	Yes	.60	36%
Iowa-Legislators	7	Yes	No	Yes	Yes	.55	30%
Massachusetts-Mass Public	4	Yes	a	Yes	No[b]	.86	75%
New York-Mass Public	5	Yes	a	Yes	No	.84	70%
Pennsylvania-Mass Public	5	Yes	a	Yes	No	.84	71%[c]
Alabama-Mass Public	6	Yes	a	Yes	Yes	.44	20%
Florida-Mass Public	4	Yes	a	Yes	Yes	.45	20%
Louisiana-Mass Public	4	No	a	Yes	Yes	.36	13%
North Carolina-Mass Public	4	Yes	a	Yes	No	.79	63%
Texas-Mass Public	6	Yes	a	Yes	Yes	.86	73%[c]
Illinois-Mass Public	4	Yes	a	Yes	Yes	.34	12%
Minnesota-Mass Public	2	Yes	a	Yes	No	.86	75%[c]
Ohio-Mass Public	4	Yes	a	Yes	No	.81	66%
South Dakota-Mass Public	5	Yes	a	Yes	No	.85	73%
California-Mass Public	3	No	a	Yes	Yes	.31	10%
United States-Mass Public	7	Yes	a	Yes	No	.72	52%

Key a = No "Political Structural" data collected for these samples.
b = Only one "Phenomenal" variable collected for these samples.
c = Differences in R^2 value from similar R due to rounding error.

207

of social-structural and political-predispositional factors as independent predictors for levels of legislative support (see Table 10.4) Some variables related to social class—class identification, income, race, or education—appear in almost every multiple regression for citizen respondents. And although the size of this relationship varies with state, its continual appearance as a significant independent predictor clearly indicates its *direct* role in affecting levels of legislative support. (A considerable indirect effect of social-structural variables also seems probable from the 13-state comparisons.) At the same time, political-predispositional variables—ideology, political participation, and relationship to the political system—also have important associations with levels of support. The cross-state comparisons underscore the importance of participation-related variables in the generation of support levels. And the striking differences among support levels for legislators, lobbyists, party leaders, attentive constituents, and the mass public in Iowa tend to reinforce these cross-state findings regarding the effects of political participation. Political predispositions thus have significant independent effects.

Based on the Iowa analysis, we conclude that certain phenomenal variables also have substantial independent relationships with legislative support. Unfortunately, the limited number of phenomenal variables available from the cross-state study restricts our ability to generalize about the impact of such variables on levels of support. Resolution of this issue must await further evidence.

Perhaps the most critical unresolved difference in our findings relates to the two somewhat competing explanatory models suggested by these data—Figures 2.2 and 9.6. If, as we have argued, the model supported by the Iowa data (Figure 9.6) is a specialized case resulting from the social homogeneity of the state, preference should be given for the original model, Figure 2.2; however, confirmation of our explanation is not obvious. For example, the appropriate explanatory model for a state that is probably as socially homogeneous as Iowa—namely, South Dakota—reveals the existence of significant indirect paths linking the independent variables with support. Further resolution of this difference is not possible within the limits of our study.

NOTES

1. These other data were collected by the Louis Harris organization for the study entitled ''The Comparative State Elections Project: 1968.''

2. In this analysis, individual responses within a state were multiplied by a weighting factor; thus the sample more accurately reflected that state's population.

3. This weighting factor for the national sample differed from the one used to derive an adequate state sample.

INDEX